VERTIGO

JOHN CRACE

For Jill, Anna and Robbie

CONSTABLE

First published in Great Britain in 2014 by Constable,
an imprint of Constable & Robinson Ltd

This paperback edition published in 2014 by Constable

Copyright © John Crace, 2011

The moral right of the author has been asserted.

A CIP catalogue record for this book
is available from the British Library.

ISBN 978-1-47211-577-5 (paperback)
ISBN 978-1-84901-946-0 (ebook)

Typeset in New Baskerville by Initial Typesetting Services
Printed and bound in the UK

Constable
is an imprint of
Constable & Robinson Ltd
100 Victoria Embankment
London EC4Y 0DY

An Hachette UK Company
www.hachette.co.uk

www.constablerobinson.com

Preface

THINGS OFTEN BECOME CLEAREST with hindsight. When I started writing *Vertigo* three years ago, my aim was simply to try to capture a lifetime's support for Tottenham Hotspur through the framework of their first ever season playing in the Champions League, and to explain how going to watch Spurs play football, far from being a pastime that made me a temporary absentee from my work and family – a view held by many, my wife included – was one that actually helped me make sense of and cope with my life.

Spurs were a club that could have been formed with the hopelessly anxious in mind. They were seldom less than entertaining and they always gave you enough hope to keep coming back, but they nearly always let you down in the end. Watching Spurs was like watching a version of my own life being played out week after week over 90 minutes. Enough highs to keep me interested and make the whole thing worthwhile, but rather more silly mistakes and disappointments. Spurs failed so I didn't have to.

In the two full seasons that have passed since *Vertigo* was first published, Spurs have done their best to make the book read as prophesy. In the first, they imploded spectacularly in the latter months of the season. Whether this was the result of manager Harry Redknapp taking his eye off the ball following his acquittal on tax evasion charges, the distraction of his being front runner for the England job vacated by Fabio Capello, the inevitable consequence of his style of managing or just an unhappy coincidence is a matter of opinion.

The uncontestable truth is that they let slip a 10 point lead over the fourth placed team, Aresenal, and were edged out of the final Champions League qualifying spot for the following season by Chelsea beating Bayern Munich in a penalty shoot out in the Champions League final. Even by Spurs' standards, it doesn't get much crueller than that. Unless you count the next season, when Spurs were again well placed to qualify for the Champions League only to falter near the end of the season and finish in fifth place, despite accumulating a record number of Premiership points. I was so certain that Spurs would mess it up that I put £100 on Spurs to finish outside the top four with more than a month of the season to go. It was the easiest money I have ever made. Sometimes, being a Spurs supporter does pay off.

And yet, as more time passes, I've come to think that, while there are still many things about the club and its supporters that remain equally true today as when the book was written, there are some things about that particular season and, indeed, Spurs themselves, which will never be the same again; that I inadvertently recorded a transitional moment in the club's history. A moment of transition that no one at the club even knew was happening.

There was an excitement to that season that will never be repeated. Qualifying for the Champions League was something everyone had dreamed of for years on end.

We'd come close – heartbreakingly close in the year of the West Ham Lasagnegate – before, and now that it had been achieved everyone was determined to enjoy every second. At times, going to White Hart Lane felt like going to a party. It was the thrill of the perennial gatecrasher finally making the guest list after years and years of being turned away at the door.

What all of us overlooked was how quickly you can get used to being on the guest list. Once you've been on the inside, the outside is never the same again. The club – and its supporters – changed from dreaming about Champions League football to expecting it. In all of our minds, we were no longer a club that was content to rattle the cages of the Big Four of Manchester United, Liverpool, Arsenal and Chelsea; we now almost believed that we were a match for any of them. The mantle of plucky underdog snatching the occasional, historic victory no longer suited us quite so well.

Far from taking a monkey off the fans' backs, qualifying for the Champions League actually made our subsequent failures to qualify even more painful. We knew what we were missing out on. Kidding ourselves that we were genuinely excited to be playing clubs we had never heard of in the Europa League was now a much harder trick of the mind to pull off. In some ways, the fans became tougher. More professional. We were less inclined to laugh off yet another game lost thanks to a dopey error with a 'That's Spurs for you'.

This new professionalism was also to be found within the club. It, too, had liked the taste of playing with the European big boys and set about the task of getting it again with a new sense of determination. Spurs had always been seen as one of the fun clubs. One of the good guys. We played football the way it was meant to be played. With style and attack. That philosophy began to subtly change. Harry Redknapp's team had tried to continue playing the Spurs Way and had failed. No matter that Spurs had still managed to finish fourth in the league, a position that would ordinarily have guaranteed Champions League football and been celebrated accordingly; it was a disaster. As far as the club was concerned, Redknapp had to go.

The choice of André Villas-Boas as Redknapp's successor couldn't have been a clearer statement of intent. Harry had embodied the club's spirit, even down to being rather more complex and serious on the inside than he often appeared on the outside. He was fun and irritating in equal measure, but never boring. You never quite knew which Spurs team was going to turn out: the one that would play the most thrilling football in the Premiership or the one that looked like it had been partying till 4 a.m. the night before in Faces nightclub in Essex. To make things more unsettling, sometimes both versions of the team appeared to be on the pitch at the same time. Even Harry can't have had much idea how his teams would play.

AVB was a very different appointment in every way. He was a technician. A man with a Project. Players, such as Benoît Assou-Ekotto, who didn't buy into the seriousness of the Project sufficiently were unceremoniously sidelined or shipped out. Rafael van der Vaart had once said that the dressing-room tactics chalkboard was always completely blank when Harry was in charge, but under AVB it was weighted down with football's equivalent of the equations needed to prove the existence of eleven universes in string theory. Harry's final instructions to Roman Pavlyuchenko before bringing him on as a substitute was 'to fucking run around a bit': AVB would have choked on that.

This new seriousness – some might call it professionalism – was evident everywhere you looked. AVB's team had a plan and stuck to it rigidly. The defence, which had always been leaky and had always relied on our forwards outscoring the opposition, suddenly became reliably watertight. Meanwhile, an attack that had used to kick the ball into the net for fun now usually only scored enough to win by a single goal. Any more was a waste of effort. It was like watching a classy Italian side. Off the field, there was also an unfamiliar sense of the club doing things 'the right, big club way'. In interviews, players seemed a little more corporate. They talked of playing in the Champions League as if it was a necessary qualification for their football CV rather than the fulfilment of a dream or a thrilling adventure. You half expected them to refer to themselves in the third person.

The change felt irreversible. The personnel might come and go, but the new seriousness was here to stay. When Harry had been fired as manager by Spurs, there was genuine concern among the fans that we might end up with someone like Mark Hughes or Sam Allardyce in charge. Competent, mid-table plodders who knew their way round the Premiership. Those fears now feel groundless and from a distant past. When AVB moves on – or is moved on – the new manager will almost certainly be someone in his likeness. Sophisticated and European.

After years of dithering, it also looked as if it was only a matter of time before a new 60,000-seater stadium, complete with the last word in corporate hospitality, escalators and supermarkets, would be built. Spurs would get their own Death Star, a physical representation of the club's ambition before which opposing teams would feel crushed on arrival. Or not. The intimacy of the old White Hart Lane would be gone and not just because the new stadium would have seats the fans could sit down in rather than be squeezed into.

What also made the season of Vertigo so special was Gareth Bale. In all the years I've been following Spurs, I've seen some wonderful players. Greaves, Chivers, Hoddle, Gascoigne... but Bale was the best of the lot. The most complete footballer. When I first saw him play after his move to Spurs from Southampton, he didn't look that special. He was best known by the fans for his unfortunate record of playing twenty-four games without being on the winning side and for his theatrical writhing in agony every time he was tackled. Redknapp likes to take the credit for realising Bale was far better suited to playing in attack than defence, which is where he started his career, but it's hard to believe that Harry had any idea just how good he would actually become. Bale would have been shipped out on loan to Birmingham in 2010 had Assou-Ekotto not been injured. And if he had gone there would have been few at the club who would have thought Redknapp had made a big mistake.

Spurs' Champions League season was the year Bale made his mark with his performances against Inter Milan. Few of us who saw him on those two nights at the San Siro and White Hart Lane could quite believe our eyes; they were performances that were so unexpected they seemed to have been summoned from nowhere. Bale had given a few hints in the preceding games that he could be good, but not that good. Even afterwards I had my doubts. Many players go through a purple patch of games before returning to normal human fallibility. I rather expected Bale to fall into this category. Someone who flickered brightly and briefly, who would be remembered mainly for two games. The front cover of this new edition is a still from a wonderful animation of Bale's San Siro hat-trick created by the artist Richard Swarbrick shortly afterwards. He, too, thought he had seen a game of one-off, individual brilliance.

Neither of us had. No one had. These games were the stepping-stones that took Bale to a new level at which he remained. Without anyone realising till much later, Bale had gone from star to superstar. Just how much of a privilege it was to see him play week in and week out for Spurs is something that's only just beginning to sink in now that he's been sold to Real Madrid. I can't believe I will ever see a better player in a Spurs shirt. He'd so seldom let you down. Opposition defences would know exactly what he was going to do but were still powerless to prevent him doing it.

My favourite memory of Bale is going to watch Spurs play away at West Ham in early 2013. Theo was driving me, Matthew and Richard to Upton Park when a VW Golf shot through some lights at about 45mph and rammed Theo's car in the side. I could see the car coming straight for me and I remember just thinking, 'Oh fuck'. There was a huge din, a smell of explosives and the inside of the car went dark. A few seconds later I heard Richard, who had been sitting in the front, say, 'Unbelievable. I'm still alive.'

As were the rest of us. I crawled out of the opposite rear passenger door and we all met up on the pavement. I had blood dripping from a cut where my head had hit the airbag and my left eye was almost closed. The car was a write-off and the police and an ambulance were called. My one fear was that the paramedics would insist I go to hospital for observation so I hung back, trying not to draw attention to myself. Eventually the wreckage was pushed to the side of the road and we were given the all clear. Gallantly, Matthew, Richard and I abandoned Theo to mind what remained of his car while we took a cab. We arrived just in time to see Bale put Spurs ahead and to win it in the last minute with the goal of the season. After all we'd been through getting there, it was the least he could do for us.

There have been other changes at White Hart Lane in the intervening seasons since *Vertigo* was written. Matthew says he has become less narcoleptic on long car journeys to away games. I can't say I've noticed much difference myself, but I suppose we will have to give him the benefit of the doubt. My daughter Anna has had a life-changing revelation and become a hardcore Spurs fan since she has been away at university in Manchester. She now comes to as many games with me as Robbie. Her first visit to Old Trafford was with me in September 2012 when we beat Manchester United for the first time on their own ground since 1989. She thought the result was quite normal.

Justin and Amici, the two people who had the seats to my left and made so many of the home games during the *Vertigo* season so memorable, didn't renew their season tickets. Or perhaps they just switched to another part of the ground. Maybe it was something I said. I still miss them.

My collection of Spurs memorabilia has also undergone a transformation. My remaining programmes have all now been sold – apart from the 1921 FA Cup final and a few from the 70s and 80s that nobody wants. They have been replaced by my almost-completed collection of banquet menus. Pride of place now goes to the dinner menu at the King's Hall, Holborn restaurant to celebrate winning the 1901 FA Cup. I can't tell you how happy owning that makes me, even if I am almost certainly the only person in Britain stupid enough to have paid so much to buy it. I also have a near complete collection of the club's official Christmas cards since the late 1950s. I'm not sure why.

Some might say these were minor changes in the club's history over the past few years. I would disagree. Sure, I go to the football hoping Spurs are going to win. That we will finish above Arsenal in the league table. That we will qualify for the Champions League. That we will win some cup or other. All these things. But they are only part of the reason I have been following Spurs for so many decades. I do it mainly because I love hanging out with Anna, Robbie, Matthew, Theo, Mat, Terry, Trevor, Richard and everyone else at White Hart Lane and I can't think of a better place to hang out with you all.

Long after AVB has taken his Project to another club and Jan Vertonghen has completed his PhD in Copernican models of the solar system – that may just be my imagination – and started teaching at the University of Brussels, the fans will still be traipsing up to N17 to cheer Spurs on. The heart of any club is not the directors, manager or players. They are merely the financial engine. It's the fans who are the heartbeat and this book was written with all of you in mind.

John Crace, 2013

5 May 2010

MATTHEW WAS LATE. THEN he nearly always is. A fixed time means nothing to him. We had agreed to meet at my work at 3 p.m. and it's now a quarter past. I eventually caught sight of him meandering up the road. He waved. I crossed the road and we hugged. He didn't apologise for being late because he doesn't think being fifteen minutes late counts as being late.

'What do you reckon?' I asked.

'We're going to win,' he said firmly. I smiled. Matthew is the only Spurs fan I know who has never lost the romantic optimism that we are going to win every game we play. Despite decades of evidence to the contrary.

'I'm not so sure.' I never am. Not least when the stakes are so high. That evening we were playing Manchester City at Eastlands. A win would secure us a place in the Champions League for the first time ever. A draw meant we would almost certainly have to win our last game of the season at Burnley. Defeat would almost guarantee City took the Champions League spot. If ever there was a game you would put money on Spurs to lose, it was this one.

While the rest of the country had been concentrating on the following day's general election, I had been thinking about why I was going to so much trouble to get home at about 3 a.m. on a Thursday morning after spending the best part of eight hours driving to Manchester and back, just to suffer the heartbreak of yet another crushing disappointment. And to fork out the best part of £100 in tickets, petrol and dodgy burgers for the pleasure.

I knew it was pointless. There was nothing I could do to affect the outcome. No one would care if I went or not. I could just as easily watch the game on TV. Tomorrow would come and Spurs would have lost, drawn or won. Just as they were always going to. Yet I couldn't not go. An action's inherent futility has never been a great deterrent to me. And for all the doubts – make that near certainties – that we were going to screw up, I couldn't shake off the niggling feeling of how good it would feel if we won and I was there. Or to reflect my negativity more accurately: how bad it would feel if we won and I wasn't there.

Not that this was how I ever envisaged our trip to Manchester back in March when I got the tickets, as the match was originally scheduled for early April. But Spurs found themselves with an FA Cup semi-final against a second-rate Portsmouth side – a game we naturally contrived to lose – and the game was put back to May, turning what promised to be merely an interesting fixture in the battle for fourth place in the Premier League table into a shoot-out for the Champions League.

First we had to get there, though, which was by no means a certainty as my car had been trying to kill me for the last three months. It had developed an intermittent habit of suddenly losing power the moment I hit an open stretch of road, making me a sitting target for any lorry that had been tailgating me. The garage had advised me not to drive it but that wasn't an option. The train was expensive, and even if we did fork out there was no chance of getting back in time for work the next day. And Matthew didn't drive.

He didn't even speak that much for long periods of time – 'I'm too tired, John. It's the twins, they're only two' – but I've kind of got used to that by now, as we've been on more of these idiot awaydays to distant football grounds than I care to remember, so I know what to expect. He may not sound it but he is very good company, especially when you get him on his pet subjects of the worst Tottenham sides of the 1990s and his misfortune at once having to spend an afternoon with Gerry Francis. He is also the only person I have ever met whose favourite band is American soft-rockers, Journey. He even had one of their songs played at his wedding, thereby ruining the occasion for everyone but himself.

After flirting with death along the early miles of the M1 as the car repeatedly slowed itself down from 70 mph to about 30 mph in next to no time, the journey became less nail-biting after Luton, and somewhere around Birmingham the talk turned back to the game.

'Do you still reckon we'll win?' I asked. Matthew's confidence usually begins to crack a little the closer we get to the ground.

'Yeah,' he says. 'We'll definitely win. Or draw.'

We then moved on to the team. Would Ledley's knee last? Is Crouchie useless? I said he was, Matthew gave him the benefit of the doubt. 'He's not as crap as he looks,' he said, gnomically. The conversation petered out; we were both too nervous to speak, and I was trying to figure out why the satnav was taking us past Old Trafford when the directions on the website suggested we should be coming into the city from a completely different direction.

No matter. We made it to the ground by 7 p.m. and bought a programme. Well, I did. I collect them.

'Maybe you should buy two,' he said. 'If we win, you'll probably be able to flog the second at a profit on eBay.' He was taking the piss so I ignored him, though the same thought had occurred to me. But I didn't want to tempt fate.

Most City fans I know can't stand their new ground at Eastlands; they reckon it's too impersonal and pine for Maine Road. But I rather like it. You can see OK, and the away fans aren't corralled into a dump as at so many grounds. City fans also share Spurs' sense of resignation and despair. Like us, they've been patronised by their more successful neighbours for years and suffered season after season of crushed expectations. Also like us, they seem to take a masochistic pleasure in it; now that the club's new owners had shown they were intent on buying in the glory, they were more miserable than ever, caught between wanting everything to change and everything to stay the same.

'You'll do us tonight,' said one City fan we passed on the way in.

'I wouldn't count on it,' I replied. We both laughed.

But one of us had to be wrong. Tonight was the night when one team had to cast off – if only for one game – its reputation for screwing things up when it really mattered. Strangely, thrillingly and miraculously, it was us. Right from the kick-off, we were unrecognizable from the Spurs team that so often turned out on these occasions. We weren't overawed, we looked as if we knew what we were doing and no one made idiotic mistakes. Nor did we lose heart when we had a goal disallowed.

'My mate says it definitely shouldn't have been ruled out,' said a bloke standing nearby, with a mobile clamped to his ear. Mates on the phone always say that disallowed Spurs goals shouldn't have been disallowed.

At half-time I looked around the ground. Not one of the 47,370 fans in the ground seemed to be enjoying themselves. There was just too much riding on the game for it to be anything other than a slow form of torture. I feared the worst, as it's almost unheard of for Spurs to string together a polished performance for two consecutive halves. Surely it was too much to expect a repeat?

Apparently not. If anything, we were better. I wasn't that bothered we hadn't scored. I'd have taken 0-0 before the game, and I'd have taken it now. Anything but lose. We could clinch qualification at the weekend. Crouch had other ideas. All night he'd been playing like an England international rather than the uncoordinated giraffe that so often shows up in a Spurs shirt, and with eight minutes to go he headed in a deflected cross right in front of us. Ecstasy. Strangers who would normally avoid each other joined in a collective embrace. For a moment nothing else mattered. My family, my friends, my work: all were forgotten in an instant of pure joy.

There was still time left to mess up as self-destruction is a long-standing tradition, but no one seemed to have told that to the City fans who made their way to the exit long before the final whistle; more curiously, no one seemed to have told the Spurs team who played out time without even hinting they were going to give it all away. It was over. We'd won, and qualified for Europe. Unbelievable.

I didn't quite know what to say. Neither did Matthew. So we said nothing. Instead, we joined in with the rest of the Spurs fans who didn't really know what to say either, singing the same fairly mindless chants – 'We are Champions League, I said, We are Champions League', 'We're all going on a European Tour' – over and over again. It was a peculiarly disembodied experience. I knew I was there, I knew we'd won and I knew there was nowhere else I'd rather be. But it just didn't feel real. I was used to being the City fan, going home moaning. I could deal with the failure. Success was just weird.

It felt like slipping through a wormhole into a new identity. Over the years, I'd got used to us winning the odd cup every now and again, but ever since shed-loads of cash had been poured into football in the early 1990s, we'd never been one of the Big Four who got to swagger about Europe in the Champions League. And in a way, it had been quite a safe place to be. Talking a good game but seldom having to play one. Pretending the UEFA Cup was really just as exciting as the Champions League.

But now we were on top of the heap, looking down, and I was feeling anxious. Having wanted something for so long, I was terrified it would be taken away. If you've never had something you never have to experience the loss. You only have to imagine it. Which is somehow better. I was also worried about what it would mean if we did keep on winning, because then the club might change character. Did I really want to be one of those fans who were relaxed about winning. Where was the enjoyment in that? Succeed or fail, either way it felt as if I was probably going to lose.

The perfect day continued perfectly. For some reason

the satnav decided to direct us out of Manchester the way it was meant to take us in.

'I've always said Crouchie was a god,' I said.

'I know you have,' Matthew replied.

Then Matthew did what he always does on the way home. He fell asleep, so it was just me and the World Service for the last 100 miles or so. Inevitably he woke up just as we got back to London.

'Great game,' he said.

'The best.'

Well, the best since I last felt like this. Only, these feelings were becoming more frequent. We had always been able to lose in style. Now, it looked as if we might even be able to win in style. How would I cope? I'd find out soon enough. Maybe I'd get used to it quite easily. I should try and enjoy it as best I could, as Spurs were bound to let me down sooner or later. They always do. That's the whole point of them.

'See you next season.'

August

THANK GOD THE WORLD CUP was over. Eight weeks of tedious hype in which the England team was built up to be world-beaters, only to play out three sub-standard games against mediocre teams in the qualifiers and to be thrashed by Germany in the first knockout stage. It was hailed as a national disaster, but we basically got what we deserved. Ask any sane football fan where England should be ranked in the world ratings, and they'd tell you somewhere between nine and sixteen. Which is precisely where we finished the tournament. You could even say we played to our potential.

But then there's often a massive reality gap between the standard of football you think you are seeing and the standard of football the pundits tell you you're seeing. The charitable view is that the experts have played the game and can spot things you can't. The more cynical explanation is that they have a vested interest in not running down their product. There's also a world of difference between those who get their football for free and those who have to pay for it.

There's nothing like shelling out for a season ticket to keep your judgement honest. When you're in for the best part of £40 a game, you're rather less inclined to make allowances for some poor love on more than £50,000 per week who is apparently having 'one of those days'; especially when to you and the people sitting next to you it's fairly clear that the little bastard isn't actually trying very hard. And, come to think of it, he didn't appear to be trying that hard the week before, either. The cameras might not have caught him having a sulk and refusing to track back, but you did. And if you behaved like that at work, you wouldn't have Alan Shearer or Andy Gray telling the world you were basically a class act.

I did, though, watch as many World Cup games as possible. As a summer TV schedule-filler it could hardly be improved upon, and it also gave me the chance to keep my Panini sticker collection going. With the exception of a few from the 1970 Mexico set – the 1958 Brazil team, Francisco Castrejón of Mexico, England's Alan Ball and Brazil's Everaldo and Leão, since you ask – I've got every sticker and every card from every World Cup Panini album. I care more about the stickers than I do the results. Sure, on balance I'd rather England won than lost, but I don't really care that much. The national team is just a sideshow for the main event: Tottenham Hotspur.

Having said that, my support for Spurs did start with a World Cup. I was nine in 1966 and football-obsessed. Like many boys that age I also thought I was fairly good at it, though probably not good enough to play First Division football. But I reckoned I could make it in the Fourth Division. After all, there were ninety-two professional clubs, and I had to be among the thousand best footballers in England, so I decided I'd do York City a favour and sign for them. But that was a career choice. I had no genuine feelings for the club, and I certainly couldn't name any of the players. Come to think of it, I wasn't entirely sure where York was. I was living in Wiltshire.

What I was missing was a team to be passionate about. The trouble was that neither of my parents was that interested in football, so there were no tribal loyalties to inherit. The field was completely clear; I could support anyone. But who? I started reading the paper the way I've read it ever since. From the back. In May 1966 the sports pages were almost as full with World Cup previews as they are now. And one man and one face stood out: Jimmy Greaves. Brilliant striker, stylishly Brylcreemed hair: here was the epitome of cool and glamour. I wanted to be Jimmy. I was Jimmy. I became Spurs.

It should have been obvious from early on that this was going to be a love affair characterised largely by heart-break. Greaves got injured in the group stages and was replaced by Geoff Hurst, who scored the winner in the quarter-final against Argentina. By the time Greaves was fit for the final, he had lost his place in the team. My dad and my sisters had gone out for the afternoon of the final, but I had made my mum stay behind to watch it on our poky black and white TV. I cried when Germany equalised with almost the last kick of normal time. I cried when England scored twice more in extra time. But I have a feeling I was one of the few nine-year-olds whose tears were also for Greaves. Hurst had scored his hat-trick.

Looking back, it seems less improbable now that I chose Spurs than it did then. Here was a side that had won the double only a few years before, a team that had followed that success by winning the FA Cup again the following season, and by becoming the first English team to win a European trophy the year after that with a 5-1 demolition of Atlético Madrid. It was a club that was for ever associated with breathtaking, attacking football. But I really didn't know any of that back then. I had as little idea where White Hart Lane was as I did about York. I'm not sure I'd even been to London then. If I had, it can only have been for the day. London was a scary place; my parents seldom visited the capital, and when they did my dad always felt the need to dress up in a jacket and tie. They certainly never dreamed of spending the night there.

But Spurs it was. I've often since wondered whether, in some cases, it's the club that chooses you rather than the other way round. It certainly seems we are the ideal psychological fit; unfortunately neither of us emerges with much credit from this. Spurs are a team with a sense of entitlement that generally exceeds their on-field successes; a team that lives off memories of past triumphs while too often falling short in the present; a team whose fans grandiosely talk of 'The Spurs Way' as a metaphor for attacking, stylish football as we slide to yet another 4-3 defeat, illuminated by massive lapses of concentration and schoolboy defending every bit as much as a lightening-quick break into the opposition's penalty area.

We celebrate the charismatic greats: the Bobby Smiths, the Jimmy Greaveses, the Martin Chiverses, the Steve Archibalds, the Glenn Hoddles, the Paul Gascoignes, the Jürgen Klinsmanns, the David Ginolas and, yes, the Gareth Bales – though many of us are still wondering if he really is the same player we saw struggle haplessly a few seasons ago. And we conveniently forget the Dean Austins, the Jason Dozzells, the Justin Edinburghs, the Stuart Nethercotts, the Paolo Tramezzanis, the Helder Postigas, the Colin Calderwoods and the Jason Cundys who played alongside some of these legends, and made watching the team for long periods of the 1990s and the early years of this century a living hell. There wasn't much of the Spurs Way about the teams of Gerry Francis, George Graham, Jacques Santini and Christian Gross.

Decades of underachievement? Tick. An heroic sense of injustice? Tick. A pathological ability to rewrite failure as success? Tick. A seemingly infinite capacity for self-destruction. Tick. Selective memory. Tick. Yes, I'd say Spurs and I were made for each other. But there's more; much more. There's also an undeniable sense of the absurd – a rich strand of comedy – written into the club's DNA. Naturally, this is not something any side is terribly keen to admit, especially when it's trying to position itself as a top-four team, but it's there nonetheless.

It's there in our choice of manager. Manchester United have Fergie's reign of Stalinist terror; Arsenal have the myopic, professorial Wenger; Chelsea – until recently – had the Italian bureaucrat, Ancelotti. We have Harry Redknapp, wide boy par excellence, under investigation for financial irregularities and a man with a gift for the one-liner. And he suits us perfectly. After decades of struggling with workmanlike Brits and minor European technicians, we're playing our best football since the Keith Burkinshaw years under a man who could have had a walk-on part in a Carry On film.

Most of all, though, there's the fallibility. Good as it sounds in theory to be a Manchester United fan, guaranteed to collect at least one piece of silverware per season, there doesn't seem to be much joy to be found there. One regulation win after another, with no one really needing to break sweat. Least of all the supporters. Where's the fun in that? Indeed, in a moment of weakness, my mate Kevin the Bright – he is very bright, despite being a Chelsea fan – recently confessed he rather missed the old days at Stamford Bridge, when his side was slipping to a home defeat to QPR on a crap pitch in front of a crowd of about 25,000, because then he was at least aware he was alive and watching a contest and not just a cog in a corporate machine bankrolled by a Russian oligarch.

Nor do I quite have the stomach for life as a Wolves fan, though I have more than a sneaking admiration for those who do. I'm just too much of a thrill-seeker; too much of an attention-seeker, come to think of it. I couldn't hack the endless backs-to-the-wall, try-to-sneak-a-goal-on-the-break afternoons, with avoiding relegation the only real aim, and the knowledge your best players will be bought by someone else the only certainty. My fragile psyche needs at least the possibility of glory; though equally it needs the probability of disappointment. It needs to be tantalised with riches and rewarded with next to nothing. In short, I need an abusive relationship. And Spurs are the perfect partner.

That's how it looks in hindsight, at any rate, though it could all be a convenient psychological retrofit. But somehow I like to think not. With their occasional high points and their many, many low points, the Spurs team have played out my life on the pitch with uncanny accuracy. They are my mirror. I watch them and I see me. And the longer it's gone on, the deeper the narcissistic attraction has become. I know that each season is almost certain to end in some kind of disappointment – years and years of following the club have taught me that – but still I keep coming back for more. And I can't imagine it any other way. Indeed, I can only see it getting worse. Having both hit the wrong side of fifty, my wife Jill and I now and again have 'the retirement conversation'. Something I do my best to curtail, because it invariably makes me look shabby. While she talks of all the things we could do together – places to visit, nights out at the theatre, that kind of thing – in my own mind I see retirement as an opportunity to go to every Spurs game, home and away, not just as many as possible, as I do now. And for some reason, my suggestion that she could come with me, and this could be a thing we do together in retirement, doesn't go down too well.

Not that retirement and existential futility were much to the front of my mind when I was nine. Indeed, life took a significant turn for the better in 1967 when another afternoon in front of the telly yielded up an FA Cup final victory against Chelsea, a triumph I suspect I took wholly in my stride. With the logic of childhood, Spurs were my team; ergo they win. End of. Sometime over the next few years that worldview must have come under threat, but what I really remember was how hard it became to support Spurs back then.

For some reason, no doubt linked both to them having no interest in football and a round trip of 200 miles up the old A4 – the M4 stopped at Maidenhead then – to a destination they were as hazy of as me, my parents managed to fend off my intermittent demands to be taken to White Hart Lane. So my support had to be conducted as a long-distance affair, something which was a great deal harder then than it is now.

Televised football was on a drip-feed. *Match of the Day* only featured one game per week – later increased to two – and was on at a time that required my mum to be in an exceptionally good mood to allow me to stay up, while ITV's Sunday offering, *The Big Match*, also only featured one game. So the chances of Spurs appearing more than once a month, at most, were slim. Nor were there pages and pages of football stories in the newspapers; it was starvation rations for a young boy. I got by on *Charles Buchan's Football Monthly*, a fairly dull magazine, even by the standards of the day, save for one thing: the small ads for old football programmes. For a few pennies – my entire pocket money, near enough – I could get the programmes to every game to which my parents were too mean to take me. I never read them that thoroughly when they arrived. Mostly I'd look longingly at the photos – the goals I'd missed – before stacking them neatly away in my bedroom.

At some point I was given a scarf, but mostly my relationship with Spurs existed in my imagination – a shimmy of emotional trickery I've been accused of many times since. I didn't have that many friends; partly because my being both a vicar's son and going to boarding school was a resistible combination to many people my age, but also because I was an awkward sod. I felt trapped in the countryside, and I wanted nothing to do with any of the outdoor activities – horses, mainly – the other middle-class kids lapped up. Nature Boy I wasn't. Rather, during the holidays, I'd spend days at home watching TV with a chair on my head. I'm still not quite sure how it got there. What I really wanted was to live in a town. Somewhere near N17, preferably.

But we did have a decent-sized garden, and with a bit of help from my dad, I rigged up a goal. The net was vitally important. Most goals on the school pitches I played on came without it. And I'd spend hours out there kicking a ball into it, dreaming I was Jimmy Greaves. Sometimes I could guilt-trip my mum into standing in goal; somehow it felt more satisfying to hit the back of the net when there was a notional goalie – even one that never dived. Best of all was when my sister, Sue, could be persuaded to join in; my sister Veronica, who was nearly six years older than me, had understandably long since decided she had better things to do than play with me. Then my mum was allowed out of goal and to impersonate Alan Gilzean on the edge of the six-yard box. The balding Scotsman would have been distraught if he'd known how many open goals he'd missed.

For about a year, my parents tried to cure me of my Spurs habit by taking me to see Swindon Town. The club may have been in the old Third Division but here at last was live football, and quite decent football at that. This was the Swindon of Peter Downsborough, John Trollope, Rod Thomas, Stan Harland, Roger Smart and the legendary Don Rogers, and this was the season they won promotion to the Second Division and beat Arsenal in the League Cup, and I went to nearly every home game. But when push came to shove, I was still Spurs. It was the Spurs results I looked out for first, and as Swindon began to struggle, my attendance petered out. I just wasn't that committed. Swindon still remain my second team; but a long way second. There's not been even a flicker of sentiment on the rare occasions the teams have played one another in the passing years.

I did finally make it to White Hart Lane for a third-round FA Cup replay against Nottingham Forest in 1975. I went on my own as I didn't have anyone else to go with, and just followed the crowd leaving the station to the nearest turnstile and ended up standing behind the goal at the Park Lane end. Forest were in the Second Division and we were expected to romp it; when they took the lead and the away fans started going mad, the bloke standing next to me said, 'Right. Let's go and do the cunts.' With my unerring ability to be in the wrong place at the wrong time, I'd managed to position myself right in the middle of the Spurs hardcore. 'Er, right,' I said, having no intention of following the mini-exodus across the terraces to where the Forest fans were grouped. A few minutes later, there was a full-scale fight taking place between opposing fans and the police. The upside was that I had rather more elbow room for the rest of the match; the downside was that we still lost.

There weren't any fights for my next two games but we lost those, too, and I'd begun to wonder if I'd ever see the team win. It was fourth time lucky, but by then I had reconciled myself to only going to White Hart Lane once or twice a season. It was just too much like hard work getting there any more often, either, from Exeter, where I went to university, or from south London, where I've lived ever since, what with unimpressed girlfriends, unfortunate lifestyle choices and, more latterly, kids of my own. I got by on the occasional hit of live action and a lot of TV, as the arrival of first the video recorder and then Sky Sports (my wife said it was her or Sky Sports; I called her bluff and she didn't divorce me) have made it fairly easy to catch at least highlights of every Spurs game. Which, for many years, wasn't necessarily a blessing.

Things began to look up in the early years of this century – if not in the quality of the live football, at least in its frequency – as the kids got older and required less looking after and I had more free time to do what I wanted, rather than hang around one playground after another pushing them on swings. More to the point, I could take them with me to the football. Or I could have done, if they had let me.

Meet my daughter Anna. Gorgeous, talented, clever. But stroppy as hell and never a girl willingly to do what she's asked. I think she must have been about ten when she realised just how much Spurs meant to me and what a foul mood I got in when we lost. Because that's when she told me, 'I support Manchester United.'

'Don't be ridiculous,' I replied. 'No one in this house supports Manchester United.'

'Well I do.'

I didn't push it. I just assumed she was trying and succeeding in winding me up, and that in a few days she'd get bored of it and see sense. She didn't. 'I still support Manchester United,' she announced some weeks later. 'David Beckham is cool.'

And that was that. Anna had found a chink in my defences and had no intention of backing down. I'd made a big error, and was going to be punished for it for years to come. I'd assumed that because I support Spurs, my children were going to do so as well. I'd lost one child but I wasn't going to lose the other. Osmosis wasn't enough; more positive action was required. So Robbie, three-and-a-bit years younger than Anna, began to be rewarded for ostentatious displays of support – many of them undoubtedly fake – with all sorts of Spurs goodies and, after a while, the occasional trip to White Hart Lane. This could have backfired badly; a nine-year-old doesn't have the concentration to last a ninety-minute game without getting a bit bored, and there were some games when I could tell he was dying to go home. Sweets helped a lot, and I got away with it. I persevered and he persevered. I made him a junior member and now he has his own season ticket, sitting next to me. Over time, I've learned not to push things. He's fifteen now and, though it seems odd to me, he's got better things to do than go to every game, especially those involving the less glamorous clubs. But that's OK, because I can always find someone else to take instead. The main thing is that he's Spurs for life.

Which brings us back to the present. In some ways, the pre-season is my favourite time of the year because it's when I don't have to feel stressed. I've managed to recover from the dramas of the previous season and the coming one is still a set of infinite untested possibilities, a time when reality doesn't need to get in the way. At the beginning of each season I manage to delude myself that this is the year we will make the breakthrough, the year we will win the FA Cup, the year we will finally qualify for the Champions League. And as last season was the year we did that last bit, you'd imagine I was full of optimism for this coming one; instead, I feel a dark sense of foreboding. The higher you climb, the further you fall. Hubris is only moments away.

Even the previous season had been a slight disappointment. I know that's not the way most people saw it, but it's the way it was for me. Yes, I was as thrilled as anyone to finish in the top four, but the game that really sticks in my memory is the FA Cup semi-final defeat to Portsmouth. The miserable tube journey that took the best part of two hours, due to engineering works; freezing to death in the ice-cold, soulless Wembley – is there a worse place to watch football in England?; the Spurs team that chose that day of all days not to bother to play; the crap pitch that led to Michael Dawson slipping on his arse and presenting Portsmouth with their first goal; the cretin of a referee who disallowed Crouch's equaliser. Fuck it, he scores few enough, so it's doubly galling when the ref arbitrarily rules one out.

Yeah, John, my friends said, but if we hadn't lost that game we wouldn't have gone on to beat Arsenal and Chelsea the following week. Possibly. But possibly not. How the hell do they know? How much better would it have been to qualify for Europe and win the FA Cup? So the Portsmouth game still rankles. And those with short memories would do well to remember what happened in our final game of the previous season, the game after we beat Manchester City. Two-nil up and cruising midway through the first half away to a Burnley side that was already relegated, the team took a collective decision to end the season prematurely and conceded four goals in the process. As I've said, triumph and disaster are never too far away from one another with Spurs.

The best bit about the pre-season is the amount of time you can waste in entirely fruitless speculation. At a rough estimate, Harry Redknapp had been reported to be in talks to bring about fifty new players to the club over the course of the last two months, including Joe Cole, Raúl, Cardozo, Forlán, Cahill, Falcao, Huntelaar, Bellamy, Parker, Fabiano, Ireland, Marin, Dzeko and Özil. We were also apparently going to swap Jermaine Jenas, David Bentley and Robbie Keane for Villa's Ashley Young and Peter Crouch for Liverpool's Ryan Babel. Of course we were. If even one of these deals came off I'd have been amazed, but that's not the point. The constant flow of disinformation is reward enough in itself, as I can spend hours avoiding the rest of my life with no real stress attached. The only confirmed deal had been to buy the holding midfielder, Sandro, from Brazil – a player no one, including the manager, seemed to know the first thing about. The club were talking him up, but then Manchester United were talking up Bébé.

The downside to this time of year is all the pre-season friendlies. I understand the point of them – get players match-fit, try out different players – but as a spectacle they offer next to nothing, as the game is played at a walking pace and with barely a competitive tackle made. Yet I still find them hard to resist. Every year, I can't stop myself looking at the fixture list and even though there's this voice yelling in my head, 'Don't do it, John. Remember how dull it was last year', I find myself buying tickets regardless. This year it was Fiorentina. 'Oooh, I've never seen Fiorentina. And my friend Barry supports them. Maybe we could go together.' The deal was done. Two tickets it was. I clicked the confirm tab on the website, and another £60 disappeared from my bank account.

It was nearly a lot worse, though. Jill's mother lives in San Francisco and as it had been about five years since we'd last visited her, we thought it was about time. By chance Spurs had also decided to make their first trip to California in ages to play the San Jose Earthquakes on the very day we arrived, and I had worked out that if we left our luggage at the airport and hired a car we could get to San Jose in time for kick-off. And I would have done it if Jill hadn't thrown a complete wobbly when I suggested it for the third time.

Checking the result that evening online, it became clear Jill had not just saved herself from me, she had saved me from myself as the game had been a sterile, lifeless, snail-paced 1-1 draw. In any case, I hadn't come away entirely empty-handed, as I'd emailed her cousins in San Jose to get me as many souvenirs from the game – old tickets, programmes – as they could lay their hands on. To the collector, nerd, saddo, call me what you will, this clobber is gold dust. Any fool can get a programme or a used ticket from a Premier League fixture – or even a cup final – on eBay for next to nothing; it's just a numbers game if you think about the quantities issued. But a friendly played 8,000 miles away from White Hart Lane in front of about 10,000 spectators, most of whom won't have been that interested in football – now that's an item worth having. And so it proved. Within days of the San Jose game being played, programmes and tickets were being hawked for upward of £20 on eBay. Not sure how many people paid that, mind.

There was a nice coda to the San Jose game, though. About a week later, Robbie and I were sitting by the hotel pool in LA, as you do, observing this hunk-like English wannabe actor prattling on in the hot tub to a couple of rather beautiful and clearly impressed women, wearing next to nothing, about how his agent had sent him for this audition and how such and such a director like totally thought he was awesome.

'The guy's a dick,' said Robbie.

'Total.'

We decided to get a little closer to the action and joined them in the hot tub. Five minutes later the hunk says, 'I can't help noticing your tattoo. [All these years later, Jill still hasn't forgiven me for getting THFC inked on to my shoulder.] I'm a huge Spurs fan myself.'

'Really?'

'Yeah. Last week I drove up to San Jose to see them play the Earthquakes. I haven't been able to get to White Hart Lane for years, and it was just awesome to see the team play again.'

Respect. A bloke who will make a round trip of nearly 1,000 miles just to see what turned out to be pretty much a second XI – most of the stars were rested – play a non-competitive match. That's dedication. We got talking about the team, our prospects and for about ten minutes became the best of mates, before he noticed that the babes were beginning to nod off and leaped out of the hot tub to give them his full-on attention.

'He wasn't such a dick, after all,' I said.

'Nah,' Robbie agreed. 'He's a bit of a player, in fact.'

Such is the power of Spurs, though I wasn't feeling much of the power when the Fiorentina fixture finally came round in early August. Barry had turned out to be on holiday and couldn't make it, and even though I had roped in my friend, John, to take his place, what little sense of purpose the match had held for me had largely dissipated before it had started. And yet I still always get that sense of excitement as I make the drive from Streatham to Tottenham. My pulse quickens and worries temporarily vanish. It still amazes me. I've had years and years of therapy, mostly dedicated to making me less self-destructive, less neurotic and generally easier to be around, and the only time when I can be certain not to be fretting about whether my family hates me, if I'm about to be sacked or about to die of cancer is during the two hours before a game and the match itself. I guess there's only so much anxiety any psyche can take at one time, and for those four hours Spurs have my undivided neurosis.

The ritual is always the same. The text alert with the team sheet comes through forty-five minutes before kick-off. I park the car near Bruce Castle and we walk the fifteen minutes to the ground, the sense of communion building as the numbers walking in the same direction increase the closer we get. I don't feel safe in many places, but I do feel safe in White Hart Lane. It's odd, I know, and probably an entirely misplaced sense of security but I feel like I am amongst friends or, if not friends, then people who wish me no harm, people who for just a few hours believe in and want the same things as me. And some are friends, people I've got to know over the years either through proximity or a shared obsession.

Not many of them were in evidence for this match, though. Season tickets don't apply for friendlies and seats had been allocated on a first-come, first-served basis, so we're in amongst strangers. It didn't really matter, though, as the game was the passionless affair it was always going to be. The main interest centred on the new shirt sponsors. For the past three years the club had been sponsored by Mansion, an online poker company. Barcelona had Unicef, Manchester United had insurance giant AIG, Chelsea had Samsung, Arsenal had Emirates airline and we had a tacky online betting company nobody had ever heard of whose sole purpose was to relieve its customers of shed-loads of cash. No one was sorry Mansion decided not to renew the deal, so now we had Autonomy. I'd never heard of them either. Apparently they are a software company, which is a step up from online gambling. And the kit looked a great deal better, too, so it was an improvement all round. The match ended with us snatching a last-minute goal to sneak a 3-2 win, so everybody left happy. Even in a game where no one is trying very hard, winning is always preferable to losing.

And so to the main event, the first Premier League game of the season. And so to the first episode of marital disharmony. Jill often affects surprise that football could possibly be more interesting than spending time with her, and maintains she had no idea what she was letting herself in for when we got married. The facts don't back her up. We met on holiday in Crete in 1982. More specifically at Gatwick airport on the way out.

Jill had planned to go on holiday with three other friends: a couple and a single man. A week before departure, the single bloke dropped out and Jill asked the couple if they knew anyone else who might be able to come at short notice. She had been hoping for someone lively and with a decent career; what she got was me. I was the only person they could find who had so little going on he could make it.

The couple spent a great deal of each day holding hands and much of the evenings in bed, so Jill and I got to spend a lot of time with each other in the bar just down the road from the apartment where we were staying. We would sit there for hours every day, getting trashed – the early 1980s weren't my finest years – and watching the World Cup on a black and white television. I scarcely missed a game. Whenever I remind her of this she insists she had no idea I had chosen the bar precisely because it was the only one that had a TV.

'Why did you think we were going to a bar where you couldn't hear yourself think for the traffic from the American naval base thundering by?'

'I hadn't given it any thought.'

'Didn't you notice the football was on?'

'Yes. But I thought it was just a coincidence.'

'Seriously?'

'I wasn't thinking straight. I had no one else to talk to and you seemed quite pretty. If a bit thick.'

I can't even claim prettiness these days, and football has remained a nagging reminder to her of how she allowed herself to be conned into having a relationship with me. Generally this causes her less distress at the beginning of the season as she's had three months to wipe clean the memory, but this year Anna's student theatre company were going to the Edinburgh Fringe for the first time, and like the good parents we longed to be we were going to Scotland to see her. The sticking point was that Jill had decided the only time we could possibly go during Anna's three-week run was the first weekend of the Premier League season. If Spurs had been away to Blackburn – no disrespect, it's just a long way away – I wouldn't have had an issue, but the first game was Manchester City at home, a key game now that City had tried to buy almost every footballer in the world costing more than £20 million – including some not worth half the money – in their desperation to qualify for the Champions League. We had reached a moderately bad-tempered compromise. She would go to Scotland first thing on the Saturday morning. I would go to the match, race straight to Gatwick and fly up separately in the evening. It sounded a fair arrangement to me, but there were still mutterings.

The Manchester City game is one I had often been to with Will, a die-hard City fan, though these outings had always been a great deal more enjoyable for me than for him, as the score had always been 2-1 to Spurs. To make matters worse he has always had to sit with me among the Spurs fans, so he hadn't even been able to celebrate the minor excitement of a City goal. Last season, he turned refusenik, saying he was sick to death of watching City lose 2-1 and missed out on the chance of seeing them lose 3-0 instead. But I was keen to get Will back in tow; City looked stronger this year, and they would be keen to get revenge for May, so a lucky talisman could be useful.

'Sorry,' he said unapologetically. 'I'm on holiday.'

As was Robbie, who was away with friends. As was almost everyone who didn't make a habit of arranging their holiday dates around the start of the football season. Which was how I came to be going with Joanna, quite the unlikeliest friend with whom I had ever gone to a football match. Joanna is very funny and great company, but her knowledge of football is almost matched by her interest – next to nothing. But her son had started to become keen on the game, she felt she should make an effort and why look a gift ticket in the mouth? Because her son supports Arsenal, for a start. When I arrived to collect Joanna there was a distinct *froideur*; her son was outraged his mother's first ever football match should be at White Hart Lane. He had a point, but there was bugger all I could do about it except get out of the house as fast as possible.

Getting into the ground itself took slightly longer than normal. Instead of the usual numbered booklets, this year's season tickets were swipe cards and no one – especially the ground staff on the turnstiles – seemed too sure how they worked. I had greater misgivings about them than most, and not just because I still hadn't wholly forgiven the club for sending out the invitation to renew my season ticket so that it arrived the morning after our clueless FA Cup exit. Impeccable timing, as ever. The problem was this. The deal with the old season tickets meant you got two cup games included in the deal, and if we played any more you had to buy them on top and got sent out a ticket. Much the same applied this year, only there would be no tickets sent out as the club could merely upgrade your swipe card online. This was obviously cost-saving, technologically efficient, environmentally friendly and all that, but it was a disaster for people like me who collect old ticket stubs. There wouldn't be many – if any – printed, and if you wanted to get your hands on them, you'd have to pay silly money on eBay. It was almost as bad for Premiership games, because club members (one step down from season-ticket holders) also got a swipe card on which their tickets could be uploaded, so there would be sod all used tickets for these matches, too. I was pissed off and undecided whether to bother collecting this season's tickets, or just concentrate on filling in my gaps from the 1950s, 1960s and 1970s.

Inside the ground, it was back to the same as we were. The same two seats in the lower east side, as last year. And, pleasingly, much the same faces as last year. There's Trevor just a few seats ago, an even more fanatical Spurs collector than myself, who I met via eBay and coincidentally turned out to sit just a few seats to my right in the same row. He's become a friend. And then there are the seven or eight blokes immediately in front and behind. I haven't a clue what they are called, but we always say hello and chat before the game and at half-time. And at the odd moment during. We have also done a fair bit of hugging over time. To my left should be Justin and Amici, the ideal football next-door neighbours; Justin remains the only person in the East stand still convinced of Crouchie's genius. But these two weren't here today. I was hoping it was because they were still on holiday and not because they didn't renew their tickets.

The game was a stalemate. Spurs dominated pretty much throughout with Bale, Defoe, Pavlyuchenko and Crouchie – yes, really – going close without scoring, while our usual comedy defending ensured it wasn't an entirely one-sided 0-0 draw. Predictably also, as Spurs failed to make their dominance count, it was the match officials who copped it for a series of increasingly doubtful decisions.

It all became too much for one bloke near us.

'Oi, lino. You're a cunt,' he shouted.

'Is the lino always a cunt?' asked Joanna.

'Pretty much,' I said.

One point isn't quite what we're used to from a home game with City, but it was a result I could live with, not just because plenty of other sides would struggle against them, but because it was a start. I know we're supposed to think of ourselves as a top-four club now, but I can't stop myself counting my way to forty: the number of points a team should need to be safe from relegation. I've followed the club for too long to take anything for granted. So one down, thirty-nine to go. I wasn't the only one pleased with the result. Joanna's son, brought up to expect three points every time Arsenal play at the Emirates, was overjoyed at what he saw as two points lost, so our friendship was restored. And Anna was great in *Clockwork Orange* the following day in Edinburgh, too.

***

It wasn't strictly accurate to say Spurs had qualified for the Champions League. What they had done was qualified to play a knock-out tie to qualify for the Champions League, though everyone rather assumed this was a formality when Spurs were drawn to play Young Boys of Bern – a team of which almost no one had heard and which, on further investigation, appeared to have made a fairly disastrous start to their season in Switzerland. The papers certainly seemed to think the result was a foregone conclusion, and even the diehard Spurs bloggers didn't think this was one we could screw up; so it was probably only me who entertained a few doubts, born more of a default pessimism than from any real sense of impending disaster. Deep down, even I thought this was a done deal.

But a first outing in the European big league since 1961 was still a game not to be missed; on past form there was a strong possibility I would be long dead before the chance arose again. Getting to Bern proved unexpectedly difficult. You'd have thought that flying to the capital of an affluent western European country would be a piece of piss these days. Try it. I typed in London and Bern into the Expedia website. Up came Lufthansa flights requiring a stopover in Munich, with an outward journey of five hours and forty minutes and a return one of seven hours, at the knockdown price of £808. It would have been a lot cheaper and almost as quick to go to New York. And that was the best offer. There was also a nine-hour each-way flight with stopovers at Hanover and Munich for £838.

Out came the map. The only cheap flights were to Zurich or Basel, both of which were more than sixty miles from the capital; either way we'd have to hire a car.

'What do you reckon?' I said to Matthew.

'Well, we've obviously got to do it,' he replied.

Matthew hadn't been waiting for this moment for quite as long as me – he's eleven years younger – but his wait had been a lot more tragic. He had been brought up in London, his father had been a shelf-side regular, he had started going to games in 1980 and, as soon as he got a job, he had got a season ticket of his own. He paid his dues every weekend throughout the 1990s when Spurs were playing some of the dullest football in the club's history.

To anaesthetise himself from the pain of the Gerry Francis years, Matthew ill-advisedly acquired an expensive personal habit that first cost him his job, then his house and, last of all, his season ticket. At least he had his priorities right. It took Matthew a good few years to reacquire the job and the life, by which time there was a long waiting list for the season ticket. In the 1990s, the club could barely give a season ticket away; when our friend, Theo, first applied for one he was invited on a stadium tour and allowed to hand-pick his seat. Now you have to pay to become a club member just to get on the waiting list. Matthew is currently number 35,000 and hanging on for a miracle. With a small annual turnover and only about 23,000 season tickets on offer in total, he could be in for a long wait.

'OK,' I said. 'There's an afternoon flight from Heathrow that gets in at about five. We should be able to make it to

Bern in plenty of time. And there's a flight back at seven in the morning, so we could save money by sleeping at the airport. There should be somewhere to kip.'

'Sounds fine. Anything you want me to do?'

'Work out the route from the airport to the ground.'

All was going well till we arrived in Basel and approached the car-hire desk.

'Do you have the directions?' I asked Matthew.

'Ah . . . the directions. Well, not exactly . . .'

That piece of foresight cost us the hire of a satnav as the car rental agent assured us he didn't have any maps detailed enough to get us to the stadium, but as we cruised into Bern little more than an hour later we were both upbeat. There had been next to no traffic and next to no signs of life in Bern. I'd had more trouble navigating my way round my mum's home town in Hampshire. We parked the car near a circus and walked towards the stadium.

'It's called the Wankdorf,' I sniggered.

'It's part of a shopping centre,' Matthew added.

'It doesn't look very big,' I said.

'And who the fuck calls themselves Young Boys?'

After an anaemic-looking sausage and a quick chat to two old Spurs friends, Rick and Neil, whom we met outside the ground, we went inside. There our complacency ended. At the other end of the near-full ground was the Young Boys hardcore: stripped to the waist, hopping up and down in unison and letting off coloured smoke flares. These were serious fans.

'Er . . . I think we might have taken them a little bit for granted,' Matthew said.

'Just a bit.'

We weren't the only ones. Within half an hour we were 3-0 down with a player sent off and it could easily have been worse. Young Boys had also hit the post, gone close on several other occasions and looked like scoring every time they got into our half. We weren't just bad, we were awful. Before the game, there had been a lot of talk about the Young Boys' artificial pitch, so you would have thought the Spurs team might have prepared for it beforehand at home. It didn't look that way. Intended passes were flying over people's heads or bouncing well in front of players and then steepling over their heads. Two completed passes were a rarity.

At 1-0 down, I groaned. Typical fucking Spurs, always have to give the oppo a start. At 2-0, I had my head in my hands. Why, why, why? At 3-0, I had all but given up. Matthew could barely watch. Only an unexpected and undeserved goal from Kaboul just before the break made half-time remotely bearable. Within seconds of the whistle, the texts from my Arsenal-supporting friends started coming in. 'Oh well, there's always next year.' I'd lost the will to respond. Or even delete.

The second half showed a moderate improvement: occasionally we managed to complete three passes, but we still didn't look much like scoring. No one could have complained at a 4-1 or 5-1 scoreline. Then, against the run of play, Pav, who had done nothing all night, scores a great goal from an acute angle: 3-2. Under the circumstances, we'd definitely take that.

The Spurs fans were kept in for half an hour at the end of the game, and Matthew and I went over to join Rick and Neil. The only feeling was relief. Somehow we had got out of jail and given ourselves a decent chance in the return home leg, but God knows how. We had been outplayed and – in truth – out-supported. The Bern fans hadn't stopped jumping and singing all night; all we could manage apart from the ecstasy of the two goals was the odd, unconvincing chorus of 'Come on you Spurs'. Even that was more than the team deserved.

'Why do we always have to make things so difficult for ourselves?' I said.

'Because we are Spurs,' said Rick, a man who has seen more Spurs games than anyone else I know.

It was about 11.30 p.m. by the time we got back to the car. Bern looked every bit as dead as it had a few hours earlier.

'What shall we do about food?' Matthew asked.

'There doesn't look to be much here. Let's stop at a motorway services on the way back to Basel,' I suggested.

The main services closed at midnight, half an hour before our arrival. Dinner was crisps, chocolate and Diet Coke. It got even worse at Basel, as the airport was also almost totally shut down and there was nowhere comfortable to kip.

'We're better off sleeping in the car,' said Matthew.

'I'm too fucking old for this,' I replied, grumpily. The car was too small to stretch out and, to make things worse, it hadn't occurred to me that even in late August the nights were quite chilly in Switzerland, and I hadn't packed anything warm to wear in my rucksack. So I got two hours' sleep at best; and froze. It was the most miserable night I'd had in years. All that went right was that the plane left on time and I was back at work feeling like shite by about ten the following morning.

'Still, it was well worth it, wasn't it?' said Matthew, as I dropped him off in Hammersmith.

Yep. It probably was.

***

There was never any danger of me sneaking up to Stoke for the following Saturday's league game so soon after a midweek jaunt to Switzerland, but Gareth Bale's double and a Spurs victory made it a satisfactory late night's viewing. Satisfactory because I didn't have to find some other rubbish on the TV; I just can't bring myself to watch *Match of the Day* when I know Spurs have lost. I know it's pathetic, but it's just too painful. In any case, the main event, the return leg with Young Boys, was just days away.

My sleep has been fairly rubbish for years; a combination of anxiety, work, depression and general neurosis means an uninterrupted six hours is worthy of high fives all round. Before a big game, insomnia is almost guaranteed. It wasn't always like this. When I was young I had the unswerving belief we were going to win, so I slept the sleep of the just. The subsequent defeat always came as a shock. As I grew older, I wised up. I learned to accept failure as the probable outcome, so never really considered the alternative. Defeat was just another day like any other; certainly not one worth losing sleep over. Then things changed again. The team started playing well enough to encourage me to believe that they might just win: more than that even, that they really ought to win, that if they didn't life would be terrible. And I started to feel my mortality. It's not a great combination. As someone who measures his life in football seasons, I can feel that time is running out. When you're young, there's always another game, another year around the corner; at my age there are fewer and fewer years around the corner and it begins to dawn on you there might be no more trophies or major thrills to be had. I might have had my lot.

It was with a sense of exhausted dread, rather than excitement, that I headed back to White Hart Lane for what, on paper, looked a doddle of a return leg against Young Boys. All we needed was a win by any score against a mediocre team. I was far from the only person feeling this way; everyone I passed looked much the same. The only small relief being the discovery that for the first time in living memory, the gents' toilets in the East stand had hot water. Hurrah for the financial pulling power of the Champions League.

I got to my seat to find Justin and Amici had renewed their season tickets after all. Good. I would miss them if they went elsewhere.

'Hi,' I said, resuming our friendship after a four-month spell on hold. 'How do you see it? Squeaky-pants night?'

'Yeah,' said Amici. 'It will be hell. They are bound to put us through it.'

'Nah,' Justin interrupted. 'We're going to cruise it. Crouchie will do the business.'

He'd said that countless times in the past, but for once he was right. Crouchie did score early on; midway through the first half, Defoe doubled the lead by controlling the ball with his hand before firing in a left-foot shot. Thankfully the ref was too dopey to spot the offence. We tried to gift Young Boys a way back into the game with some witless defending, but the Swiss couldn't take advantage and

Crouchie scored twice more as we cruised to an easy 4-0 win.

'Go Crouchie,' Justin shouted.

'Go Crouchie,' I echoed. The giant had done it, after all. The man who could barely buy a goal in the Premier League was unstoppable for both England and in Europe. I could only imagine it was because international and European football are generally played at a much slower pace, so Crouchie's poor first touch doesn't matter that much when he's got enough time for a second. Anyway, what the hell. Tonight Crouchie was a god, though I was left feeling emotionally short-changed. Here we were, finally achieving something I'd dreamed about for years and I just feel a bit 'so what?'. Was this it? It somehow all felt a bit anticlimactic. Was there nothing I couldn't spoil for myself?

***

It wasn't just me who knew how to spoil things. After qualifying for the Champions League, and getting a dream draw against the champions Inter Milan and the anonymous Werder Bremen and FC Twente, everything came down to earth with a bump against Wigan. Here was a match that not even I had pencilled in for anything less than three points.

The previous year we had won the game 9-1, a match I will never forget. Not for the scoreline, nor for Defoe's five goals, but for Scharner's handball – an offence so obvious it was seen by everyone in the stadium apart from the match officials – that preceded Wigan's solitary goal. This was an injustice not to be ignored: so while Spurs happily continued to clock up goal after goal, the main thing of interest to the fans in my block – and, I would be willing to bet, elsewhere – was booing Scharner every time he touched the ball and cheering the ref ironically when he got a decision right. It was an object lesson in fan power, in fans setting their own agenda for the after-noon's entertainment. And an object lesson in the Spurs' fans perverse ability to focus on the one thing that's going wrong.

On this day, though, in the following season, just about everything that could have gone wrong did go wrong. A year or so before, Robbie had impressed me with a sto-icism beyond his age. We were leaving the ground after an excruciatingly dull 0-0 draw at home to Hull, and I was dreading him saying he wasn't going to come again for a while if he had to watch that all over again. I'd always thought that I got rather more out of our trips to White Hart Lane than he did: fathers tend to have a much bigger investment in spending time with their teenage children than their children do in spending time with them, and the style of the 0-0 draw, as much as the scoreline itself, could have tipped him over the edge. Instead, he said, 'I rather enjoyed that.' It seemed unlikely but he appeared to mean it, and I wasn't about to contradict him. And while I did feel a little guilty that I had managed to lower a thirteen-year-old's expectations to such a level that a crap game was enjoyable, it was undoubtedly a seminal moment in our football relationship. He was now a Spurs fan through and through. We would be going to games together for years to come.

Not even Robbie could find a kind word to say about this Wigan game, though. It was beyond awful. The players seemed barely familiar either with the ball or with each other. I'd seen more accomplished performances for free on Tooting Bec Common. The feeling in the stands was that the team had been spending rather too long celebrating their Champions League success – no season is complete without some of the team being papped falling legless out of an Essex nightclub at 4 a.m.

We might have put up with it if the score had stayed at 0-0. But with eighty minutes played, Wigan suddenly twigged that it wasn't a mirage and we actually were playing far worse than them. At which point, Rodallega ventured out of his half for the first time and kicked the ball speculatively towards the Spurs goal. Cudicini, playing instead of the injured Gomes, hopelessly mistimed his dive and the ball bounced over him into the net. Game over.

After the match, Harry moaned about the fans booing the players off the pitch, saying we'd got spoiled by success. I felt the boos were deserved. They weren't for the defeat itself – heaven knows, most of us have seen enough of those over the years – but for its manner. The team was just unprofessional, with half the players looking utterly incompetent and the other half as if they wished they had stayed in bed. What's not to boo?

There are still a few old-school fans who believe booing your own team is the ultimate no-no, but they are becoming much thinner on the ground now it is ever harder to maintain the pretence that we are all involved in a two-way relationship with the club. Long gone are the days when players grew up near the club, stayed for life and felt a shared empathy with the supporters. There are a few – Michael Dawson, Heurelho Gomes and Gareth Bale in particular – who make noticeable efforts to bridge the gap, but we all know they are still mercenaries on borrowed time whom we can enjoy until they move onwards or downwards. Long gone, also, are the days when the club needed to go out of its way to court its fanbase to fill the ground; there's a waiting list of about 30,000 for season tickets, and it's growing by the year.

The sad reality is that the club doesn't need me. If I don't renew my season ticket, there are thousands of others who will be thrilled to take it off me. But – for a whole load of worrying reasons that will become apparent over the course of the season – I do seem to need the club. I am stuck, mostly happily stuck – entirely of my own volition, I should add – in a hopelessly one-sided relationship with my football team. Cheering and booing are, both literally and metaphorically, the only voice I have. And I'm in no hurry to give up 50 per cent of what little power I do have any time soon.

September

THE GOSSIP LINE WAS working overtime on the morning of 1 September. Every Spurs fan seemed to have something to say about the club's signing of the Dutch World Cup star, Rafael van der Vaart from Real Madrid just before the transfer window closed at midnight the day before. It was all positive. And why wouldn't it be? The Dutchman is a class act. That he was a total outlier, someone who hadn't been linked to any move in the closed season, someone who wasn't even officially available until mid-afternoon on 31 August, whom we had grabbed from under the noses of the top clubs in Europe for a bargain £8 million, made it all the sweeter.

Predictably, all the other transfer rumours had turned out to be the footie porn most of us suspected them to be at the time. Well, all except one. William Gallas. His signing on a free transfer did not get quite the same reception. Not because at thirty-three he was coming to the end of his playing career, but because he was coming from Arsenal.

It's at times like these that I wonder whether I really am Spurs through and through, as I'm not at all sure I quite hate Arsenal enough to qualify. Don't get me wrong:

I take nothing but pleasure in their defeats, and some of my greatest memories are of our victories over our north London rivals and I certainly never take anything for granted. When we were 4-1 up with ten minutes to play against them in the Carling Cup semi-final a few years back, and the rest of the crowd was already celebrating, I was telling my mate Terry they could still sneak a draw; it was only when Steed Malbranque tapped in a fifth in injury time that I felt secure enough to join in the festivities. I also happily join in the odd bit of Arsenal baiting – 'If you hate Arsenal, stand up' – and I try not to forget to send texts to my sister, Veronica and other Arsenal-supporting friends to share a laugh over the more ridiculous Wengerisms. But there is something of the pantomime about it all; my hatred just isn't that visceral.

There's been nothing fun about watching Spurs be mostly outplayed by Arsenal for the past fifteen years or so, but I do have a grudging respect for them. I know it's anathema, I know it's wrong, but I can't help it. They pass the ball well and they play good, attacking football, the sort that many Spurs fans claim as the trademark of their own club, despite the evidence before their own eyes. For long periods of our recent history we were playing precisely the dull, unimaginative football which was supposed to be Arsenal's house style. And we weren't even doing it very effectively.

My proper football hatreds – every fan should have them; *Schadenfreude* can offer rich pickings when your own team is struggling – are Manchester United and Chelsea. Is there anything more nauseating than the way Fergie expects the whole world to defer to him? The man hasn't spoken to the BBC for years now, after some perceived lese-majesty. And most people do fawn to him, with match-day commentators referring to him continuously as Sir Alex. What's going on? Fergie is a working-class Scot supposedly without a Tory bone in his body; surely he can't insist on his title being used on every occasion? His players get much the same treatment. I've no time for Joey Barton but Paul Scholes is every bit as dirty a player, and while Barton gets universally reviled Scholes is championed as a consummate professional. Talk about double standards. And before anyone accuses me of sour grapes, I felt this way long before Carrick – so sad he hasn't really progressed as a player – and Berbatov signed for United from Spurs.

My issues with Chelsea centre almost entirely on John Terry, or JT as he apparently likes to be called. The man who ostentatiously kisses his badge and likes to say he has Chelsea and England written on his heart. In the past four years, Spurs have had two tense 2-1 victories over Chelsea at White Hart Lane; both times the home team joy was doubled by Terry getting himself sent off.

As you can see, my football hatreds are all fairly petty and based on little information and extreme prejudice. In fact, they are hardly real hatreds at all; rather, they are more like pet hatreds, a way both of generating interest in games in which Spurs aren't playing, and extending my support for the team in its absence. It makes those 'Big European nights', as ITV and Sky like to call them, which don't feature Spurs, so much more enjoyable. The commentators have this idea that the entire country is behind Manchester United, Chelsea or Arsenal in games like these; that we're all against Johnny Foreigner. I'd be willing to bet the actual ratio is about 20:80, with the being those home-team fans who couldn't get to the game. Everyone else will be rooting for the oppo. The biggest disappointment of the recent Manchester United and Chelsea Champions League final was that both teams couldn't lose.

Other games are only a little more problematic. How do I choose between Stoke City and Everton – two teams about which I feel largely indifferent – when they play each other? Simply by studying Spurs' self-interest. I check out which team's loss would most benefit us, and support the other one. It's hardly rocket science. I do have a slight preference for London clubs, though, which, given that West Ham are also meant to be a bitter rival after Arsenal, again probably makes me a lightweight fan. All I can say in my defence is that it's motivated entirely by self-interest. It's got nothing to do with some tribal north–south divide. I don't want these other London clubs to win anything; I just don't want them to be relegated. I enjoy my away games at Upton Park and Craven Cottage. They are easy to get to, and require almost no negotiation with Jill.

All this is the kind of stuff that floats around my head to keep me amused between games. And there are no limits. My mind will always find more than enough footy crap to fill dead space and, as with the universe, that dead space seems to be still expanding as I undoubtedly think a great deal more about football now than I did ten or twenty years ago. Nor is it as if I think of nothing else: I think about family and friends, politics, literature, TV . . . all sorts; and I'm not aware of thinking about any of these any less. Rather the opposite.

I don't drink, so I guess I spend more time fully conscious

than a lot of people, but that doesn't feel like a sufficient explanation for why football takes up so much airtime in my head. Nor does the fact that every passing year means I have acquired more useless knowledge to think about. All I can say is that it is a much-needed displacement activity from being me, and one that is a great deal less self-destructive than many I've tried in the past. Transferring my own existential neuroses, disappointments and sense of futility to Spurs works well: even if we're playing well, we're only one game from it all going pear-shaped.

It also helps that my relationship with the club – apart from the scarf, the replica shirt, the memorabilia collection and the season tickets – takes place largely in my head. How I think about the players has changed in some respects since I was a kid; back then my heroes – Greavsie and Big Chiv (Martin Chivers) – were my avatars, running around doing what I wanted to do but couldn't, and even the lesser mortals who played with them I held in awe. Now, the mystique has gone. Mostly they exist fondly in my mind as talented, wayward, unwittingly comedic adolescents who are just as likely to do something idiotic as they are to create moments of genius.

They all have their little defining tics: Heurelho Gomes, aka the octopus, the goalkeeper with Teflon hands; Alan Hutton, the full-back who looks as if he'd get in a fight with his reflection; Benoît – Benny – Assou-Ekotto, whose right leg is redundant; Wilson Palacios – the Wilce – for whom no game is complete without a booking or a misplaced back pass: Tom Huddlestone – Hudd the Thudd – who can't run or tackle; Jermaine Defoe – Easy-O – who can't pass; and Aaron 'Azzer' Lennon who can beat four men before running into the corner flag. I could go on.

Yet in some way nothing has changed. I actually know as little about the current team as I did of teams past; I can work out the basics of who is confident, who is gobby and who is a bit of a slacker but, beyond that, what's really going on in the players' lives and minds is a mystery to me. And I prefer it like that. I don't want to read a nice, sanitised 'At home with Peter Crouch and Abbey Clancy' or even a not-very-nice, unsanitised 'Away with Peter Crouch and Monica Mint'. I want them to exist off the pitch largely as figments of my imagination, where I can bend them to my will and they can create havoc as extensions of my psyche. It's sometimes the closest they ever get to playing as a team.

Back in the real world, Redknapp's new signings were looking a better and better deal by the minute. There had been no Premier League action on the first weekend, as the football world was obliged to stop for some dreary qualifiers for Euro 2012, but that had not stopped two key Spurs players, Defoe and Dawson, from getting badly injured while on England duty. Yet another reason why international football is so often a curse.

I've always rather enjoyed the drive to Birmingham. The M40 is the most civilised motorway I know: it always seems to have far less traffic than other routes, and the miles tick past satisfactorily. It's being in Birmingham that's the problem. This isn't a dig at the city; I barely know the place apart from its football grounds. It's just that whenever I've gone to see Spurs play against Birmingham City or West Brom – for some reason I've never made it to Villa Park – they've invariably been fairly useless. It's as if the players arrive at St Andrew's and the Hawthorns and think, 'Nah, we don't fancy this much. The ground is a bit rubbish [they do have a point], the crowd is small, we'll probably be put last on *Match of the Day*, so we can't be bothered.'

So expectations weren't high when Matthew and I made it to the ground about three-quarters of an hour before kick-off. At least, mine weren't. No one else appeared to be thinking about the game in hand. There was a large Spurs contingent already there by the time we arrived, and they were all buzzing at the prospect of the first Champions League game away to Werder Bremen in a few days' time. Most of the chat was about how to get a ticket. Under UEFA guidelines, Bremen had only made 2,400 tickets available to Spurs fans, and just about everyone wanted to see our first ever game in the Champions League; the tickets had been allocated to season-ticket holders with the most loyalty points – in this case, a staggering 450-something points – so most people, myself included, had missed out. Still, that didn't seem to have deterred a lot of fans who were busy checking out the chancers who had gathered around the away end to hand out flyers offering cheap coach deals to Germany.

'Let's just get there,' was the general feeling, 'and we'll work out how to blag our way in on the day.' It seemed like a long way to go to watch the game in a German bar to me: I'd already decided to hang on for Milan. One man who was never going to have to hang on for anything was Rick, a friend who has barely missed a home or away game in decades. He has more than 1,200 loyalty points, more than he could ever possibly need for anything; he is a man who deserved Champions League football more than the team. With his distinctive full head of brilliant-grey hair, Rick is an unmissable figure in any Spurs crowd.

'Hi, John,' he said. 'You going to Bremen?'

'Couldn't get a ticket. Do you know of any going spare?' It seemed dumb not to ask on the off chance. If Rick couldn't hunt down a ticket, no one could.

'No, but I'll ask around.'

The Spurs fans weren't the only ones with one eye on Bremen: the team did too, given the way they played against a less skilled but bigger-hearted West Brom team that was clearly fed up with yo-yoing between the Premiership and the Championship and was buggered if it was going to be pushed around by some poncey Londoners who considered themselves too grand for an old-fashioned scrap.

As had become customary on my trips to Birmingham, Spurs cruised into a 1-0 lead, squandered several chances to increase it and then had a collective snooze to allow West Brom back in and equalise. We were just lucky their second-half finishing was as abject as ours and they didn't sneak all three points. It wasn't the 1-1 scoreline that was so depressing – though we had chucked away the other two points – it was the manner in which we played. Only Kaboul, Modrić and van der Vaart played with passion; everyone else looked short of confidence, energy and motivation.

A familiar feeling of resignation swept over me at the final whistle. Why had I bothered to come all the way to Birmingham yet again when I had predicted the likely outcome? And why did some of the players look so unconcerned when they left the pitch after playing so far below their potential? I guess they had a nice bath, a quiet snooze in a luxury coach and a night out clubbing to look forward to.

JOHN CRACE

Even so, an away draw isn't as bad as a home draw, and there is something very special about away games. I love the sense of heightened tribalism, of being an oppressed minority, of standing up throughout the game, of singing mindless, posturing chants – 'Just like a library', 'Your support is fucking shit' – that are meant to wind up the home crowd but never do. The sense of being a member of the Yid Army.

This is a tricky one, a circle I've never quite managed to square. I wouldn't dream of using the word Yid in everyday life, but somehow in the Spurs context there's a parallel universe where it doesn't feel offensive. It's certainly only ever used in Spursworld as a term of approval. Traditionally, Spurs have always been a club with strong Jewish ties, and Yid Army is seen as a badge of honour and for the crowd to roar 'Yiddo, Yiddo, Yiddo, Yiddo' is the highest accolade a player can achieve. But is intentionality enough? Those I know with Jewish cultural ties are split; most, like me, perform the mental gymnastics that allow us to ignore the racist connotations; a few find it wholly unacceptable.

Leaving an away game is almost always a source of irritation. Unless you've won; then you will put up with anything. The West Brom game was no exception. There are usually far fewer exits at the away end – presumably clubs are less concerned about away supporters burning to death in a fire – so there's always a long wait to escape, even if the police haven't decided to hold you back on the assumption you can't wait to get out of the ground and cosh a few home-team fans. At West Brom it is even worse, because rather than just letting you nip round the side back to the car, you are forced to take a half-mile detour through an industrial park. So I wasn't feeling that jolly by the time we made it back to the car.

'If we continue to play like that, we're going to be fucked,' I said to Matthew.

'Don't worry, we're playing Werder on Tuesday,' he replied.

'I know. But we still need to concentrate on the league.'

'Here we come. Champions League next week.'

'Yes, but we'll be back in the Europa League next season if we don't finish fourth.'

'Fuck me, you're depressing, John.'

Like almost everyone else, Matthew wasn't to be denied his European dream. Once more, I was the lone voice of negativity. I tried to affect something more upbeat, but Matthew was already asleep.

I turned on Radio 5 Live in time to hear Harry saying he'd had to take Rafa van der Vaart off midway through the second half because he was knackered and not yet up to the pace of Premier League football. If a few other players had tried as hard as Rafa then they'd have been exhausted, too.

***

It wasn't quite as I'd imagined it. Spurs' first proper game in the Champions League – even I'd now got round to partitioning the tie against Young Boys into a half-world where it probably never really took place, or if it did then it certainly wasn't as important as I'd thought at the time – and I was watching it at home, in Streatham, on my own. Robbie had to be out, Jill and Anna made sure they were out, so there was just me and the TV. It was all wrong. This was supposed to be the big communal event, a celebration of arrival on a bigger stage, and I was lying on the floor. I always seem to end up watching televised matches lying down, as the tenser I get, the more gravity seems to take over. Normally I reach this point sometime in the second half – usually at about the sixty-minute mark – but this was such a big game I was on the floor from the start.

It was all wrong on the pitch, too, though in an unexpectedly joyous manner. Rather confirming my theory that success had rather gone to some of the players' heads and they were too grand for the run-of-the-mill matches, their first thirty minutes of the Champions League were marked by near-perfect football. We were 2-0 up inside fifteen minutes, and could and should have been 3-0 up within half an hour if we'd been just a little more clinical.

We were cruising. Then, with two minutes to go till half-time and the match commentators saying, 'Spurs want to make sure they don't concede before the break', Benny Assou-Ekotto (he can be relied on for one moment of madness a game) and Cudicini gifted the Germans a goal back before the break. It was all the encouragement they needed. They scored again early in the second half, and from then on it was backs-to-the-wall stuff. It was agony watching it on my own, with no one to share the misery. I spent as much time watching the little clock in the top left-hand corner of the TV as I did the game. Seventy minutes? Surely we'd played more than that? Eighty minutes . . . I would rather have fallen asleep for the last ten minutes and woken up when it was all over. I didn't quite know how to feel when it *was* all over. A good away point earned, or two chucked away? It was certainly a decent start to the campaign, but a more seasoned team would surely have closed the game out from 2-0 up. Fuck it, though. Who wanted to follow a well-drilled professional side, when you could watch Spurs blow hot and cold? I tried to text a couple of mates to make myself feel part of the tribe, but Vodafone's universal network coverage only intermittently extends to inside my house and there was no reception. So I watched the news instead.

***

There was more regret on offer at White Hart Lane a few days later at the Wolves game. Without telling Robbie – he gets very pissed off with me chatting to friends about 'boring old tickets and programmes and stuff' while he has to stand around getting bored – I'd arranged to meet Pete before the game to collect a used ticket from the Werder game that he'd saved for me.

'How was it?' I asked.

'It was great,' he said. 'Top atmosphere, and the Germans were really friendly.'

Rather different from my experience of watching it alone on TV.

'I'm jealous.'

'You should have come. There were loads of people selling tickets outside. You'd have got in easily.'

After all that fussing, all those conversations with Matthew about whether we should chance it – we'd decided that if we did and didn't get in, we'd have to lie to our wives and say we did otherwise they'd have both gone apeshit about us spending so much money to watch the game in a German bar – and finally opting to do the sensible, grown-up thing, it turned out we could have just showed up on the day after all.

My mood wasn't improved when I saw Amici. He, too, had made it to the Bremen game – 'I couldn't not go, could I?' – though he probably remembered rather less of it than Pete. 'I was completely bladdered,' he laughed. Just about everyone but me, it felt, had managed to get to Spurs' most important game in years.

But the thing about important games is that they often don't seem quite so important looking back as they do looking forward. You get yourself into a right state beforehand, talk a load of shit about 'season-defining games' and then it's over, and there's another 'season-defining game' on the horizon. You'd have been hard pushed to call the Wolves game a season-defining game, but there was pride at stake as Wolves – Wolves! – had done the double over us the previous season, and we badly needed a result to kick-start our Premiership bid.

It also felt good to be back at White Hart Lane after a three-week break. There are times in the season when the fixtures pile up, and I find myself schlepping up to N17 twice a week so often that I take it all for granted, but for the Wolves game it felt fresh once more. I'd missed the crowd, the noise and, above all, the sense of belonging.

For as long as I can remember, I've felt apart from things. As a child, I felt on the outside among kids my age both at home and at school; it was as if these were worlds from which I was mainly excluded, worlds where I hovered in a half-life at the fringes, hoping to be allowed in. For a brief period while I was at university, these feelings largely vanished, only to return when I was chucked out into the real world. One by one – a couple with narrow-eyed ambition, most with extreme reluctance – my friends knuckled down and got proper jobs, until I was the only one left hanging around doing next to nothing. I can't say I really wanted a job, but I certainly didn't want to be doing bugger all, either; it was more that I had no idea what you had to do to get a job. Part of the toolkit was missing. Mind you, substituting its absence with a lifestyle that was irreconcilable with having a proper job probably didn't help much.

Anyway, that's a different story. The thing is that I've always wanted to belong to something, though only up to a point. I've never been prepared to buy into any organization without retaining an opt-out clause to think and say whatever I like. Understandably, membership is non-negotiable for most organizations; you're either in or out. But with Spurs I can belong entirely on my own terms. I can go as often or as infrequently as I like, I can cheer, boo or keep quiet and I can buy as much or as little official merchandise as I want without anyone saying a word or thinking less of me.

Like all clubs, Spurs does have its own official party line and, like many clubs, it has its own *Pravda*, the magazine *Hotspur* that exists purely to disseminate the idea that all is for the best in the best of all possible Spursworlds, but no one I know takes it all seriously – though I did mistakenly once subscribe to it for a year before I realised I seldom got round to opening it before forwarding it to my friend Eric in Singapore in exchange for him sending me programmes and ticket stubs from Spurs pre-season jaunts to the Far East.

In fact, it often seems as if the most loyal supporters –

those who have been following the club the longest – are usually the most independent of thinkers about the club. Whether this is a function of age, cynicism, wisdom or resigned Zen-like stoicism born of years of crushed expectations is anyone's guess, but it certainly provides amusement.

Shortly before the Wolves game I received an email from two friends, Mat (not to be confused with Matthew) and Keith, saying they had come up with a variation of the Fantasy Football games that run in most papers. Like many brilliant ideas, it was startlingly simple. Their game was called Fantasy Fuckwit and rather than reward brilliance, teams and players would be awarded points for losing matches, getting booked or sent off, lack of effort, hopeless incompetence (missing an open goal, for example), bad haircuts and moronic goal celebrations; and you'd pick your team based on those you thought most likely to be the worst offenders.

It was also a much more faithful reflection of how most regular supporters both watch and enjoy the game. Of course, I love it when we win, when we make a five-pass move from our own penalty area that results in a goal. But face it: how often does that happen? If you're really, really lucky, once a game. Which means there's another eighty-nine minutes and forty-five seconds to get through when the beautiful game isn't quite so beautiful, and then you have to find your pleasures elsewhere. So that's when you have those conversations about Gareth Bale's pointy haircut (has he ever used a mirror?), how Crouchie continually gets outjumped by defenders three inches smaller than him and why Gomes insists on punching balls that are easier to catch. And though these conversations do come with groans of frustration as standard, they also come with affection. It's a strange mental split: while I want the players to be faultless, to dazzle me with skill, it's their fallibility for which I love them; it's what makes them human. Their ability to screw up is just about the only thing we have in common.

Fantasy Fuckwit also lent itself to a very different form of match report, though one rather more recognizable to most long-term habitués of the erstwhile terraces. And if the papers had written up the 3-1 victory over Wolves in Fuckwit style, this is what you might have read.

A late three-goal rally saved Spurs from a host of unwanted Fuckwit points – though their performance was a long way from the depths of the home defeat at Wigan and the second-half catatonia at West Brom – and it was Wolves who came away with this week's honours.

Not that Wolves played that badly. They weren't nearly as dirty as their early-season billing had suggested – always a slight disappointment in Fuckwit football – and had Ward not scythed down Hutton in the penalty area to get himself on the Fuckwit score sheet, they could easily have left White Hart Lane empty-handed.

And it wouldn't have been a total surprise. This season Spurs have shown every sign of believing they are too grand to play unglamorous teams whose names begin with a W – half the players have looked like they couldn't wait to head for an Essex nightclub, the other half have looked like they never left – and with West Ham to come

next weekend, their supporters were rapidly losing faith. Not least after watching an atrocious
Robbie Keane – not even Celtic would want him
on current form – squander two clear chances to
give Spurs a two-goal lead midway through the
first half. No prizes for guessing who won the
three points for most disappointing player.

Mind you, Tom Huddlestone did his best to
run him close. Hudd the Thudd seems to have
started believing his press that he is the best
passer and striker of the ball in the Premiership;
unfortunately, at the moment he doesn't always
pass the ball to his own players, he doesn't score
goals and he certainly doesn't seem to have realised his job in midfield also requires him to run
from time to time.

Elsewhere, the Spurs line-up showed signs
of losing some fuckwittery. Kaboul – normally a
banker for the catastrophic – has been admir-
ably committed and consistent; Hutton, who last
season didn't seem to know his left foot from
his right, virtually won the game single-handed;
and even Lennon seems to have emerged from
his coma, creating more in the ten minutes he
was on the pitch than he has all season. At this
rate, Spurs could soon go scuttling down the
Fuckwit league.

***

In recent years, Spurs have had to find their crumbs of
comfort in the Carling Cup, getting to the final twice

in successive years – winning one and losing the other. So while my more complacent Arsenal- and Chelsea-supporting friends have been conditioned to get a bit sniffy about this competition, I've always had rather a soft spot for it. Three wins and you're in a cup semi-final.

This year, though, according to the official Spurspeak coming out of White Hart Lane, was the club's date with destiny; the fiftieth anniversary of the league and FA Cup double, the year when we cemented our place at Europe's top table. Naturally, then, it was the year we decided we couldn't really be bothered with the Carling Cup. This looked a poor decision on all counts. As someone who believes – with plenty of documentary evidence after watching Spurs for years – that if something can go wrong, it will, it seemed wrong to invite defeat so early in the season. It also felt just wrong when our opponents were Arsenal. Most of all, though, it was like being mugged by the club. Season-ticket holders get two cup ties included in their package deal, of which this was one: to be told the manager didn't think it was a priority and was going to send out a weakened team was taking the piss. We'll take your money but we can't promise to try very hard. Thanks.

No matter. In the ritual pre-game build-ups, Harry promised to send out a second-string side, and he duly delivered. Wenger, his Arsenal counterpart, did just about the same. Where he differed was that having also promised to give the reserves a runaround, he played a virtual first team instead. It was Harry's turn to feel mugged. The game went to extra time but the result was never really in doubt. We were outplayed for most of the game, and the 4-1 scoreline was fair enough.

It was also the night when Spurs fans finally felt embarrassed for Robbie Keane – the striker who used to huff, puff, argue with his shadow yet still score crucial goals for us before he left to seek glory at Liverpool. He was back within six months, having failed to set Anfield alight, and the spark had gone in White Hart Lane, too. His performances had been getting poorer and poorer, and it looked as if his spirit was broken. Not even Robbie believed in Robbie any more. He did score early in the second half – a miskick that must have surprised him every bit as much as it did everyone else – but nothing else went right.

'I can't watch this,' Amici said to me. 'Keano's completely lost it.'

'I know,' I replied. 'It's awful.'

'I wish he'd just leave. I know it's harsh, as he's been great for the club over the years and I don't want it to get to the stage where we have to boo him.'

Everyone else felt the same way. Fan loyalty has a breaking point, and it came in a game for which we were being charged top dollar to watch a player earning £65,000 a week appear short of pace and out of touch. Mind you, I only had myself to blame for not getting more for my money. I've only ever left one match early before – and that was when Arsenal scored in the ninety-second minute to go 3-1 up and I just couldn't bear the celebrations – but this time I left with ten minutes to go when we were 4-1 down. We'd used all our substitutes, half the team could barely run because they had cramp and Lennon, our most attacking player, was playing full-back. Someone was taking the piss.

The one highlight was my accomplice for the night. As

it was a midweek school day, Robbie was banned so his ticket went to my daughter's boyfriend, Ollie. While Anna was growing up, I had tried to blank out the thought she might ever have a boyfriend, and on the rare occasions when I had thought about it I'd just assumed I was always going to hate him, whoever he was. On principle. But now she was eighteen, and she had Ollie. And it wasn't that awkward or difficult, especially when she eased the pain by telling me he was also a Spurs fan. She has better taste than I would have predicted. What's more, she wasn't the only one who got to hug him. When Keane equalised, we fell into each others' arms.

Mind you, I'm not sure Anna was wholly thrilled. Before the game, she had demanded to know why I was taking Ollie and not her.

'Because he's a Spurs fan and you have no interest in football.'

'What's that got to do with it?'

'Um . . . just about everything.'

'Well, it's just wrong. I'm your daughter and you've never taken me . . .'

'I have offered many times.'

She ignored that.

'People will think you like Ollie more than me.'

'Then come to a game with me soon.'

'All right then, I will.'

Things were looking up. At this rate, I might even persuade Jill to come to White Hart Lane someday.

***

What a difference a day makes. Having shrugged off

their Carling Cup defeats with affected insouciance for years, my Arsenal-supporting friends had miraculously recovered their interest and I got into work the following day to find several emails forcefully reminding me of Spurs' capitulation the night before. It was no more than I expected. In fact, I'd have been disappointed if there had been none, because that would have meant they felt sorry for me – that they felt my pain – and were trying not to hurt my feelings. There's nothing worse than being patronised. I'd much rather the other team's fans took the piss out of a poor Spurs performance than applauded sympathetically at the underdog's gallant efforts at damage limitation. Actually, there is one thing worse; the oppo being so sure of the result it doesn't feel worth crowing over.

These ritualised abusive exchanges between friends are all part of the fun, and they mean nothing as no one takes them that seriously. You accept the victories as if they were your own triumphs in which you personally played a crucial role, and distance yourself from the disasters with the resigned gallows humour of 'What can you expect from a bunch of headless chickens?' Win or lose, you wear your scars with pride, a witness to your loyalty and, all too frequently, your masochism.

Gloating was far tougher ten or fifteen years ago when only the wired geeks used email. Friends could make themselves curiously absent for a few days, and even if you did hunt them down you thought twice about rubbing their noses in it. What is intended as a (relatively) harmless needle in email can escalate to a declaration of war in a face-to-face conversation or phone call. It's also a great deal easier to knock out a few lines of email and send it to several people at once. There's even an online etiquette. The winner indulges in some mild triumphalism, the loser replies – you've always got to reply; there's no point trying to pretend you didn't receive the email or deemed it unworthy of an answer because then you've lost – either with a gag or a polite 'Fuck off'. In response to Patrick's morning-after email, obligatory for an Arsenal season ticket holder, I did both.

As most clubs have become steadily more and more corporate, modern technology has been a life-saver for those of us who choose to support our teams on our own terms. Hardly a day passes without someone on our group email sending round a bit of club gossip, but the crowning glory of the week is the Spurs Podcast – usually presented by comedian Phil Cornwell – and run on a shoestring budget from the basement of talent agent Mike Leigh's central London office and broadcast via the internet to 10,000 listeners each week. It's democracy in action: Phil and Mike are diehard Spurs fans, and the show is an irreverent celebration of the heroic and absurd in all things Spurs. It's like listening to your mates talking football in the pub. Only a lot funnier and more interesting.

To be invited on the show is to feel you have arrived as a Spurs fan. The first email invitation I got from Mike a year or so back was a moment of pure joy; the second that arrived after the Carling Cup exit was just as good. I said yes immediately; on the off chance I had something planned, I would cancel it.

'Great,' said Mike. 'Phil's away, so it will be me presenting. Paul Hawskbee from Talksport is the other guest.

We'll meet at the pub across the road from my office at seven.'

We were meeting at the pub for the very good reason that the comedian Alan Davies was recording the Arsenal Podcast in Mike's office immediately before we were due on – further proof that these days old enmities exist more as convenient caricatures to get the pulse racing rather than as expressions of heartfelt animosity. Out of curiosity, I listened to the Arsenal Podcast a few days later; it was similar to the Spurs Podcast in all but one respect: it just wasn't as funny. I say that not to diss Davies – he's a very funny man – but because I've noticed that almost every Arsenal fan I know seems to have a sense of humour failure when it comes to discussing their team. Then I guess they've never really needed one. Rather, they adopt the air of their manager and talk very intensely about different formations and their strongest line-up as if they were hammering out a Middle East peace settlement. On the Spurs Podcast, any talk of tactics generally ends in less than a minute with 'Yeah, but the real question is what hairstyle Benny will have this week. We always lose when he has it tied up in a bun.'

I missed the away game at West Ham. When I check out the fixture list before the season starts, I try to pencil in this match as a definite. Travel is easy, and we've always done well whenever I've gone. But this year I had a work event in Scotland so Upton Park was a no go. By all accounts I made the right choice. I'd been worried about this game – when am I not? – as West Ham are another mediocre team beginning with W. Sure enough, having deservedly spent the last month propping up the bottom of the Premier League, the Hammers ground out a 1-0 victory as Spurs had an utterly predictable collective bout of narcolepsy ahead of their first Champions League home tie. I did wonder if the result would have been different if I'd been there; but then Benny probably did have his hair in a bun anyway.

There was only one empty seat at White Hart Lane for the arrival of Dutch side FC Twente. The one next to mine.

'Where's Justin?' I asked Amici.

'Stuck in a tailback on the M25.'

It was a close run thing for a few others, though, as the new swipe-card system for season-ticket holders had a fit of the yips and several hundred fans near me were stranded outside the ground for half an hour until someone got round to fixing the problem. They were spitting blood at half-time. I would too if it had been me. You wait fifty years for a game like this and you miss a third of it because someone screwed up the IT.

I suspect it had all felt a bit different down at Stamford Bridge the previous night, when Chelsea had played Marseille in their Champions League match.

'To be honest,' Kevin had told me, 'very few of us can really get too excited about the competition until the knockout phase in the New Year. Loads of season-ticket holders can't be arsed to go, and the club has to flog the tickets off cheap to fill the ground.'

That's the reward for umpteen consecutive years of top-level European football, I guess: apathy. There was nothing like that at White Hart Lane. This was a game no one wanted to miss; tickets had been priced in the top band, and the club could easily have sold half as many again. And those of us who were in the ground knew better than to expect an easy ride. Only a good save from Gomes prevented us from going 1-0 down after ten minutes, and when we were awarded a penalty towards the end of the first half, van der Vaart, our Mr Reliable of the season so far, had his effort saved. It felt as if it was going to be another of those long nights of frustration.

Minutes into the second half, though, the wonder Dutchman made up for his miss with a stunning goal, and shortly afterwards the Norwegian referee gave us the softest of penalties. Two in one game. For most teams, a penalty is a gimme; at Spurs it's fifty-fifty. I've lost track of the number I've seen us miss. There were four or five in the previous season alone. It's hard to believe we actually won the UEFA Cup on penalties back in 1984.

Pav didn't miss, but that didn't mean we stopped trying to make life unnecessarily difficult as van der Vaart got himself sent off and Twente pulled one back.

'I can't bear this,' I said.

'Nor me,' said Matthew. When he had lost hope, it usually meant we were a goner. Unbelievably, the ref gave us a third penalty – even softer than the last one – and equally unbelievably, Pav scored again. Bale added a fourth, and we were home and dry.

Joint top of our league with the holders Inter Milan after two games – it somehow didn't feel right. We weren't meant to go round thrashing the Dutch champions 4-1 when we kept losing to teams like Wigan and West Ham. There was a delighted, yet subdued, atmosphere in the ground when the game ended. I wasn't the only one who was confused by what they had seen. It hadn't been in the script.

Three days later I found out that Justin didn't get home till 6 a.m. the following morning, having been stuck in a jam on the M25 for over twelve hours. That wasn't in the script either.

October

'YOU KNOW SOMETHING, DAD?'

'What?'

'You're weird when you watch football.'

'How do you mean?'

'You make these really odd groaning noises the whole time.'

'Do I?'

'Yeah. And you're so tense. When you're not shouting or having a moan about Crouchie, you're in a world of your own.'

It was half-time at the Villa game. We'd started in our usual post-European trance and had predictably gone 1-0 down inside fifteen minutes. Nor had we much looked like equalizing until van der Vaart scored just minutes before the break. To me, it was no wonder I was so tense.

On the best of days, when we're 3-0 up and cruising, I'm still rigid with anxiety, lost in a world of football heaven and hell, a distorted, suspended world where all my other neuroses are drowned out and I get time off from myself for ninety minutes. Work worries, health worries – you wouldn't believe the amount of times I've supposedly had cancer – family worries: everything retreats into a submerged subconscious and gets put on hold for the duration of the match as I latch on to something temporarily more important to worry about. You could call football my respite care. Perhaps not one most shrinks would recommend. And today, very definitely, was not the best of days; Spurs needed all the concentration and energy I could summon to compensate for the effort that many of the players so obviously weren't making.

'I'm sure I don't groan,' I said, striving to retain some dignity.

'Yes you do.'

'How does it sound then?'

'Like a groan, you moron.'

'Do an impression of it, then.'

'Nnnnnnnnnnnnnnnnnnnggggggggggghhhhhhhhhh.'

'That's not a groan. It's more of a low hum.'

'Yes, Dad. Sure it is. Call it a hum if it makes you feel better. Though it's definitely a fucking groan.'

'Do you think anyone else notices?'

Robbie looked at me as if I was an idiot. 'Well if I can hear it, why wouldn't everyone else?'

He had a point. It didn't bear thinking that Justin and Amici also thought I was weird. Best to ignore it. I tried another tack.

'But it is a pretty tense game. Don't you think?'

'Not really. We started poorly, but we're back on terms and bossing the game.'

Robbie was beginning to sound a bit like Harry Redknapp.

'Hardly bossing. Villa could easily still sneak this.'

'Not a chance. We're definitely going to win.'

Now he really did sound like Harry.

I've always wondered where Robbie gets his optimism from. Ever since he was born, he's always expected good things to happen to him. And if something does go wrong, he'll be momentarily surprised but he'll take it in his stride, confident that normal service will swiftly be resumed. None of the rest of us, Jill, Anna or I, has an optimistic bone in our body. Nor have we ever had one, though I don't think Jill or Anna have quite so many doggedly negative ones as me. That's just the way it is. I didn't start out with some childlike Panglossian belief that everything was for the best in the best of all possible worlds, which was steadily kicked out of me by a lifetime of failure and disappointment. My pessimism was hotwired from birth. My earliest memories are of expecting the worst to happen and being moderately surprised by the few occasions when it didn't, and nothing much has changed over the last fifty years.

That said, I wouldn't want to let Spurs completely off the hook for their contribution to my fragile mental health. Pick out almost any season and I can instantly recall several harrowing disasters that have tenaciously etched themselves into my memory. And they aren't necessarily the big games, the cup finals and semi-finals that ended in defeat, or the last game of the season loss to West Ham that kept us out of the Champions League a few years back, though these are carefully stored to be retrieved at will. Nor are they always the most obviously heartbreaking: like the time we were 3-0 up against Manchester United at home and went on to lose 3-5. Or the time we were 3-0 up against a ten-man Manchester City and lost 4-3. Rest assured, though, those memories are there to stay, too. It's the little games, the ones most people in their right mind have airbrushed out of their lives, the 1-0 home defeats to Wolves, Wigan and Hull – these are the games that really haunt me on a sleepless night.

I can't pretend that any of this is rational or even-handed. After all, Spurs win their fair share of games, sometimes more than their fair share and, as I've already made clear, I don't have the kind of gritty 'fuck you' mindset to support a club that plays ordinary football and bumps along in the lower divisions. The problem is that the victories – even the big ones – feel so ephemeral; the sense of joy they bring metamorphoses instantly into one of relief and thence to emotional oblivion. Their memories survive, but they are largely dead memories. If someone mentions a game we won, I might well be able to remember the score and replay the goals in my head but I struggle to recapture how I felt. With the losses, I instantly reconnect with the despair.

There was a study I came across a few years back that concluded Spurs were the most stressful Premier League team to support. The researchers had gone through all the relevant stats – conceding goals in the last ten minutes, turning winning situations into losing ones – and had apparently worked out that Spurs were the club most likely to confound expectations and give you a heart attack. Now I've no idea how rigorous a piece of science this was, but it sounded entirely plausible as it mirrored my own experience exactly. In any game when we go a goal up inside ten minutes, I automatically fear the worst. Rather than thinking, 'Great, we can go on to score a couple more and kill off the game by half-time,' my instinctive reaction is

'Oh no, we've somehow got to hold on for another eighty minutes.'

I know I'm not the only person who feels this way. During one game last season when we had managed to take an early lead, Amici turned to me and said, 'OK, John, the game can end now. The ref can blow the whistle. I've had enough.' Like me, he'd have happily foregone another seventy-five minutes of football in return for the guaranteed win. It is insane, of course: no one in their right mind would willingly fork out £40 or more for a match lasting just fifteen minutes. But there are plenty of us in the East stand who would do just that in return for a certain three points and lower blood pressure. Talking of which, there have also been countless games when the last half-hour has been nothing short of a living hell – as we either try to defend a narrow lead, retreating ever further backwards into our own half, or swarm forwards in search of an equaliser or a late winner. In every single one there comes a point where I'm tempted to leave because the tension is unbearable; what I'd really like is for an anaesthetist to put me out until the final whistle and to be told the result on waking up. Anything but having to live through every agonizing second. And yet, I can't leave. I'm rooted there, like a rabbit waiting to be knocked down in the road. The bottom line is that I need the suffering to feel the pleasure.

Only there wasn't that much suffering to be had against Villa in the second half. Van der Vaart showed another touch of class to wrong-foot the Villa defence with just under twenty minutes remaining, and for once we rarely looked like letting the opposition back in. It wasn't commanding, but there was more than a hint of a most un-Spurs-like display of determination. If we couldn't win, well, then we'd win ugly. Even more remarkable, in van der Vaart, Bale and Modrić we had three supremely gifted footballers who were prepared to run themselves into the ground in pursuit of the cause. No one at White Hart Lane had seen anything like it for years. We were used to heroes like Hoddle, Gascoigne, Lineker, Klinsmann and Ginola, who regarded physical exertion as an insult to their talent.

'I told you we were going to win,' Robbie reminded me on the walk back to the car.

'Indeed you did,' I smiled.

'It was never in doubt.'

Wasn't it? Maybe Robbie had been right all along. Maybe it had been obvious we were always going to win. Maybe it was my natural pessimism that was out of synch with the season. Maybe this year it really was going to be different.

***

Even though he's never seen Spurs win at Craven Cottage – two draws, including a thrown-away 3-1 lead, and a loss is his tally so far – the away game at Fulham is always Robbie's favourite match of the season. He likes the fact that it's only a short drive from our home in Streatham; he likes the walk along the river through the park; he likes the food – it must be the only football ground where you can get an organic lamb and mint burger from a stall outside; he likes the friendliness of the Fulham fans; he likes the homely, ramshackle feel to Craven Cottage; he likes the way the whole stand at the Putney End feels like it's imminently about to collapse when the away fans start bouncing up and down to celebrate.

The away game at Fulham is also my favourite game of the season. My reasons are rather more straightforward. In fact, there's only one that counts. It's my favourite because it's Robbie's favourite. Now he's fifteen, I realise I'm on borrowed time with Robbie. He has his own travelcard, he has his friends and the weekends are pretty much his own. I can no longer boss him around the way I did when he was younger; if he comes to the football, it's because he wants to. Like most teenagers, he can be fairly stroppy at times. So I have to watch my step, as I'm fairly certain he doesn't share the same vision of the future as me. My hope is that Robbie and I will be going to football matches together for as long as I'm still standing, and it may yet happen. But if it does, it will almost certainly be because it has happened without Robbie giving it much thought, because most normal blokes in their late teens and early twenties only want to hang out with their dads now and again. Supporting the same club guarantees nothing; he could end up sitting with some mates in a different part of the ground.

Being a dad to Robbie these days feels like steering a fine line between control and neglect. Get too hands-on and he acts like I'm some kind of psycho who's permanently on his case; too hands-off and he thinks I don't give a toss one way or the other. And if I look too much like I'm trying too hard to find that perfect balance, he'll say, 'Great attempt at perfect parenting, Dad. But sadly, not quite good enough.' Teenagers can be very cruel, and Robbie doesn't miss a thing.

So Fulham at Craven Cottage is always a thrill because

it's a game Robbie wants to go to every bit as much as me. We share the excitement from the moment we leave home, rather than, as is more usual on football days, from the time we arrive at White Hart Lane. These details matter, because I'd like Robbie to look back in years to come and treasure these moments as much as I do.

Even now, I can still clearly remember two games my dad took me to as a kid. The first was a rearranged game between Swindon and Barnsley. We'd had tickets to go to the original game that was called off because the pitch was frozen, and there was no enthusiasm from my parents to take me to the rescheduled game on a cold midweek evening. I'd tried to make the case, but my mum had to work and my dad ... well, he just wasn't interested. An hour or so later, I overheard my parents in heated conversation: they didn't have rows, and this was as close as they came.

'Why won't you take him?' my mother said.

'Because it's late and I've got things to do,' my father replied.

'No, you haven't. You just don't want to go. When was the last time you put yourself out for him?'

I sneaked back to my room, making sure they didn't know I had heard them.

Ten minutes or so later, my dad called up to me.

'Come on, John. Grab your coat and scarf. We're going to the football.'

I acted surprised. 'Are you sure? I thought you had things to do.'

'I'll do them tomorrow. Let's go.'

'Wow. Thanks, Dad.'

I can't remember what we talked about in the car, though I suspect it was not very much as my dad wasn't a great talker. But I can guarantee neither of us mentioned he was only taking me because he had been bullied into it by my mum. It wasn't the family way. My guess is I told him how grateful I was a couple more times – partly because I was, but mainly because I was anxious to maintain the pretence that he was taking me of his own free will – before we lapsed into silence. As for the game, I remember it better than the dozen or so other matches I went to at the County Ground that season. Swindon won 2-0 on a near-waterlogged pitch, thanks to two second-half goals from the now long-forgotten, balding Peter Noble. I was ecstatic; my dad, I would think, was bored to tears.

Ever since the World Cup final in 1966, it had been my dream to go to Wembley: to see the twin towers, to be part of a crowd of 100,000 and to see my team walk up the thirty-nine steps to the royal box to collect a trophy. Then, one day in March 1971, my dad said he was taking me to Wembley; to see the Amateur Cup final between Dagenham and Skelmersdale.

'Great, Dad,' I said. 'Thanks.'

I even sort of meant it. I loved him for trying, but was upset that he just didn't quite get that the Amateur Cup final didn't make the grade for a fourteen-year-old as a prime Wembley experience. I'd seen enough Third Division games at Swindon, and had been following the Saturday teleprinter on the television for long enough by then to know my Burys, my Hartlepools, my Macclesfields and my Plymouth Argyles. Hell, I even knew my Queen of the Souths and Cowdenbeaths. But Skelmersdale and

Dagenham were complete unknowns. And the Amateur Cup? Who cared? When I told people at school I was going, their answers were a uniform, 'Why?'

We were sitting in the Skelmersdale end – it turned out my dad had answered an advert in *The Times* placed by the Skems – and as we also had an Austin Maxi, and Dagenham was the home of Ford, we were honorary northerners for the day. We went home happy with a 4-1 win. We were even sitting close enough to the royal box to get a good view of the players picking up the cup. But I felt semi-detached from the event; it wasn't how Wembley was supposed to be. Sure, the stadium was impressive, and if I closed my eyes I could imagine it as I had seen it on television just two months earlier, when two late Martin Chivers goals had won the League Cup for Spurs against Aston Villa in front of a full house; but when I opened them, the ground was less than half full, the crowd echoed instead of roared and I just didn't really care enough who won.

I've thought about this game often since then. I've felt bad for being so ungrateful to my dad. He probably knew only too well this wasn't the real Wembley thing, but also realised he wasn't the type of dad who had the connections to pull a couple of cup-final tickets out of the hat. He was just a West Country vicar and this was the best he could do, so he did it. It was his token of love, which I only grudgingly accepted.

We never went to Wembley together again after that; in fact, I'm not sure we went to another football match together. I was an increasingly difficult, monosyllabic adolescent, desperate for independence yet terrified of it, who continually adjusted the bar so it was always set at a height my dad was bound to fail. There was nothing he could ever do to prove himself to me, so he probably stopped trying too hard. It was a bit of a mess. We didn't row; we just didn't speak that much. There was the understanding of love without much mutual understanding. That only came years later, towards the end of his life.

So my own memories of going to football with my dad are bittersweet, a legacy I'm anxious not to repeat with Robbie. In some ways, I'd almost rather he forgot the individual games we've been to together and for them all to merge into one uber-memory, a general sense of connection that we shared, something we enjoyed together, a sense we did things together because we both wanted to rather than because one of us was making a special effort. And to do that, I've always known I have to let him have his own relationship with Spurs, one founded in his own personality and experience. So I've always tried to go easy on him, always offering him first refusal on any game but never forcing the issue if he said he fancied doing something else. Well, not too much.

At the Fulham game, it finally felt as if my approach had paid off. Teenage boys are a self-conscious mob, and Robbie had never been big on singing at games; he'd stand up, cheer and give me a hug when we scored, but for the rest of the game he'd sit pretty much in silence. But this afternoon, I became aware of a low growling noise beside me. It was Robbie singing, 'We are Tottenham, super Tottenham, we are Tottenham from the Lane'; not very loudly, certainly not in tune – then no Spurs fan ever is – but definitely audible. It was one of my happiest moments at a football ground: singing alongside my son at Craven Cottage.

Bizarrely, we even got a result. The game had started badly with skipper Ledley 'Oh Ledley, Ledley, he's only got one knee, he's better than John Terry, Oh Ledley, Ledley' King going off injured yet again. For several years now, he'd managed to turn out sporadically and play brilliantly despite his knee being so knackered he could barely train, and every time he was taken off now, I couldn't help wondering if I'd ever see him play for Spurs again. And I also wondered how I and he would feel if he didn't. I, no doubt, would be a bit sad for a moment, consign him to my memory Hall of Fame and then devote my thoughts to his replacement. But what would he think? At fifty years old, with his knees totally arthritic, barely able to walk and with only a few of the fans having a clue who he was, he would be dragged out for his once-a-year half-time matchday presentation at White Hart Lane – would he still think it had all been worthwhile?

It soon got worse as Fulham took the lead after some characteristically dopey Spurs defending. Astonishingly, Fulham repaid the favour less than a minute later. Two even more remarkable things happened in the second half. For a player who is supposed to have one of the most cultured right feet in the premiership, Hudd the Thudd does seem to miss the target more often than not. But today he didn't, a strike from outside the area finding the bottom corner. Except the linesman flagged for offside. Normally that's that, but for once the referee overruled the lino after the Spurs players protested. I couldn't tell one way or the other, as it was down the other end; what I did know was that this kind of blag only happened to the likes of Manchester United and Chelsea. Maybe we were a top-four team, after all. The stands bounced satisfactorily (for Robbie) and unnervingly (for me) as we hung on to win 2-1. All in all, a near-perfect day.

***

Ever since the Champions League draw had been made, there was only one tie I really cared about. Sure, along with everyone else, I'd talked piously about making sure we didn't take Werder Bremen or FC Twente for granted, blah, blah, but what I really thought were that these were precisely the kind of club we had been playing in the UEFA Cup for years on end, and no amount of piping the Champions League theme tune through the PA system or fluttering the Champions League flag in the centre circle before the start was really going to change that.

Inter Milan, though, were a class apart. A team with history and one of the European greats; better still, they had won the tournament the previous year. Football just didn't get better than this. Spurs were going to be playing at the San Siro. All my life I had waited for a moment like this, a chance to see my team play in one of the most famous stadiums in the world against one of the most famous teams in the world in the biggest club tournament of all. We had played there once before back in the 1970s – a UEFA Cup semi-final against AC Milan – but I hadn't gone: I was still at school and barely left my bedroom, let alone the country. Besides, it had only been the UEFA Cup.

This time, I had to go. There could well be no second chance: I'd be long dead if I had to wait as long again for Champions League football. There would be no half-hearted attempts or missed opportunities as there had been with the Bremen game. I would be there. It proved to be easier said than done, as virtually every other Spurs fan had made the same promise to themselves. My friend Celia at work was even planning to arrange a week's holiday in Italy with the Milan game as the focal point.

To no great surprise, it soon became clear that you would again need a ridiculous amount of loyalty points to be guaranteed one of the 5,000 tickets Milan had allocated to the away fans; I and thousands of others were going to be disappointed. It was immensely depressing – not to mention annoying. The San Siro is massive; it can hold more than 80,000 spectators, and everyone knew that it would be little more than half full. To put it bluntly, the Milanese just weren't that interested in Spurs. Force-fed a diet of Barcelona, Bayern Munich, Real Madrid and Manchester United over the course of more than a decade, the Milan fans couldn't get too worked up over a team of which most of them had barely heard. We knew that, the Milan fans knew that and the clubs knew that; yet still Milan refused to increase the away-ticket allocation, pleading policing difficulties despite there being several empty sections of the ground.

It was Pete, another Spurs fan I'd come across through collecting old programmes and tickets on eBay, who came to the rescue, pointing me in the direction of a website selling tickets in the neutral area. He also sorted out the travel arrangements.

'Don't go direct to Milan,' he said. 'All the airlines have put their fares up for this game. The normal return fare is under £100 at this time of year; the cheapest I can find is well over £450. So I've worked out we're better off flying Ryanair to Bologna and taking the high-speed train to Milan.'

You know you're in trouble when you have to fly Ryanair anywhere; to have to do so going to a city you don't even want to visit sounded like pure masochism. But I trusted Pete. He was acting as his own one-man tour operator for his party of twelve, and had spent days researching the trip. If there was a better way he would have found it. So I unofficially became the tour guide for my own squad.

There were three of us this time. Matthew, you've already met. The new recruit to our travelling line-up was Terry. I've known Terry for more than twenty years; our families have been on holiday together and he's one of my best friends. I would also reckon that nearly ninety per cent of our conversations have been about sport. He is a sport and Spurs obsessive, though since he took himself off to live in the sticks he hardly gets to White Hart Lane these days. He does, though, have the uncanny knack of being able to track down tickets to all big sporting events. I've lost count of the number of cup finals and test matches he's managed to wangle his way into over the years. Needless to say, he'd got his Milan ticket sorted weeks ago through a good friend of his, Marco G., an Inter supporter.

'We could go together, though, I suppose,' he had said when I had rung to ask him if he fancied coming. 'Could you book the same flights and trains for me?'

This wasn't so much a request as an order. One of Terry's nicknames is Skip, as he's been captain of our fairly useless nomadic cricket team ever since it played its first match about thirty years ago, and he's been telling us all what number we are going to bat, where we are going to field and if there's any likelihood we are going to get a bowl every summer ever since. Terry, it should be noted, always stands at slip, even though few of us can ever remember him taking a catch there, and he always opens the batting. To be fair, he is one of the best batsmen, though that isn't saying a great deal and the rest of the team has lost count of the number of times we've been bored out of our minds watching him grind his way to a slow fifty in thirty overs, leaving the remaining six or seven batsmen, who've probably travelled for over an hour for the pleasure, ten overs between them to lose their wicket slogging in order to try and post a remotely competitive total.

My only real talent for cricket is sledging my own team – abusing your friends is so much more entertaining than having a pop at the oppo. I am what Terry patronizingly calls a 'handy fifth-change bowler', i.e. someone to whom he can throw the ball when the game is already lost as everyone wants to go home asap, and a number-nine batsman, though I have been known to go in as high as seven when batsmen higher up the order have either pulled a hamstring (not uncommon) or have fallen asleep (increasingly common).

The cricket team, then, is Terry's personal fiefdom – as was our football team, from which I retired ten years ago with dodgy knees and from which everyone else, much less fit than me, I should point out, hung up their boots three years ago after one of our opponents had a near-fatal heart attack on the pitch. In return for doing nearly all the organizing and delegating, Terry gets to call the shots. And as I still harbour aspirations of becoming the regular number seven – a position traditionally awarded on whim and patronage rather than merit – I was hoping that getting Terry to Milan and back within just over twenty-four hours would earn me a few brownie points for the following summer.

'Turn off the light and stop making such a fucking din,' said Jill as I got out of bed.

'Have a good time, too,' I replied.

Getting up at 3 a.m. wasn't my idea of fun either, but when Ryanair insists on flying from Stansted at seven there's not a lot of choice. I shouted at Terry and Matthew to get up and we were on our way. In silence, as both promptly went straight back to sleep in the car.

Stansted was teeming at five in the morning, with roughly half the passengers wearing a Spurs shirt and flying to anywhere in northern Italy. Here were thousands of fans like us who had also decided they were going to do whatever it took to get to Milan. It could almost have been life-affirming if there hadn't been massive queues for everything.

Matthew's wife calls our trips to away games 'mini-breaks'. I think of them more as endurance tests, away-days to find out how much physical and psychological pain – step forward Ryanair – I can put myself through within a short period of time. And more often than not, we suffer in near silence – even to the extent that Matthew, Terry and I sat in different sections of the plane as we all wanted an aisle seat so that we were in with a chance of surviving the flight without having a leg amputated.

I've made it sound like we are a group of typical middle-aged, middle-class men hovering somewhere in the middle of the autistic spectrum. But that's not quite fair. I'm actually quite good at emotions, as are Terry and Matthew.

I've done time in mental hospitals, I've been in therapy for over twenty years, I can recognise a feeling when I see one – especially the bad ones, I'm an expert in them – and I'm very happy (bad choice of word; perhaps I should have said willing) to talk about them. Indeed, my wife often wishes I would stop. But football is our brief time out from all that, a time when everything gets sublimated to the common cause of getting to and from a match. Winning is merely an added bonus, which is just as well when you're playing Inter Milan in the San Siro. There's no long-term, deep-rooted psychological avoidance going on; we know we'll get back to whatever else it is we're worried about soon enough. So try to think of it like going to a health spa. Only without the pampering.

Pete caught up with us on the train from Bologna to Milan. He had taken his tour-guide duties rather more seriously than me – or perhaps he had more serious doubts about the mental competence of some of his companions – and had printed out detailed instructions of everything, from what ticket to buy on the metro to what tram to take to the San Siro. As I hadn't realised Milan had an underground system, this was face-saving information.

'So we'll take the metro into the centre of town, pick up the tickets and then meet the two Marcos for lunch,' I said. Neither Matthew nor Terry bothered to respond to what clearly struck them as an inane statement of the obvious.

'Ciao, Terry,' said Marco G. and Marco A., as we arrived at the restaurant.

'Ciao, Marco, ciao Marco,' Terry replied. 'Meet John and Matthew.'

Terry is one of the best-connected people I know. I've been on a near-deserted beach with him in the middle of nowhere and he's still managed to bump into someone he'd met years before. The two Marcos didn't quite fall into this category. Terry had known Marco G. for more than thirty years and Marco A. for about half that time, and had twisted their arms into putting him up for the night in his own presidential suite in Marco G.'s apartment, while Matthew and I were shoehorned into sharing Marco A.'s spare room. And very decent it was, too. It just wasn't a presidential suite, Terry.

There were no problems of loyalty, though, with Marco A. He was an AC Milan supporter and wanted nothing more than Inter to be thumped; for tonight he was happy to be an honorary Spur. Not so with Marco G. He was Inter through and through, but distressingly unbothered about his club's challenge in the night ahead. He was very funny and extremely charming, but his subtext was unmissable; that Spurs were a second-rate club hardly worth his attention and if we hadn't made it out to Milan, he wouldn't have dreamed of paying to watch such a C-list game. He spoke for the entire city.

The two Marcos had to go back to work, so the three of us had an afternoon to kill. There we were in one of the most stunning cities in Europe, and what did we want to do? Well, I wanted to find the Inter Milan club shop to see if I could buy any clobber it had produced to mark the game, but not only did it turn out this wasn't a game that Inter thought worth even a programme, the shop itself seemed to have been closed down. Or possibly relocated. No one seemed to know, or care. In England, even a lower-league club has its own shop, hawking all varieties of tat; it seemed the Milanese were too street-savvy to fall for marketing hustle.

I then said I'd like to see La Scala. Terry and Matthew looked at me as if I was mad, and adopted their long-suffering 'we're going to be really indulgent on this occasion but you owe us' faces. I've been an opera lover for years, and have always wanted to go to the world's most famous opera house. So this was important to me. The building was locked up when we got there, but it was thrill enough just to be outside the building and imagine the great nights I had missed inside.

'You had enough yet?' said Terry after we'd been at La Scala for less than two minutes. 'Matthew and I are bored.'

Still, it was a rather more impressive piece of sightseeing than the rest of the fans had achieved. We made our way to the huge square outside the cathedral to be greeted by the Yid Army in full force. It wasn't the most edifying of spectacles. It looked as if every fan had made a beeline for the square from the airport several hours previously and set up shop with industrial quantities of lager. Most were now pissed out of their minds and singing the offensive Sol Campbell chant that was banned in the UK, while the Milanese gave them a wide, disapproving berth. I guess it was one way of killing time in a stylish, sophisticated city that you don't know and in which you feel insecure and threatened by its foreignness, but it wasn't mine. I could feel my effete middle-class liberalism seeping out of every pore.

'Wow,' cried Matthew, as we got to the San Siro. 'We've just got to have a stadium like this. It's got to be worth a goal advantage every game.'

I felt much the same way. There was nothing beautiful about the San Siro; it was just breathtakingly immense, a vast, fascistic slab of concrete that screamed, 'You are a speck of dust who will be crushed underfoot' to all visitors. We were so overawed, we didn't say a word till we had found our seats among the neutrals. Or rather, among a cabal of Spurs fans. As expected, the ground was half empty, but something like 14,000 Spurs fans had made the effort to come. Almost all the noise was coming from the Spurs fans, with the Milanese maintaining a complacent quietude. This was a chorus I could join in.

The players looked equally as overawed when they walked out of the tunnel, and played like it. Within minutes we were a goal down. The Italians cheered for a bit at that. Within ten minutes, we were two down. The previous season, Gomes had become a local hero, the fans' favourite, and had won my own unofficial accolade as 'best shot-stopper in the Premiership'. He had the club's best terrace chant of, 'I love you Gomes, You are the love of my life, Heurelho Gomes, I'd let you shag my wife, Heurelho Gomes, I wish I was Brazilian too'. This year, though, his keeping had shown signs of reverting to the idiosyncrasies of his early days with Spurs; this night was a case in point, as he unsubtly assaulted Jonathan Biabiany in the box to get himself sent off and concede a penalty.

Within fifteen minutes, Stankovic had scored a third, a goal the Inter fans could barely be bothered to cheer as all their pre-match forecasts of the one-sidedness of the contest had been borne out.

'This is as bad as the Bern game,' I said to Matthew.

It wasn't. It was worse. Crouch had a free header inside

the six-yard box and ballooned it over – a miss that had the Inter fans, who weren't used to his goal shyness, sniggering – and then Samuel Eto'o added a fourth.

'It could end up 7-0,' I said at half-time.

'Or 8-0,' Matthew added. 'This could be the worst night in our entire history.'

'It would be nice if we could just get one goal back. I'd like to see us score at the San Siro.'

We did rather better than that. Early in the second half, Bale picked up the ball deep in his own half, carried on running, past Zanetti, past Maicon, past Samuel, before hitting the ball left-footed past a stunned César. We went mad, singing 'We're going to win 5-4' while the Inter fans smiled at us underdogs, almost pleased we had a magic memory to take home with us. Then late, late in the game Bale scored twice more – one a carbon copy of the first – to make the score 4-3. Suddenly it was the Inter fans who were on the back foot, screaming for the ref to blow the final whistle. It was their team who was hacking the ball away aimlessly, and had the match gone on for another ten minutes we might have even won 5-4.

It was a wonderful, thrilling, ridiculous finale. The sort that only Spurs seem to make a habit. It was also, as Marco G. was quick to point out afterwards, 'still a defeat. And Inter cannot play as badly as they did in the second half again.' But some honour had been restored. Our ten-man Spurs had outplayed the best team in Europe for the second forty-five minutes, and proved that both the club and fans had a right to be there. We weren't imposters. Better still, Bremen and Twente had played out a draw in their qualifier, leaving us still in second place and with a decent chance of making the knockout stages.

But best of all, I had fulfilled a lifetime's ambition of seeing Spurs playing at the San Siro, and I hadn't been let down. Before the game, I'd have settled for a 2-0 loss, a scoreline that wouldn't look embarrassing. Coming back from 4-0 to 4-3 with a world-class hat-trick thrown in was something never to forget. I suppose a 1-0 win would have been even better, but that really would have been Fantasy Football.

The plane was a great deal quieter on the way back than it had been on the way out, but I did get chatting to the bloke sitting next to me. He and his dad were none too happy.

'Guess what?' he said.

'What?'

'We missed the second half.'

'Serious?'

'Yeah. My dad wasn't feeling too well at half-time and we were 4-0 down, so I took him back to the hotel.'

There wasn't a lot I could say. I went back to my book.

As I dropped Terry off at a tube station in central London later that morning, I thought it was time to chance my arm.

'Great game, wasn't it?' I said.

'Yes.'

'Um . . . Do you think there's any chance I could bat at seven next year?

Terry said nothing for a while before replying.

'No, not really. You're more of a natural number nine.'

To add insult, three days later I got a £60 ticket and a three-point penalty for driving at 31 mph over Tower Bridge at 3.47 a.m. when there wasn't another car in sight.

Still, I'd got lucky in Milan, and that's what really counted.

***

Almost inevitably, a reaction kicked in soon afterwards. Having spent so many years imagining Spurs playing in the San Siro, achieving that milestone left me feeling somewhat empty. I'd been there, I'd done it, the game – at least the second half – had lived up to expectations, and yet I was left with the niggling sense of 'Was that it?'

But then, I often feel that way. My overwhelming reaction to every book I've ever written has been disappointment – a sentiment possibly shared by publishers and readers alike, though for rather different reasons. While I'm in the process of writing, there is still the sense of possibility; but once the book finally appears it feels somehow dead. There's a brief week or two of good-for-the-ego attention and then it's largely forgotten, gathering dust somewhere in the Amazon warehouse. And every time I'd wondered whether the amount I had been paid had been worth all the effort. The having of the dream often seems so much more rewarding than its fulfilment. Back in the early 1980s, I queued up for hours to get a ticket to see one of the world's greatest tenors, Luciano Pavarotti, perform at the Royal Opera House in Verdi's *Un Ballo in Maschera*. As the opera reached its climax with the death scene, Pavarotti fell to the stage and bounced; half the audience, myself included, tittered. Three hours of sublime music undone in an instant.

The practicalities of dealing with the hollowness of disappointment are simple enough: you just shift the goal posts. With Pavarotti, I simply promised myself I would only ever listen to him on record, and save my cash for live performances with Plácido Domingo. With the San Siro ticked off, I could switch my focus to the Bernabéu and the Camp Nou. But the emotional fallout was harder to deal with, because with every shift there comes a sense of compromise, a feeling you are having to fool your psyche into finding new reasons to stay alive.

Yet there was undeniably a San Siro-shaped hole in my life; even if I did get to see Spurs place Barça or Real Madrid in their own stadiums in the Champions League sometime in the future, it would never match the thrill of the first time in Milan. It's just the way it is. Sleeping with Sienna Miller is probably quite exciting the first time, I should imagine; after that it probably just feels routine. Possibly even toxic.

I wasn't the only one to be having an adverse reaction to Milan. Every Spurs fan had known Gareth Bale was fairly special ever since the February of the previous season, but now the media had caught up and the papers couldn't get enough of him, bigging him up before the home game against Everton. Typically, he had one of his quieter days, though if Spurs had had a striker in form – or, as Amici said to me at half-time, any kind of striker – we might have come out comfortably on top. As usual, we only had Peter Crouch. To be fair, he did manage to get some part of his body to make contact with the ball to lay on an equaliser for van der Vaart once more, but Harry Redknapp's post-match assertion that Crouch and van der Vaart were developing into one of the Premiership's top strike forces was a startling piece of news, when everyone sitting near me was under the impression that we had missed loads of clear-cut chances and that 1-1 against a mediocre team was yet another two points dropped.

The only person to go home vaguely happy was my friend, Alex, who came along when Robbie had to cry off; partly because he doesn't get to many games, but mainly because he is one of the few people I know who takes more perverse pleasure in things going wrong than I do. For him, the general levels of post-Milan inertia within the team – crowned by Crouch's rendition of Bambi – were a piece of postmodern football performance art. Something to be treasured, rather than mocked. I just wish I could have seen it the same way.

**

Confession time. I've only ever been to Old Trafford once, and that wasn't for a football game. It was back in the early 1990s when I'd just started my career as a writer, and had landed a plum gig writing a book to tie in with the second series of *Cracker* – part of which involved interviewing Robbie Coltrane. After countless calls with the programme's fixers, a date was finally arranged for me to come up to Old Trafford where they were filming on location and chat to Coltrane once he had finished for the day.

I got to Old Trafford on time, but it soon became clear that the interview wasn't going to happen any time soon as the filming was running hopelessly late. So I hung around to watch. For a while I couldn't believe my luck. Here I was, watching Robbie Coltrane filming the best cop show on television. But after viewing a couple of takes of Coltrane doing the same thing over and over again, only for the director to insist on doing it once more exactly the same, I rapidly grew bored and wandered up some steps into the stands to take a look at the pitch itself. I was amazed by the size of the ground; it dwarfed any other club ground I had been to. It made White Hart Lane look like the County Ground at Swindon.

Having tortured myself enough, I went to rejoin the film crew, where my eye was caught by an intense-looking, shaven-headed short-arse. He spotted me looking at him, came rushing over, squared up to me and poked me firmly in the chest.

'What the fuck are you staring at?' he yelled.

Several members of the crew pulled him off me and the producer came over to calm things down.

'Don't take it personally,' he said. 'He's the actor, Robert Carlyle, who is playing Albie, the killer in this episode. He's a wee bit method in his acting.'

A wee bit of a prat, if you ask me. But the encounter has scarred me, because ever since I have identified Old Trafford as a place where I am going to be abused for no good reason. Which, as it goes, pretty much describes Spurs own experiences of the ground. Unfortunately the team doesn't have the option of not turning up – even if it's often looked as if they haven't bothered over the years. For some reason, we invariably go to Old Trafford in a craven state of mind. We expect to be beaten, and invariably we are. On match-days, I doubt it even occurs to Fergie or the United fans that they are going to lose. It's just a question of turning up to collect three points.

And even on those rare days when we do look like we believe we have a right to play at Old Trafford, something always goes wrong. There was the disallowed Pedro

Mendes goal which was a yard over the line. There was the match we were two goals up in at the fifty-minute mark, and the referee was conned into awarding a penalty and sending off Gomes. The shock sent the team into freefall; they played like headless chickens for the rest of the game and lost 5-2.

For all these reasons, I'm a reluctant traveller to Old Trafford. Each year I say to myself, 'Maybe this is the year I should go. We can't go on losing there indefinitely, and it would be a shame to miss out when we eventually do win.' But each year I can't make a good enough case why this year should be any different to the previous twenty, and the idea of paying £40 to one of the richest clubs in Europe for the pleasure of being turned over either by United or the referee sticks in the throat.

As it happened, we were turned over by both United and the referee. We were already 1-0 down, having allowed Vidić a free header, when the referee, not content with allowing Nani to handle the ball, let him kick it into an empty net when Gomes tried to take the free kick that should have been given. Some of the pundits tried to claim it was legitimate and that Gomes should have played to the whistle, but this was a piss-poor argument. The only judge of a fair decision at Old Trafford is whether the referee would dare make the same call against Manchester United, and the chances of a ref risking a post-match bawling-out from Fergie were nil.

So stuffed again, and my decision to watch the game from the floor of my Streatham living room was absolutely vindicated – though I remained in a foul mood for the rest of the weekend. We may have been the talk of Europe with our Milan second-half comeback, but we didn't seem to be presenting too many problems to teams in the Premiership. Harry talked breezily about it being early days in the season, but mid-table is mid-table. And just because it's where I always feared we might be right now, it didn't mean I was enjoying it.

November

OUT OF THE WOODWORK they came. Emails, phone calls, apologetic half-conversations at work. The return leg against Inter Milan was suddenly the hottest ticket in town, and dozens of people were on the scrounge. It was a strange feeling. I'd lost count of the number of times in the past when I'd had a spare ticket to a game and could scarcely give it away. Jerry had once refused to go to a match as a matter of principle because it was still officially the cricket season; Tom had preferred to go swimming. They were the exceptions: most people couldn't even be bothered to come up with an excuse. I've never really understood it. I know a midweek game against Middlesbrough on a cold night in February isn't the most thrilling of prospects, but the mere fact it is being played at all makes a pointless February weekday worthwhile. Any day when Spurs are playing is better than one when they aren't. At least up until kick-off.

Pleasing as it was that no one was that interested in whoever Chelsea, Arsenal or Manchester United were playing in the Champions League that week – I knew how they felt – I couldn't help thinking my personal space was being invaded. White Hart Lane was my semi-private

communion and I didn't really want a whole load of
neutrals, seduced by a Bale hat-trick in Milan and Spurs'
growing reputation for playing attacking football from
media pundits who must have missed some of the dreadful league games I had been forced to endure, taking an
interest in the game. I preferred us as outsiders looking
in, and the idea of the club being the centre of so many
people's attention made me feel uncomfortable.

There was never a chance of me having a spare ticket
for the Milan game. Despite it being a midweek night in
term time – normally his mother's kiss of death – this one
had been earmarked as a Robbie game from the off. It was
just too important a game and I – and Robbie – wanted
him to be there. Some finessing of the travel plans were
required to get it past the thought police.

'It's the biggest game of the season,' I said. 'He can't
miss it.'

'There seem to be an awful lot of the biggest games of
the season,' Jill replied.

This wasn't a direction I wanted the conversation to go
in. Best to keep it non-committal.

'Mmm.'

'Mmm what?'

'I'll make sure he's got all his homework done, and I'll
tell him not to be too grumpy in the morning.'

'I'm still not happy . . .'

She seldom is, though this wasn't the time to point that
out.

'So it's a deal. Great. Thanks, babe.'

'Um, let me . . .'

'Relax. It will be fine.'

I shouted upstairs. 'Oi, Robbie, Mum says you can go.'

Before Jill had a chance to put the record straight, Robbie called out. 'Thanks, Mum. Love you.'

Four words that work every time. It was now a deal. The boy will go far.

I wasn't the only one to be feeling unexpectedly chipper. For as long as I've known him, Bob at work has always been even gloomier than me about Spurs' prospects. Just about the only times anyone can remember him smiling are when he has something disastrous to report. 'Did you hear that Lennon is out for four weeks?' he'll say with a grin. 'We're screwed now.' He also takes a keen interest in the declining form of Wilson Palacios. I've always had a soft spot for the Wilce. He came into the team at a time when it would collectively wilt if it started raining or the temperature fell below a balmy 15°C, and cheered everyone up by indiscriminately clattering opponents and displaying a willingness to pick up a yellow card in injury time, long after the game had already been lost. The trouble with Wilce is that as the team began to improve, he didn't. He still had the unerring knack of mistiming a tackle – it was now becoming a race to see how soon Harry had to substitute him in case he got sent off – and every other pass he made went to the opposition. The less said about his shooting skills the better. In short, he was becoming a liability; hence Bob's current fascination with him.

But for a few brief days, Bob had things on his mind other than injury crises and Wilson's decline. Like the rest of us, he'd been caught in the carnival spirit of the Milan game and was looking forward to taking his ten-year-old son to his first evening kick-off. 'I couldn't not take him,' he said. 'It might never happen again.' By the sound of it, he'd had a very similar conversation with his wife as I'd had with mine.

There was something vaguely unreal about the excitement. It was one of those rare occasions when being there was almost enough in itself. After a lifetime of waiting, we were going to play Inter Milan at White Hart Lane. Nothing could stop us. All that was required was for each of us to make it to the ground intact – I drove with more care than usual on my way up – and an ambition would be realised. It would be nice if we played well, but it wasn't essential. This wasn't related to my usual dose of pre-match pessimism; if anything, I'd seen enough at the San Siro to believe we could compete. It was more that on this night, winning or losing was less important than just being there. As long as we weren't outclassed, I could live with any result.

There was only one team outclassed; and it wasn't Spurs. Right from the off, the game had a fantasy quality. Normally it takes a while for the crowd to find its voice. There's a quick five minutes of 'We are Tottenham, super Tottenham' and then it all gets a bit subdued, as if we're waiting for the players to inspire us. This time, the noise never stopped. I looked to my right to check on Robbie. He was on his feet, arms stretched out, singing tunelessly. And loudly. There was none of the tentative growling I'd first picked up at Fulham. This was a full-on, unselfconscious chant, the first of his life. I turned away, keen not to let him know I'd been staring at him.

On the pitch, the same Disney film-script boxes were also getting ticked. Everything we tried, worked; the lesser mortals played like kings, and our kings played like gods. By half-time we were 1-0, and no one could quite believe what we were watching. It wasn't the scoreline in itself so much as the manner of the lead. And it quickly got better. Bale had already been running the Brazilian defender Maicon ragged, and Amici and I had spent half-time wondering why on earth Inter didn't do what every other Premier League club had taken to doing and have two men mark him. The best we could come up with was that the rest of the Milan defence had had enough of being embarrassed by Bale in the San Siro, and had decided the best way to protect their reputations was by giving Bale a wide berth. Still, no one in the ground was complaining when he ran past everyone and whipped in a cross that even Crouchie couldn't miss.

Normally when Spurs are 2-0 up, they try to do what other professional teams do: shut up shop and close out the game. Except we are hopeless at it, invariably defending deeper and deeper until we concede a goal and then panic as the opposition goes all out for an equaliser. This time, though, we just kept going forward. It was glorious to watch. Even when a mistake let in Eto'o to make it 2-1 we kept attacking, and a couple of minutes before the end another Bale run from the halfway line gave Pav a tap-in and we were out of sight. After indulging in a few verses of 'Taxi for Maicon', the crowd moved on to 'Gareth Bale, Gareth Bale, He was born to play for Spurs'. It wasn't true, of course. Bale is fit, fast and never stops trying, qualities that haven't always been endemic in past Spurs legends. But tonight was a time for celebration, not quibbling.

On the way out of the ground, we met Mat. He looked shell-shocked. He held out his hands and shrugged. 'I just had no idea we could play that well,' he said. Nor did I. And neither, I would guess, did the players themselves. For one night only they had been given a rare glimpse of what it was like to play near-perfect football, and would probably spend the rest of their lives trying to find that magic again and wondering just why it was so hard to recapture.

Robbie was in no doubt about what he had seen. 'That was just fucking incredible, Dad,' he said. 'I can't imagine a better game.' He was probably right. I kept my mouth shut, choosing not to point out this meant his life as a Spurs fan had peaked when he was fifteen. There was plenty of time for him to realise that later. Or maybe he would, like me, come to see the Milan game as something so out of the ordinary it could be recompartmentalised as paranormal.

The following morning, I got a call from Adrian. 'That Bale, he's unbelievable, isn't he?'

'Yes,' I said, waiting for the follow-up. Adrian wouldn't have phoned just to tell me Bale was unbelievable. Even though he was a Manchester United supporter, he'd long clocked Bale's progress.

'Um . . . So what is it with Bale's tats?'

'What tats?'

'You know, the tattoos on his legs.'

Fantastic. He'd mistaken the black strapping on his thighs for a tat.

'Oh, them? They're tribal art. They symbolise the warrior. Bale says that ever since he had them done, he feels invincible.'

What the hell. After the way he had played the night before, it was near enough the truth.

***

There was never a chance of me going to Bolton. It's a real schlep to get to, the ground isn't that nice and, more importantly, we always seem to play badly against them on their own ground. I've never quite worked out why. It just seems that whenever the team arrive at the Reebok Stadium they take one look at the pitch and reckon they are going to get a bit too muddy. Or maybe that's doing Bolton a disservice. Maybe they just know that a bit of muscle and a few tasty challenges in the first half-hour will see off a bunch of soft Londoners. Either way, we usually manage to look like we'd rather be almost anywhere else. Which is how many of us Spurs fans have also come to feel about the fixture.

This year, there were even more compelling reasons to avoid the game. The papers had been full of our brilliance for a couple of days since the Milan game, and were predicting we'd outclass Bolton, seemingly unaware we usually followed up a European match by looking like a total rabble in the next game. And then there was the time of kick-off. Spurs and lunchtime kick-offs are rarely a good combination, as for the first half most of the players tend to look as if they have barely got out of bed. We just stand around, rub our eyes and let the other team run at us. Only if we're by some chance holding them to 0-0 at half-time are we in with a shout.

No chance this time. Bolton were 2-0 up and out of sight by half-time – more through our own haplessness than their own creativity. Not long into the second half Bolton scored a third, and though Spurs did sneak two back towards the end, we were overstretched going for an equaliser and gave away a fourth in injury time.

Watching all this on TV didn't make it any less painful. And seeing what we could do when we bothered made it even more frustrating; if only we'd started the match playing like we did during the last fifteen minutes we'd have won comfortably. After the game, the Spurs message boards were polarised between 'It's a bad day at the office, forget it' and 'How fucking dare they?' I was more of a 'How fucking dare they?' man, myself. Each defeat hurts, even when it's expected. And when it's a self-inflicted defeat, I'm pissed off.

A few days later, we got a variation on the 'it's hard to lift yourself after a big game' excuse after the Sunderland home fixture, the highlight of which had been Trevor telling me that the programme for the Inter Milan game had sold out and people were wanting silly money for them on eBay, and asking had I bought any extra to flog? Of course I hadn't. Almost everything I've ever bought as an investment has lost money. I'm probably the only person in Britain with an endowment mortgage who hasn't thought about suing for mis-selling – for the very good reason that the person who sold it to me was me. My nine months as an insurance salesman in the mid-1980s weren't the highlight of my career.

There were a few boos – not mine this time; I didn't have the energy even for that – as the teams went off with the score 0-0 after a first half of little passion, played largely at training-ground pace. The tempo picked up a little in the second half, and for a glorious three minutes Justin was crowing about Crouchie's genius after he had teed up van der Vaart for the opening goal. I was so relieved to be ahead I almost found myself agreeing with him, but then our defence was caught snoozing, Sunderland equalised and that's the way it stayed.

As usual on the way home, I had Radio 5 Live on in the car and sure enough Harry had something to say. He'd given the fans Champions League football and they were an ungrateful load of bastards – or words to that effect – for moaning about a 1-1 draw.

You couldn't have asked for a better example of the divide between those who make a living out of football and those who spend rather too much of their time and cash watching it. The moans weren't for the draw; as at Bolton, they were for the manner in which we played, a kind of 'Couldn't really be arsed, oh well, never mind there will be another game along soon' mentality. And maybe that's how it is for professional footballers; it's not a game, it's a job and there are some matches where you're not feeling much like working and you take your foot off the pedal.

But as a fan, I just don't get it. One of the reasons I started watching football was because I wasn't good enough to play it to a decent standard and I was in awe of those who could. I'd have traded a lot to have been able to play just once in front of a crowd of 35,000, with several million watching later on TV. And even if I was having a dog of a game, I'd have run myself into the ground, out of fear of being embarrassed, if nothing else. Come to think of it, I used to run myself to a standstill back in the days when I had two good knees and played park football in front of a crowd of zero. We all did. It wouldn't have occurred to us not to. A football game was one of the highlights of the week – a break from not doing very much (in my case) or from a dreary day at the office (for everyone else). Why would we waste the time by counting the minutes to full-time? So here's a deal, Harry. You make sure each and every one of your players plays with commitment and desire for ninety minutes, and I can promise not to moan, whatever the result. Well, not much.

***

There are also losses off the pitch. The only reason I am now able to go to virtually every home game – and quite a few of the away ones – each season is because the kids no longer need such close surveillance. It's a strange one. I've always adored Anna and Robbie, and it has been a privilege to watch them grown up, but their early years weren't always the most thrilling. Being woken up at all times of the night wasn't the issue: my insomnia had been doing that to me for years already. It was the mindless production-line repetition. Reading them the same story night after night: their choice not mine. Going to the same park time and again to push them on swings: their choice not mine. Crap children's TV, the endless going through their tables with them – 'If two times three equals six, how can three times three possibly equal ten? What do you get if you add three to six?' 'Eight, Daddy' – the piles of plastic cluttering up the house, their friends bursting into tears the moment their parents left them at our house for a play date. That sort of thing.

I wasn't the most patient of dads, but I got on with it and did my bit. If I didn't think about it too much I even enjoyed some of it, but life became much more rewarding when they got older and I could have a decent conversation with them. There was at least the possibility of finding an activity that both of you might want to do. There was also a brief window when they were compliant enough to do a few things if I leaned on them a bit and offered enough bribes. With Robbie, it was playing football. As my own undistinguished playing days had long since ended on the operating table, the next best thing was for Robbie to play vicariously for me. So for a couple of years he played in goal – his preferred position – every weekend throughout the winter for a local south London club side.

He did sort of enjoy it, too, as they weren't a bad side – they reached the cup final both years – but then some of the other boys, along with most of the dads (myself included), started taking it far too seriously by trying to make the team attend midweek training sessions and shouting at everyone throughout the game. As far as Robbie was concerned, the fun was over. He liked playing – he still does for his school team – but fulfilling the grandiose, frustrated managerial ambitions of a bunch of middle-aged dads wasn't on his agenda. So one day he just said he'd had enough and was going to take up mountainbiking instead. And that was that.

I had tried something similar with Anna. She'd shown promise as a runner at school, and since I'd also once fancied myself as a runner, I took her down to train with the local athletics club. It wasn't a great success. She made a lot of friends, but there was a big difference between being able to run faster than everyone in her school over almost any distance, and racing against some of the best runners in her age group in London. It all got a bit too serious a bit too quick.

The main sticking point, though, was that running was my idea, not hers. She wasn't the one who had once fantasised about being Steve Ovett; nor was she overly grateful when I gave her the Paula Radcliffe autobiography for

Christmas one year. The miracle was that she stuck it out for two years and was still talking to me by the end. If only intermittently.

And that was my problem. With Robbie, I'd managed to limit the feelings of loss associated with his growing independence through a shared love of Spurs. We had something we enjoyed doing together, and it created an important connection – for me, at least. But with Anna I was rather adrift. She now had her own dreams. She had a serious passion for drama – she got top billing in most school plays and joined a semi-professional theatre company – and all I could do was admire her talents from afar. And wonder where she got them from. So there was nothing now she really wanted me for beyond some arm's-length moral support, the frequent lift and the more frequent cash hit; and knowing that was how it was probably meant to be – she knew I loved her enough for it to be safe enough for her to ignore me – was little consolation. I missed spending time with her.

From time to time, she would wind me up by asking why I never invited her to come to Spurs with me, even though we both knew the answer; she hated football. So from time to time, I would make a point of asking her and she would make a point of looking at me as if I was an idiot and saying, 'Why on earth would I want to do that?' You could call it honours even; or, if you wanted to give it a more positive spin, keeping the channels of communication open.

I admit to taking a perverse enjoyment that her boyfriend Ollie was not only a Spurs fan, but a man after my own heart who considered following a game via a live blog on the BBC website time very well spent. The idea of him

grunting non-committally as he stares at the screen praying the next update will be a Spurs goal, while she tries to
makes conversation with him, strikes me as some kind of
poetic justice. An even more unexpected upside of their
relationship was to come. She refused to admit it, but,
as mentioned, she was unquestionably put out that Ollie
had got to go to a Spurs game with me before her. Even
though she didn't actually want to go, the natural order
had somehow been disturbed.

So the next time Robbie couldn't make it, I asked her
if she wanted to go. She paused a while and said, 'Yes. But
I want you to know I'm doing you a favour.' Whatever it
takes. A home game against Blackburn isn't always the
easiest sell to a neutral, but luckily Anna knew – and cared
– so little about football, she was entirely indifferent to the
quality of the opposition. She just had two basic ground
rules.

'I won't be singing,' she said.

'No problem,' I replied. 'That will suit us all.'

'And I don't want you hugging me if we score. That
would be embarrassing.'

Blackburn may not have meant much to Anna, but it
did to me. It's often the games we're expected to cruise
that make me the most nervous, because the expectation
is so much higher. Winning this kind of game is only ever
experienced as relief rather than joy; a potential banana
skin missed. Fortunately, Spurs did their best to settle the
nerves with an early goal.

'I told you not to hug me,' said Anna as I began my
usual celebrations. It made me think. Whenever I've gone
to a game with Matthew and we've scored, I've always
given him a hug too, but I don't think he's ever initiated a

hug with me. He's never pushed me away, mind. Perhaps football fans divide between the huggers and the huggees.

The match should have been over by half-time as we missed chance after chance, including a penalty. I've lost count of the number of penalties I've seen us miss over the years, but it's reached the point where – after a moment's euphoria at being awarded the decision – some of those around me can't bring themselves to watch when the kick is taken. I've often wished I hadn't either, but I find myself transfixed. 'Surely we can't miss another one,' I say to myself as whichever striker has drawn the short straw runs up. Only to hit it wide or straight at the keeper. When the Carling Cup final against Manchester United went to penalties a few years back, a couple of people sitting near me left before they started.

'We're going to lose, and we'll only get caught in the crowd for the tube if we hang around,' they said. They were right on both counts. It took me hours to get home.

Pav missed the penalty, and no one on the pitch or in the crowd was that surprised.

'Ah well,' said Justin.

'Ah well,' I replied.

Pav did redeem himself by scoring shortly before the break, but a 2-0 scoreline means nothing at White Hart Lane.

'We're doing OK, aren't we?' Anna asked during the interval.

'I suppose so. But . . .'

We scored twice more early in the second half, and even Crouchie got on the score sheet with his first league goal of the season. A tap-in.

'I told you he'd come good,' yelled Justin.

It didn't seem the moment to point out that almost anyone – apart from Wilson Palacios – will score if you leave them on the pitch for long enough. And besides, at that particular moment, I loved Crouchie as well.

At 4-0 up with ten minutes left, even I didn't think we could screw things up, though we did manage to take the gloss off the victory by conceding two late soft goals.

Still, a win was a win, even if, as expected, it was accompanied only by feelings of disaster averted. And I had got to hug Anna four times: I even rather think she had got used to it by the end.

'So did you enjoy it then?' I asked as we left the stadium.

'More than I expected,' she said.

It was a start.

'Would you come again, then?'

'Yeah. But it does feel a bit weird hanging around with a load of sad, middle-aged blokes.'

That's my life rubbished, then, though I'm not sure Justin and Amici would be thrilled to be described as middle-aged. I guess when you're eighteen anyone over the age of thirty is ancient.

We walked on in silence through the crowd.

'I am curious about one thing, though,' she said.

'What's that?'

'How come you get so much pleasure out of something that gives you so much pain?'

It was a good question.

***

The answer wasn't long in coming. Any away game against Arsenal always feels like the inscription above Dante's gates of hell: 'Abandon all hope, ye who enter here.' No Spurs fan has ever seen us win at the Emirates for the simple reason that we never have. Then most fans, myself included, never saw us win when Arsenal's home ground was Highbury as our last away victory was sometime back in the early 1990s. There have been a few draws that we've celebrated as wins – most notably a couple of years back when we scored two injury-time goals to draw 4-4. But, let's face it, when you've reached the point where you're forced to delude yourself that a draw is as good as a win, then you're clutching at straws.

Which pretty much described my state of mind on the morning of the match. Although our away record against Arsenal has always been as piss-poor as against Manchester United, I've found it much harder to stay away. I've even once gone with an Arsenal fan and sat in the home fans section when I couldn't get a ticket. Never again. I came within nanoseconds of being lynched before my friend pulled me back into my seat when Berbatov equalised. And we went on to lose. Of course.

It helps that the Emirates is a lot closer to home – there's no three-and-a-half-hour gloomy car ride home to worry about – but the Arsenal game also has a much more visceral pull. However much I may hate Man United and Chelsea on a day-to-day basis, no game brings out my feelings of resentment and sense of underachievement more than the local derby. It could just be that there's no other game that shapes your identity so clearly; it's certainly one of the only games where rival fans are regularly, openly anti-Semitic. On several occasions I've been part of a crowd of Spurs fans that has been greeted with the hissing sound of the gas chamber by Arsenal fans. That focuses the mind. Or it could just be, as Matthew insists, that I'm not a proper north Londoner – he went to a predominantly Arsenal-supporting school where he claims he probably received more anti-Semitic abuse as a kid than many Jewish people get in a lifetime – and that I'm actually just in denial.

I guess what I'm really talking about here is fear. Where Man United and Chelsea bring out the more surface layers of *Schadenfreude*, Arsenal brings out a more primal sense of dread. I may detest losing to United, but I fear losing to Arsenal. There's more at stake: the all-too-frequent defeats are the stuff of nightmares rather than anger. A sense of diminution. The certainty of being patronised.

So, to my lucky shirt. I'm a milch cow for the club and an embarrassment to my wife, but I insist on buying the new first-team shirt every season: I've now got so many, I can vaguely pass them off as a collection rather than the sad annual ritual it actually is. And because the club was a bit late off the mark in selling this year's design, it turns out that I've not actually seen Spurs lose when I've been wearing it. Some dodgy, depressing draws, certainly; but no actual defeats. Part of the reason for this non-losing streak is that I never wear it to away games – apart from Fulham as their supporters aren't very frightening – as I'm a bit of a pussy and don't want to get beaten up. But for the Arsenal game I decided to make an exception. The shirt was on a good run and a draw would be a more than acceptable result. If the price of getting a point – and, yes, that was the summit of my ambition – was to turn myself into a potential target, then it was one worth taking. Either the shirt would lose its semi-canonised status, or the team would owe me.

Tickets were hard to come by for this game – they always are – so I was on my own for this one. Or rather, nearly on my own. I'd agreed to meet my friend Patrick, an Arsenal season-ticket holder, at his home before the game and walk on down to the Emirates with him. At the very least, he would give me and the shirt some diplomatic protection.

Patrick was not nearly as stressed about the game as me. But then, if I was an Arsenal fan, I might have felt the same way given our relative track records. Where I had done little but think about the game since I had woken up, he had been out and about doing worthy things with his kids – like taking them to the last library still standing in Islington – and was completely unbothered that he had kept me waiting on his doorstep for at least twenty minutes. Then we were both kept waiting for another twenty minutes by his wife, Anna, who had been out seeing a friend and was due back to take control of the kids.

'She always does this,' he said. 'She tries to cut it as fine as possible so that I'm starting to get anxious about missing the kick-off.'

My own anxiety had been in full flow for some time, although it was reassuring to know football provoked tensions in other households than mine. But sure enough, as Patrick predicted, Anna materialised moments before panic set in, and we made it to the ground with seconds to spare.

'See you at the end,' Patrick said. 'We'll meet out the front by the cannons.'

Within minutes of the start, I was wondering why I had bothered. We quickly went a goal down after two of our players managed to get in each others' way and could easily have conceded several more before we inevitably leaked a soft second. Two-nil down at half-time. We had barely strung two passes together, let alone created a chance. In short, we were awful and I knew exactly what was coming next. A text from Patrick that was trying not to be too smug: 'What's going on? We haven't even had to break sweat.' I've lost count of the number of texts like that I've had over the years from rival fans. I used to just ignore them until I decided that was rather playing into their hands, as it could be taken as a sign they had got to me. So instead, I've taken to replying with abject misery: 'We are totally useless. I want to kill myself.' That usually guarantees an end to any exchange.

Then the miracle. First the knee-high-to-a-grasshopper Defoe outjumped a defender several feet taller than him to head a ball through to van der Vaart. A neat pass to Bale, a delicate flick with the outside of the boot and we were only one down. Next, a penalty that we didn't actually miss. And finally, after one sublime Gomes save and another horrendous Arsenal miss, Kaboul headed in a free kick with four minutes to go; at which point some huge bloke behind me launched himself off his seat and almost knocked three of us over.

'Sorry,' he grinned. 'I got carried away.'

We all did. I was in shock. All the more so as we managed not to throw it away by conceding an equaliser before the end. This was better than beating Inter Milan. There was no history with the Italian club; winning against Arsenal felt as if some ancient wrong had been righted; as if N17 had been tilted a little more towards the sun. The Emirates rapidly emptied while the Spurs fans were held behind. We wouldn't have left anyway; we wanted to enjoy every last second.

A chant began. 'Who's the fat boy, who's the fat boy, who's the fat boy over there?' I looked up to see a lone Arsenal supporter, a dead ringer for James Corden, rooted to his seat in the tier above, looking hollow-eyed out towards the pitch as if, were he to stare for long enough, time would be reversed and his team wouldn't have thrown away a two-goal lead. For a moment I felt sorry for him: not for being fat, but because in the past I had so often been that bloke, wondering where it had all gone so horribly wrong.

Then I thought, 'Fuck it, I bet he's taken the piss out of me for losing once or twice,' and I joined in, though not before taking his picture on my phone. I wanted a memory of the day, and he seemed to sum it up as well as anything else. Besides, when we'd been on holiday in the United States in the summer, Anna had spotted the real James Corden on Muscle Beach – yes, really – looking ridiculous on a Segway and sneakily papped him, so it felt as if I was continuing a family tradition.

Patrick was looking thoroughly fed up by the time I finally caught up with him after the game. And not just because he'd had to wait forty minutes for me to leave the ground. It was some kind of justice for him, keeping me waiting before the start.

'I just don't know what happened,' he kept repeating.

'It's all down to the shirt,' I explained.

***

I've lost count of the things I've ruined for myself. Holidays where I've spent most of the time worrying about something that was almost certainly never going to happen, rather than trying to have a good time with the family. Evenings out that have been poisoned by ridiculous rows over things I don't really care about. A lifetime spent dwelling on the negative; the internet is a goldmine for this – if you write for a newspaper, it takes you next to no time to find someone who hates you. Not that concentrating on the downside is invariably a bad idea; for one thing, you're less surprised when the worst does happen but, more importantly, I might have turned out to be a Manchester United supporter if I hadn't always done so. At any rate, I thought I had seen every variation on spoiling things. I was wrong. There was one more: indifference.

A win over Werder Bremen in our last home Champions League game would ensure qualification for the knockout stages in the New Year, with a game to spare. It was a great deal more than any of us had dared hope at the beginning of the season, and I swear I was as hyped-up and tense when I left the office on the evening of the game as I had been for the match against Inter Milan. But within minutes of getting to the stadium, it was clear almost no one else felt the same way. The atmosphere was almost completely dead. There was no sense of anticipation. Everyone seemed to think the game was a done deal. True, Werder Bremen had been spectacularly crap in their previous games, and their one good defender was suspended, but it felt more as if the old grandiosity of the Spurs' crowd was back in style. Having craved Champions League football for more than a decade, we were already taking it for granted. If we weren't playing Inter Milan, it was hardly worth bothering.

Matthew put a more positive spin on it.

'We're just exhausted after Arsenal,' he said. 'The fans have nothing left to give.'

'You mean that five days later, we're only just coming out of intensive care?'

'That's exactly what I mean.'

'No achievement is greater than beating Arsenal.'

'Winning the Champions League.'

'No.'

That was an end to it, as far as Matthew was concerned. The lack of atmosphere in the ground was entirely down to collective Emiratic Post-Traumatic Stress Disorder rather than complacency.

'We're definitely going to win this,' Matthew announced a few minutes later, sounding suspiciously complacent.

'That's what you always say.'

'But this time I mean it.'

'He's right,' Amici interrupted. 'We can't lose this.'

'And is Crouchie definitely going to score, too?' I asked Justin.

'Of course.'

Normally Justin says this with a smile. This time it was said with conviction. I felt out on a limb. Werder Bremen wasn't just a passion-free zone, it was an irony-free zone.

You can usually count on Spurs to respond to the mood of the crowd. If everyone's tetchy, so is the team. If everyone is half asleep, so is the team. It was just as well tonight was an exception, otherwise the ball would have barely left the centre circle. As it was, we started playing quick, neat football and were a goal up inside six minutes, which was the cue for brief hysteria before the crowd retreated once more into its coma. Everyone who had always known we were going to win had been proved right, and there was no real need for anyone to pay much attention. Especially when Modrić added a second just before half-time.

'We're cruising it,' said Matthew.

Even I, who can see disaster coming from any angle, had to agree. We were pissing it, and we continued to do so in the second half. No one is ever surprised when we miss a penalty, but this time no one was even that bothered when Bale hit a tame effort straight at the German keeper because it didn't really matter much one way or another. It was a bloodless night, rounded off by Crouchie making it 3-0 with another tap-in. Justin didn't even bother to indulge in his customary triumphalism; his pre-match prediction hadn't been the usual article of faith, it had been a statement of fact. Long before the end, fans began to drift away to miss the rush, secure in the win.

Strange night. We had reached the knockout stages at the very first attempt. We'd even qualified before Arsenal, who would have to sweat on their final game. Officially – at least for a year – we were now one of the sixteen best teams in Europe, and everyone seemed to be reacting as if we had just beaten Rotherham in the third round of the Carling Cup. Maybe, I wondered on the way home, it had been me who had been out of synch all along. Maybe we really were one of the top sixteen teams in Europe, and the pre-match torpor had been nothing less than the chronicle of a victory foretold. It was a peculiarly disturbing thought.

There was a vaguely similar feeling at White Hart Lane four days later for the Premiership game against Liverpool. True, Liverpool had been having a poor season so far and we had beaten them the year before, but I belong to the generation of fans that have been scarred by defeat after defeat against the Scousers over the past few decades. I will never forget the game at the start of the 1978–9 season. It was the year after we had been promoted back into the First Division, the year we had astonished the world – and me – by signing Ossie Ardiles and Ricky Villa, two of the Argentine World Cup winning squad. It was meant to be the year we revisited the old Spurs way of the early 1960s. Four games into the season, we were annihilated 7-0 at Anfield. I've never taken a game against Liverpool for granted since.

Yet a lot of other people seemed to be doing just that. It wasn't quite the same sense of entitlement as for Werder, but there was a definite mood around the ground that the three points were ours to lose. I should learn to be more trusting of the wisdom of crowds, though when we were 1-0 down at half-time, had missed yet another penalty – Defoe this time – on the hour mark and Crouchie had missed an open goal shortly afterwards, my pessimism appeared justified. Redemption came with Martin Škrtel nudging in an own goal. It's usually Carragher who scores own goals against us, but we will take what we get. Then, with seconds of added time remaining, Lennon ran through the Liverpool defence and thumped the ball past Reina.

Joy or relief? It was hard to tell the difference. I don't suppose it mattered much to anyone but me. But then, I might have been the only person experiencing cognitive dissonance. For as long as I could remember it had been Spurs conceding late winners and equalisers. It had been our trademark. Now we were scoring them regularly against everyone else. We were winning games we normally lost. The team had departed from the usual script, and I wasn't at all sure how to deal with the new one. Then perhaps they didn't either. Maybe we would both just have to ad lib for a while.

December

WHEN THE SEASON'S FIXTURE list comes out in the summer, everyone's first port of call is to pencil the glamour games – Manchester United, Arsenal, Chelsea and any local derbies – into their diaries. I'm as guilty of it as anyone, but it's one of the more pointless activities of the year. Because there's no chance of me missing them. Whatever day they happen to be scheduled for, I know I will be there, even if it means cancelling some prior engagement.

You could argue that family relations might be improved by giving advance notice of key games so that everyone is aware well in advance that I'm unavailable on those days, but there's some dangerous flaws in that logic. The first is that all fixtures are only provisional anyway: come the end of the season, what with teams involved with cup replays, matches cancelled due to bad weather and kick-off times and even match-days changed to suit TV schedules, there are nearly always rearranged key games and committing yourself to certain times and dates too early is asking for trouble.

The other obvious drawback of giving advance warning of key games is that it draws unwanted attention to the possibility there may be un-key – and therefore missable – games. The last thing you need is to leave the door open for your partner to say, 'If you're going to the Liverpool and Chelsea games, surely you wouldn't mind if we went away the weekend Spurs are playing Blackburn?' I know I'm going to go to as many games as possible throughout the season – Jill even knows I'm going to go to as many games as possible throughout the season – but the only realistic way of achieving this is for us both to pretend that I'm not, and that every weekend is open to possible negotiation. However, I have begun to wonder if Jill hasn't started to use the system against me: a couple of times this year she's announced on a Friday morning, 'I hope you've remembered I'm going walking with Simone this weekend,' when it's the first I've ever heard of it.

So the games for which I really keep an eye out when the fixture list comes out are the away games that will require hard graft. Though I do have my limits. I've never yet made it to Sunderland: not just because we almost always lose there and it's miles away, but because it's a complete nightmare to get to as you have to change trains twice. And hanging around on freezing-cold stations is an acquired taste. It's the games in the Midlands that test me, because there's no real excuse for not going as I can't really claim they are too far to get to. I just have to pray they are played towards the beginning or the end of the season, when the temperature is significantly above zero. Invariably, though, there's always at least one in December. This year it was Birmingham City.

I knew what I was in for. Maybe I've been unlucky, but every time I've seen Spurs play at St Andrew's it's been a dour, dull game, heavy on robust midfield challenges (from the Birmingham side, at least) and short on flair and creativity. In other words, it's another of those grounds where, if you're being polite, you'd say we underperform, and, if you're me, you reckon we rather lose the will to live. Add in the fact that, unusually for the first week of December, the country was blanketed in snow and shivering in sub-zero temperatures, I wouldn't have been altogether sorry if the game had been postponed. Till sometime in May.

It wasn't, of course, and to make matters worse the car that had been trying to kill me for some time was back in the garage for the second time, since the only thing the mechanics had managed to do the first time was bugger up the satnav so it appeared as if I was driving across the football pitches on Tooting Bec Common when I was on Streatham High Road. Their explanation for this was that 'a fox must have climbed on the roof and eaten the aerial' on the day they returned the car. And it would cost another £200 to be fixed. Great. So that meant I was forced to take the other, older car that struggled to go much above 65 mph and had a front-left wheel that squeaked alarmingly.

Matthew, though, was in a surprisingly good mood when I picked it up.

'You're in the car of shame,' he observed.

'I know. It's a drag.'

'No. It's great.'

'Why?'

'Because it increases our sense of suffering. We've never particularly enjoyed a trip to see Birmingham before, and we're even less likely to now.'

The logic was faultless and, as so often in the past, Matthew used the outward leg of the drive to inform me of the differing merits of the various Journey line-ups over the years. The general gist of which seemed to be that they've been getting steadily worse, though they're still utterly brilliant and streets ahead of any other band that had ever played. Of more relief was that it had stopped snowing so the motorway was totally clear, and we arrived at the ground with ninety minutes to spare.

'Let's get something to eat,' I said. 'I'll ask the car-park attendant to recommend somewhere.'

'Your best bet is the cafe in Morrisons,' he said.

'You're kidding, right?'

'No. Seriously. Trust me. It really is the best place round here.'

It was certainly popular. There was a curious mix of families taking time out from their shopping alongside a horde of Birmingham and Spurs fans with any rivalries put on hold over a plate of scampi and chips. It felt old-fashioned and safe. I'll go there again next year.

It was the game that was the let-down, though my ability to be disappointed despite the result being entirely predictable – 'we'll go 1-0 up and be cruising, fail to take advantage, doze off in the second half, look like we're going to hold on and concede a late equaliser,' I had told Matthew confidently on the way up – does make me question my sanity, as it seems I can hold two contradictory beliefs at the same time. Somehow, despite the overwhelming expectation of disappointment, I can't erase the last vestige of hope. It's the same listening to the result of a third-round FA Cup tie between Manchester United and Scunthorpe. When the inevitable score comes through – United 3, Scunthorpe 0 – I can't help feeling an opportunity has been missed, not because I'm a fan of what TV commentators call 'the romance of the Cup' and 'plucky underdogs', but because United have escaped embarrassment.

But there you go. I was disappointed when the game turned out almost exactly as predicted. I don't make any great claims for prophecy, here. It was a prediction based entirely on experience and probability; the year before, Matthew and I had gone to the same fixture at roughly the same time of year and we had dominated the game, gone 1-0 up, nodded off and conceded an injury-time equaliser. Just as we have done so many times in the past against less fancied, less talented opponents who are more up for a scrap on a cold winter's day. The only difference to the scenario this time was that Birmingham equalised in the eightieth minute, leaving us a sweaty ten minutes when it appeared possible we would surrender all three points.

The one person who was satisfied with the result was Matthew.

'That was a truly noble experience,' he said.

'It didn't feel that way to me.'

'I'm talking about the quality of pain we suffered. It's what we came for.'

It was certainly what we got. As ever, Matthew slept the sleep of the righteous martyr on the way back down the M40. The car of shame can't pick up Radio 5 without repeated bursts of white noise, so in between the odd clear minute of the desperate and the damned talking nonsense with Alan Green, I had little choice but to concentrate on the squeaking front wheel and pray it didn't fall off. It didn't. And that, along with the scampi and chips at Morrisons, was probably the day's highlight.

***

Within days, hypocrisy was alive and well. Having moaned to a semi-comatose Matthew about how some of the team didn't seem to give a toss at Birmingham, I was guilty of precisely the same attitude towards our final Champions League qualifier away to FC Twente. For almost the first time ever, I couldn't really care whether we won, lost or drew. We had already made it to the knockout stages regardless, and that was enough: coming top of the group would be an added bonus but I wasn't going to lose any sleep if we didn't. A fatal lack of ambition, or being thankful for what I've got? You decide.

Maybe I'd have felt differently if I'd gone to the game, but there was never a chance of that. The Dutch ground only held 24,000 spectators, Spurs were allocated just 1,200 tickets and I was well down the pecking order. So it was a another night in front of the TV, made curious because I've felt more tense hoping Arsenal or Chelsea lose a Champions League game than I did that night. Without the adrenaline and the anxiety, it just wasn't the same. I got a bit excited when we went a goal up three times and a bit annoyed when we conceded an equaliser three times, but these were more Pavlovian than heartfelt responses. Watching the game in this way may have been good for my nerves, but it wasn't nearly so much fun. Yet maybe there was a lesson for me: while I was busy not being bothered, so were Inter Milan, who were unexpectedly imploding 3-0 to Werder Bremen to gift us top spot in our qualifying group. Perhaps it was contagious.

If it was, I was definitely not infectious by the weekend for the game against Chelsea. There was a time not so long ago when I used only to feel dread of these games, as so often we would end up on the losing side and I'd be bombarded with abusive messages from my friend Kevin, who never misses an opportunity to kick a Spurs fan when he's down. But in recent years, things have looked up rather, with a few victories made all the sweeter by John Terry managing to get himself sent off twice, so now the feelings of dread come tinged with a sense of expectation. Which is somehow worse.

Robbie feels rather differently about the Chelsea game, as he's only ever seen us win at home against them and he had every confidence he was in for a repeat performance.

'Of course, we're going to win, Dad,' he said.

'You're beginning to sound like Matthew.'

'Trust me.'

'You're definitely beginning to sound like Matthew.'

But his optimism was catching. After looking like run-away champions at the end of October, the Chelsea owner, Roman Abramovich, had managed to torpedo his own team's morale by sacking assistant manager Ray 'Butch' Wilkins, and ever since they had looked vulnerable. Better still, from my point of view, was that Harry had decided to start with Pavlyuchenko up front instead of Crouch.

'I'm not happy about that,' said Justin.

Everyone else was. Pav is one of those players that are almost certainly a manager's nightmare, because he often looks a bit moody, doesn't get stuck in and, well . . . to the ignorant, like me, can look a wee bit lazy. So Harry has always seemed reluctant to play him. But he has the knack of scoring goals and for that I – and most of White Hart Lane – will forgive a lot. Within half an hour Pav had obliged by hitting a left-foot shot between Petr Čech and the near post to put us one up.

'Sweet,' said Robbie.

That was as good as it got, though. Halfway through the second half, Drogba equalised with a shot that squeezed under Gomes's body and from then on, we were hanging on for a draw. It almost got worse in injury time, as Gomes inexplicably assaulted a Chelsea player heading away from the goal to concede a penalty. To everyone's surprise and relief, the Brazilian Octopus redeemed himself by saving it.

'I suppose it's a sign of how much we've improved that a draw feels like a disappointment,' said Mat on the way out.

That, I suppose, was the measured, objective assessment of the game. Mine was, 'Thank fuck I was wearing the lucky shirt.'

***

A few days later I rang the ticket office.

'I've got an unusual request,' I said.

'Fire ahead.'

'You know we've got swipe-card season tickets this year . . .

That was dumb. Of course she did.

'Yes.'

'Well, I collect match tickets and I was wondering if there was any way you could print out tickets for the games I've already been to this season.'

A pause.

'You mean, you want tickets for games that have already been played?'

'Precisely. You'll be able to work out which ones from my card.'

'I can't say anyone's ever asked me that before.'

'I'm not altogether surprised. But can you do it?'

'I don't know. I'll have to ask. Hang on a moment.'

She was gone several moments.

'I've had a word with the manager. He's not sure, but if you come in one day when we're not busy, we'll see what we can do.'

At least there was hope; it was better than I feared.

I started collecting things as a kid. Brooke Bond tea cards, stamps, old pennies, Biggles books, World Cup Panini stickers, Esso World Cup plastic figurines and, of course, the Spurs programmes I'd got from *Charles Buchan's Football Monthly*. You name it, I almost certainly had a small hoard of it somewhere in my bedroom. If a child did that kind of thing nowadays, he'd probably be taken to a shrink and diagnosed with an obsessive compulsive disorder, but back in the 1960s and 1970s it was considered relatively normal. At least, in my family.

The collections petered out as I reached my late teens. I took driving lessons within weeks of reaching seventeen, passed my test a few months later and bought an old beaten-up mini off my sister; I now had an exit from the sleepy Wiltshire village where my dad was a vicar and my life could begin. I did make it to university, but after that things went downhill. My idea of what having a life meant didn't really coincide with anyone else's, and the highlight of my twenties was selling ice creams on Oxford Street. I did try to get slightly more interesting jobs, but I was beyond clueless. At one interview I was asked, 'Why do you want this job?' I replied, 'I dunno. I don't, really.' The nadir was working on commission for a dodgy life-insurance set-up, during which, as I have mentioned, I managed to mis-sell myself a crap mortgage endowment policy.

Things improved in my thirties. I'd finally worked out

that one of the secrets to life was not actively trying to kill yourself, I was making a decent living as a freelance writer (it's one of the few jobs where no one ever asks you to explain the ten-year hole in your CV), I was married, had two lovely kids and a room where I worked at the top of the house with a pile of stamp albums, Panini stickers, Brooke Bond cards, old pennies and football programmes stacked up in the corner, though I dare say if they had been worth anything I'd have flogged them some time in my twenties. The Biggles books were on the bookshelf, by the way.

And then my dad died and left me £20,000; more than enough for a decent holiday, but not exactly a game-changer. It wouldn't buy a new house or pay off the mortgage. My wife was in no doubt what I should do with it.

'You need to put it in your pension. You've got next to no savings at all.'

This was true; my most recent pension projection, based on the £100 per month I had been salting away for the previous few years, suggested I was in line for an annuity of just under £1,000 per year by the time I retired, a sum even I could tell would barely keep me in Mars bars. The way I saw it, though, was that tossing another £20,000 into the pot was not going to make much difference to a pension fund so substantially underfunded as mine. So I ignored her.

I'm not sure exactly when I decided I'd spend the money on adding to my collections. Or even if it was a decision in the normal sense of the word. I definitely didn't discuss it with Jill. My recollection is that I was looking through an old stamp album and thought it would be nice to buy one or two of the more expensive stamps that I'd always wanted as a kid, but had never imagined

I would be able to afford. I'm fairly sure it was meant to be a one-off thing – a sentimental nod to my father who gave me his old, worthless stamps when I was a child – but things rather snowballed. Or to put it another way, I kept on buying more and more stuff so that, by default, my collections became my pension. Which is one of the few financial decisions I've never regretted, because had I dumped the £20,000 into my pension it would almost certainly be worth half that now if my friends' pensions are anything to judge by. As it is, I'm fairly sure my clobber is worth at least as much as, if not more than, I paid for it, so my own mismanagement of my assets has for once proved significantly less disastrous than leaving it to a professional to fuck it up for me. It's also worth pointing out that I'm much happier spending cash on stuff I can see and want than having it siphoned off via direct debit for some anonymous suit to play with, so my collections, aka my pension, now benefit by considerably more than £100 per month. Though how much more you'll have to guess, as I've made a point of never telling Jill. There are limits to her tolerance.

My collection of Spurs memorabilia expanded rapidly when Robbie started coming to games with me. Every match I would buy a programme from the same seller on Tottenham High Road and, when we got home, I'd put it away neatly and unread in Robbie's bedroom cupboard. It wasn't long before there was a huge heap of them and I imagined that they mattered to him, a visible, physical reminder of time spent together. Then one day I realised he didn't give a toss about the programmes, and that he'd be a lot happier if they weren't cluttering up his room. At which point I transferred them upstairs to join all my old ones from the 1960s and 1970s that were gathering dust in my study.

None of my collections have ever started out with a proper plan: I've just bought things fairly indiscriminately – call me a sucker – until I've worked out exactly what it was that I did want to collect. So I began with the vague idea of setting out to get a programme from every game the team had ever played. It wasn't long before I began to run into massive problems. You can pick up most programmes from the late 1960s onwards for next to nothing – as usual, it turned out that none of the ones I had kept for the best part of forty years had any real value – and soon I had boxes and boxes of them filling up my study and spilling out on to the landing. The main problem, though, was that the early ones – from the 1910s, 1920s, 1930s and 1940s – were expensive, ranging from about £40 for the later ones in average condition to upwards of several hundred quid for the early ones. And that's if I was lucky enough to find them. I could spend a lifetime bankrupting myself and never get close to completing the collection.

I needed to specialise. A logical first step was to start with all the games Spurs had played in European competitions – the European Cup, the Cup Winners' Cup and the UEFA Cup – since they had first qualified in the early 1960s. It seemed a reasonable ambition; it also turned out to be a pricey one. The point about old programmes is that it's not always the big games – the finals – that are the most expensive, because they tend to be played in big stadiums and a lot of people buy programmes as souvenirs. So there's plenty on the market. There are exceptions, mind. A programme for the second FA Cup final played at Wembley in 1924 will cost you a lot more than the one played in 1923 because, after the success of the previous year, the organisers got greedy and doubled the price of the programme; most fans said thanks but no thanks, and thousands of programmes were pulped. But as Spurs weren't playing in either of these cup finals, who really cares?

The tricky games are the away games – especially those played behind the former Iron Curtain, as very few Spurs fans made the trip. It took me an age to find the programme for the away leg of the 1963 Cup Winners' Cup semi-final against OFK Belgrade. It took even longer to find one at a price I was willing to pay; and that was a great deal more than I wanted to pay. When something is vanishingly rare, all it takes is one other bidder to push the price sky-high. Come to think of it, a programme doesn't even need to be rare for the price to rocket. Chris Williams, who runs the auction house, Sportingold, once told me that some years back there were only two people who seriously collected sporting memorabilia from their club – I think it was Mansfield Town, but I can't be sure – but they hated each other and would regularly try to outbid the other on everything. For a while, prices for anything from this club were astronomical. Then one of them died and they fell again.

There's not much chance of that happening with Spurs, though, as the club – along with Manchester United – is one of the most collectible. No one has ever been able to explain exactly why. I prefer to think that Spurs fans have a keen sense of history; Chris Williams, a Manchester City fan incidentally, reckons it's just that Spurs fans have deep pockets. Either way, the upside is that there will always be a market for my stuff; the downside is that there's often a lot of competition. It took me several auctions to find the OFK away programme at the right price, though looking back it might have been that it took several auctions for me to reconcile myself to paying so much. Still, I got there in the end.

Then there were the other cup competitions. It seemed silly not to try to complete the full run of matches in the years we won the FA Cup or League Cup. Again, I baulked at handing over the far too much I had to pay for the 1921 FA Cup final, but needs must and all that, though I've still drawn the line at the many thousands of pounds a programme from the 1901 FA Cup final would set me back. Well, I say I've drawn the line, but it's a totally theoretical line as I've never actually seen a 1901 programme at auction and, if I did, I couldn't guarantee not to take out a bank loan to fund it. Interest rates are still very low . . .

Tracking all these programmes down was a slow process, so it seemed silly not to use the downtime to fill in a few of the other cup runs. Getting to the semi-final isn't so bad, after all. Then I became interested in friendlies, especially the ones played in odd parts of the world that very few Spurs fans were likely to have seen. Who would have gone to see Spurs play Liverpool in Swaziland in 1984? Or Western Australia in 1976? My favourite is still the programme from Spurs' trip to play Torpedo Moscow when the Cold War was at its coldest in 1959; I haven't a clue what it says because it's in Russian, but it's a mini-masterpiece of Soviet art.

After a few years of all this, with still more programmes cluttering up the house despite my efforts at rationalization, it was time to call a halt. And so I started collecting old match tickets because they took up less space. A whole season's worth of tickets could fit easily into one medium-sized brown envelope, and there was no need to set any limits; all the tickets from every game the club had ever played would fit inside one box. Finding them was another matter: before all-seater stadiums became standard after the Hillsborough tragedy, most people either had season tickets or just paid cash at the turnstile. And of the comparatively few people who did buy seats on the day, most never bothered to keep their old stubs, which made the tickets much rarer than programmes. With my unerring instinct for haemorrhaging cash, I'd stumbled on a yet more expensive obsession.

I can confidently say the collection will never be complete. My earliest ticket is from the 1921 FA Cup final; only the insurance company and the vendor know how much I paid for that, but I've no regrets as I've never seen one on sale since. Then there's a twelve-year gap to the 1934 third-round FA Cup tie against Everton. And that's it for the 1930s. From the 1940s I have just two tickets; the home league game against Fulham in the 1947–8 season and the away game against Arsenal the following year. The 1950s are only slightly less threadbare with just twenty or so tickets across the decade, but then the collection bulks up exponentially – apart from the double-winning year of 1960–61, which is still a bit thin as tickets from this season are like gold dust.

So there's plenty of room for growth. How much is anyone's guess. It seems reasonable to hope I might one day have a full set of everything from 1960 onwards, but were any tickets printed for all the missing games before that? And if they were, has anyone bothered to keep them?

Probably not, though there's always the tantalizing thought that someone has a drawer full of them stashed away somewhere. It probably seems odd, but it's this uncertainty that generates much of the pleasure; the not knowing if I'm ever going to find what I want. If I knew that what I want is definitely out there somewhere, and that if I only had enough money and looked hard and long enough then I could fill in all the blanks, then it wouldn't be nearly so much fun. You see, it's the gaps in my collection that keep me going because the actual tickets are fairly dull in themselves. There's a momentary excitement when a new one I've bought at auction turns up in the post, but to be honest once I've looked at it for a few minutes, added it to my catalogue and then put it away in its relevant envelope, I've exhausted most of the fun I'm likely to get from it. Only Matthew has ever expressed any interest in seeing my collection, so few tickets ever make it out of their brown envelope, and even he got bored after a few minutes and couldn't resist a sarky remark.

'Brilliant move, John,' he said. 'Everyone knows the stock market is permanently fucked. You're definitely going to clean up.'

Collectors often like to justify what they do. It's an investment. It's an important archive. Blah, blah. I've done it myself when forced into a corner by my family. They and I know that's bollocks, really. Collecting is fundamentally a pointless activity. You can't argue your way round that. I once got chatting to a trainspotter at Clapham Junction for an article I was writing, and asked him what his goal had been when he started out.

'To clear BR,' he replied. 'To see every piece of rolling stock in the country.'

'And have you done that?'

'Yeah. It took me years and years, and I had to sneak into a shed at Doncaster to tick off the last one.'

'How did you feel then?'

'Fantastic. For an hour or so. And then I felt a bit disappointed. As if my life had lost some of its purpose.'

'So what did you do?'

'I decided to start again.'

And he was very happy with it, ticking off for a second time all the rolling stock he'd seen before. At first, I thought he was a bit nuts but by the time I got home I reckoned, 'Fair play.' Because almost everything anyone does in their spare time – and a fair amount they do in their working life, come to think of it – is a bit pointless. Collecting is just another way of filling in time, like watching TV, reading a book or listening to music, which I also spend a lot of time doing, and who is anyone to judge which is the most worthwhile?

I'd willingly concede that collecting feeds an obsessional part of my personality, but compared to almost every other habit you can acquire this one is fairly benign, and I still get a visceral kick from looking through eBay listings or auction catalogues. However, increasingly relief comes as polar opposites: relief that I've got everything on view and won't be tempted to shell out cash, or relief that I haven't got everything . . .

Most auction houses specializing in sporting memorabilia are run by enthusiasts who got fed up with being treated like shit by the big auctions on the rare occasions they branched out into this area, so they tend to be smallish, informal affairs. The first one I went to was Sportingold, held in one of the function rooms at Northampton Rugby

Club on a freezing-cold winter's day. It was a steep learning curve. Inside were seventy or eighty men. Men mostly the wrong side of fifty. Men who were badly dressed. Men who didn't appear to have glanced at a mirror before leaving home. Or ever, possibly. Men like me. While most people would probably have gone to some lengths to avoid them, I had been travelling for the best part of two hours on an icy Thursday morning to join them. It was a moment of disturbing self-recognition; one best treated by sliding into blanket denial and a cup of coffee.

I then wandered over to the viewing table and opened my catalogue. Winding myself up by looking at something I couldn't afford seemed a good place to start, so I asked for Lot 634, a programme for the 1915 FA Cup tie against Sunderland. Nice. Very nice. Its estimate was £300 to £350. Sod it – maybe I'd just slap it on the credit card. I put a question mark against it in the catalogue. Then it was down to the serious business: a programme for the away game at Everton from the 1960–61 double season. A must, as it was one of the ones I was missing. Then there was a fabulous sixteen-by-twelve-inch black-and-white photo of the triumphant Spurs team holding the FA Cup at Wembley in 1961, signed by seven of the players. Also a must.

I had history with Lot 668, the programme for a 1970 friendly against Valletta in Malta. I'd only seen it up for sale once before, and I had missed out. I wasn't going to make the same mistake again, which naturally meant I would pay far too much for it. Finally, there was the away 1972 UEFA Cup game against Romanian side UT Arad. There are two versions of this programme: one printed in red, the other in black. I already had the red one; this was the black.

Well, that was the plan. No one sits next to each other at football auctions – buyers of sports memorabilia clearly work on the principle of Schopenhauer's porcupines; close enough to keep warm, but far enough apart to avoid the intimacy of spiking one another – so I found a lone seat and waited for the bidding to start. I managed to resist the 1915 FA Cup programme – largely because it went for a lot more than its estimate – and then settled down for the rest. It took a long time; with some 1,700 lots the auction went on for the best part of eight hours, and I found myself getting bored. So I started bidding for stuff that I had expressly told myself not to, just to fill in time before the lots I had really earmarked came up. And with two of the three, I ended up paying more than I meant to, because there was just me and this other bloke bidding by the end and it seemed a shame to drop out. And I was buggered if I was going to stop.

The only upside was that the auction went on so long, I had to leave before the UT Arad programme came up. I left an-over-the-estimate bid with the auctioneer, and wasn't altogether disappointed when he told me the next day I had lost out. I'd already spent a great deal more money than I'd intended. So now I just bid online as it involves no travel, reduces the temptation to bid on stuff I don't really want and makes it sometimes easier to drop out when the bidding gets out of hand. I still can't believe how much I paid for a pair of home and away tickets for Spurs versus Northampton in 1965–6 season – the only season Northampton played in the First Division. It was the away ticket that was so rare. The one consolation was that there was someone else out there willing to pay just £10 less.

For all its nerdiness, collecting Spurs memorabilia has turned out to be a surprisingly social activity. If you exclude Robbie, that is. I've learned never to tell him I'm planning to meet one of my fellow collectors before a game as he goes berserk, ever since he was forced to listen to me and another bloke witter on for half an hour while he ate a dodgy burger. I now know it's far better just to take him by surprise; the rows are so much shorter. And he could learn so much . . .

There's Simon, who sits in the Paxton Road stand at White Hart Lane. With highlights of an 1898 share prospectus, an almost complete run of club handbooks from 1904 and a complete run of programmes from the double season, his collection makes mine look amateurish. Simon has rather taken me under his wing, advising me on prices and bidding. 'Always hold back right till the last minute,' he says. 'And if the price goes too high, let it go. Chances are another seller will see there's a market and put a similar item up. With any luck, you'll get it cheaper next time.' I can't say I always follow his advice. There's Pete H., who I often bump into at the Hay Literary festival; there's Pete C., who has provided an invaluable service as a European-tour travel agent this year.

And then there's Trevor. We met online – this sounds dodgy but bear with me – via eBay, and, as I have mentioned, it turned out he had a season ticket in the same row, five seats along from me in the Lower East stand. So we chat every game. Trevor just likes collecting, so once he's completed one line of Spurs memorabilia, he'll flog it to fund a new line. He recently got me interested in cup final banquet menus. Take the 1971 League Cup final: Les Scampis Newbourg, washed down with Liebfraumilch

Crown of Crowns 1967, followed by dancing to live music from The Gaylords. This isn't Spurs memorabilia, it's social history. Trevor also had a great run of 1940s and 1950s season tickets – fabulous, old Bakelite badges rather than the booklets they moved on to in the 1960s – that it took me the best part of a season to persuade him to sell to me. He's now trying to sell me a Jimmy Greaves tankard. I'm resisting.

And for all its inherent pointlessness, collecting Spurs memorabilia does have meaning for me. It's a way of collecting my own life and giving it some order. It helps make sense of a past that never really had a sense of purpose. I've never had a life or career plan; I've just gone with the opportunities that presented themselves. It's not that I'm not ambitious or competitive: I am. It's just I've never had the organizational skills, the self-confidence or the self-discipline to do much about it. My tickets and programmes don't just fill in the gaps between the matches I did see and those I would like to have seen, they fill in the gaps in my life; the things I would like to remember and those I would prefer to forget. They put the years back into order in one brown envelope after another. And as for all those Spurs items I've got from the years before I was born? Let's call that connecting with my collective unconscious.

***

Ten days or so before Christmas, another mini-email storm broke out. 'Hi,' they all said. 'I've got a couple of spare tickets for the away game at Blackpool going cheap. Any takers?' As if.

I'd initially been tempted by the Blackpool game, as I'd never been to their ground at Bloomfield Road and, to be brutally patronizing, I wasn't entirely sure there would be another opportunity the following year as, despite their decent start to the season, I wasn't convinced they would stay up. So it was more a box to be ticked than a game to be enjoyed. But once the temperature stubbornly refused to rise above zero at the start of the month, it had become obvious there was next to no chance of the game being played on 21 December, as Blackpool was the only club in the Premiership whose pitch had no under-soil heating, so I hadn't bothered to get tickets. I rather suspected the emails were coming from those who had been a bit slower to see the writing on the wall.

Then Christmas had more to offer than a postponed away game at Blackpool. In my day job I'm often asked to do an end-of-year book round-up: the highlights of the year, what I'd most like to be given for Christmas, etc, etc. It's always tempting either to come up with something that makes you look ferociously intelligent, such as 'the marvellous new biography of Tolstoy' which actually is rather good, or something by one of your mates, like Patrick Barkham's *Butterfly Isles*, which is also very good, by the way, in the hope they might one day do you a favour and recommend one of yours. But the previous year, I'd decided to be honest. The book I had most wanted was *Big Chiv* – Martin Chivers's autobiography. Not because I necessarily expected too many great revelations – football biographies rarely offer them – but because Chiv was such an important part of my childhood, and to relive it through him was like being guided by a ghost of Christmas past.

Everything seemed to be there. The early days. The rows with Bill Nicholson. The stunning last goal in the first leg of the 1972 UEFA Cup final against Wolves; I can still remember listening to that on a crackly radio commentary. But it wasn't all there, because as with so much of my involvement with Spurs over the years, my relationship with Big Chiv had been almost entirely in my imagination. My fondest memory of Chiv didn't even rate a mention in his book, because to him it was inconsequential or long forgotten.

It was a Good Friday in the late 1960s and that afternoon Spurs were due to play Leeds, the best, hardest and most unpleasant team around at the time, who didn't care if they played you off the park or kicked you off it so long as they won. Which they usually did. But first my mum and dad had insisted I go to church for an hour.

'It will look bad if the vicar's son doesn't make an appearance on Good Friday,' they had said.

'I doubt anyone will notice.'

'You're going.'

I wasn't old enough or stroppy enough to argue. But I was mighty pissed off. I didn't like going to church at the best of times, partly because I wasn't very religious but mostly because I was embarrassed my dad was a vicar. I feel bad about it now, but that's how it was. Of all the jobs a dad could have, being a vicar was the least cool I could possibly imagine and I hated feeling so exposed. Going to church on a Friday when I knew I'd be made to go again on Easter Sunday felt like a humiliation. So I did what I've often tended to do in similar situations ever since: I complied with passive-aggressive silence. And spent the entire hour bargaining with God to let Spurs win that afternoon, and for Greaves or Chiv to score in exchange for my being sat in a pew against my will. Later that afternoon I lay out in the garden listening to sports reports on the radio. Spurs went up 1-0 through Greaves. Yes! Leeds equalised. What was the fucking point of church? Then Big Chiv scored the winner. Thank you, thank you. It was almost enough to make me believe in God. Almost, but not enough. I always have been an ungrateful little sod.

This year's must-have book was *And Still Ricky Villa*. Matthew and I had laughed when Ricky had been introduced to the crowd at half-time during one of the home games earlier in the season, partly because he now looked in worse shape than either of us, but mainly because we both knew we would be unable to resist getting his book. Ricky was and is a legend; a legend based entirely on about five seconds of pure magic that ended with him scoring the winning goal in the FA Cup final replay against Manchester City in 1981; a goal that Matthew insists is partly his as he was at Wembley that night.

It's strange really because mostly Ricky's career at Spurs had been a bit of a disappointment. He'd scored on his debut in 1977 and we all thought, 'Yes, he's a superstar,' but then he'd faded and been entirely eclipsed by his fellow Argentine, Osvaldo Ardiles, whom we'd signed at the same time. It had almost begun to feels as if Ricky's prime function at the club was to stop Ossie feeling homesick. Then he scored that goal and everything changed. If he hadn't scored that goal, there would have been no memories and certainly no books.

There's something almost cruel about it; not to Ricky, who openly acknowledges the debt he owes to that goal, but to all the other Spurs players who have been largely forgotten. Especially Mark Falco, because I still feel guilty about him. Falco regularly used to score about twenty goals a season, a tally of which any striker can be proud and one we would have happily killed for this season when Defoe, Pav and Crouchie lost their radar, but we all used to hate him. I can't even remember why. We would jeer when he screwed things up, and there would be a huge roar when he was substituted. Whatever next year's Spurs must-have book is going to be, it's not *My Life* by Mark Falco.

The hints were duly observed and a signed copy of *And Still Ricky Villa* appeared under the Christmas tree. And was finished by the next morning. Boxing Day is always a tricky day. If we're playing at home – or away in London – then Robbie and I can make it past the recriminations of abandoning the rest of the family and get to a match. I'm not sure Jill or Anna actually want to do anything with us, but there is a point of principle at stake; one that precludes me from travelling to Birmingham. So the away game against Aston Villa was out. Not that I got much credit for the sacrifice I made by not going, as apparently it was extremely rude to abandon our guests who had come for the day by disappearing to watch the game on television. Still, much to my surprise, we won despite Defoe managing to get himself sent off, thanks to two goals from the by now near-divine, 'His missus is a model, He's better than Waddle, He's as good as Hoddle' Rafa van der Vaart.

Two days later we faced Newcastle at home. There was a wonderfully relaxed feeling about the ground as we got to our seats. Everyone had had a few days off and there were handshakes, 'Happy Christmases' and hugs all round, even from those who generally limited their acknowledgment to me to just a nod. It was a lovely moment, because I felt closer to these people – many of whose names I didn't know and in all probability never would – than some of my neighbours I see most days out in the street in Streatham; a closeness born of having shared so many intense feelings throughout the season. Suffering, mainly.

The festivities ended with the kick-off. Many teams had come to White Hart Lane with the sole objective of stopping us playing this season – it's standard practice for less talented players to try to unnerve quicker and more skilful ones by out-muscling them – but Newcastle were something else. Right from the start their midfield made one heavy clumsy challenge after another, and the referee did nothing about it. So I suppose it was all legal, but it didn't look that way. If anyone in my son's school team had made just one of those tackles it would have been a straight red; and if you behaved like that in the street you'd be done for GBH. I know football has always had its hard men, and Spurs have had their fair share – step forward Dave Mackay – but the game is so much quicker now than it was even ten years ago, and this one felt positively lethal. Going to watch football is, by definition, a voyeuristic pursuit, but this match felt almost obscenely so as the possibility of someone's career being ended seemed uncomfortably real. It was like hanging around the A&E department of a hospital hoping for some car-crash victims to be wheeled in.

Until well into the second half, it looked as if Newcastle's tactics were going to pay off. Spurs had been unsettled and, with the game still goalless, were once again down to ten men after Younès Kaboul had finally lost his temper and threatened to headbutt one of the opposition. Then justice prevailed when Lennon broke away down the right-hand side.

'Fuck me,' said Amici, as the ball flew into the far corner of the net. 'I didn't know he could kick the ball that hard.'

'Nor so accurately,' Justin added.

For once we weren't made to sweat it out till the final whistle as, with about five minutes to go, Bale ran away from the Newcastle defence to add a second. We did know he could shoot that hard and that accurately.

At the end of the game, I watched amazed as the players indulged in their own customary post-match handshakes and hugs, having spent the previous ninety minutes either trying to do some serious damage to one another or to avoid it. I dare say there might even have been a few 'Happy Christmases' too if I had been able to lip-read. And it all looked just as genuine as the pre-match hugs among the crowd. There are some things a fan will never really understand about professional footballers.

'Have a good New Year,' said Trevor on the way out.

Up in the mix for fourth place in the league and in the knockout stages of the Champions League? Yes, there was a distinct possibility he would. But me? I doubted it.

January

THERE MIGHT HAVE BEEN a time when I enjoyed New Year, but if there was I don't remember it. The older I get, the more I have a sense of time passing, of a promise that will be for ever unfulfilled, rather than one of a slate being wiped clean, where past sins and failures can be forgiven or forgotten. Yet even as a child I thought of New Year as a time of ending rather than beginning, a day that said goodbye to Christmas and marked the countdown to another school term.

Hard to believe, but Spurs had always been one of the few antidotes to this negativity. This wasn't because there was any real belief that things would come good – though in some seasons it had felt hard to think they would get much worse – nor even because there was the possibility they might. In fact, winning has sometimes been a mixed blessing; after we beat Chelsea to win the Carling Cup in 2008 and secure qualification for the UEFA Cup, the team seemed to regard it as job done and sleepwalked through the final three months of the season. It was more that in football terms, New Year was very much a halfway mark, not an ending; and whatever happened in the next five months there were still the fixed waypoints of twenty or so more games. I couldn't count on the results, but I could count on the games being played.

You can never eradicate all traces of hope in football – at least not before kick-off; you'd never get out of bed otherwise. But I'd learned to restrict my optimism, such as it was, to an ad hoc basis; the thought that any one game might somehow be special, that we would play like gods, but that no conclusions could be drawn from the outcome. Every match was like returning to Year Zero, where I tried to cast off the learned disappointments or triumphs of the previous ones, and start again from scratch, praying that the hours I had often spent just getting to the match would offer enough in return.

This year was a bit different, though. It wasn't just the plainly delusional, like Matthew, who now expected us to win. Diehard pessimists and TV pundits were now expecting us to win. There was a belief we had turned a corner, that we were no longer the perennial underachievers who occasionally flickered brightly, but genuine contenders who could mix it with the best of the best. We'd been here before, of course. There had been a couple of years in both the early 1970s and early 1980s when it felt as if we had great teams in the making, but neither quite went on to fulfil their potential. Maybe no Spurs team ever could, forever being found wanting in comparison to the double-winning side of the early 1960s, but it didn't stop the expectations resurfacing.

And they were infectious, for even I was no longer just crossing my fingers and hoping: I could see we did, undeniably, have one of the best squads, playing some of the best football in the country – at least up till the moment when we were meant to get the ball in the net – and I had begun to find myself looking at the fixture list and, in unguarded moments, thinking, 'We ought to beat this lot.'

It's a great deal more fun watching your team on the up rather than on the slide. The 1976–7 season in which we were relegated is imprinted in my memory, and my collection of tickets from the following year we spent in the Second Division is particularly precious to me – not just because attendances nosedived, so tickets are scarcer, but as a safeguard against complacency: I will never take it for granted that we won't have to play Mansfield Town in the league again.

But it's not always as much fun watching your team on the up as you think it will be. There's the obvious anxiety of disappointment; the higher the expectations, the greater the potential for tragedy. More than that, though, is the worry that the price of becoming one of the Big Clubs is that the character of the team will become unrecognizable from the one I've always supported. It almost can't be any other way. As hard as my long-standing Manchester United, Chelsea and Arsenal supporting friends try – and they do try – to pretend that nothing much has changed over the years, it's obvious to everyone else it has. And so have they. When you've grown so used to success over such a long period of time, when a season in which only qualifying for the Champions League is considered a disaster, then you've almost certainly lost touch with what first made you a football fan because your experience is so radically different. And I don't want to lose that feeling. Then – and here's another heresy – I'd have given a lot to have the past ten years as supposedly disappointing as that of Arsenal. I guess it's an irreconcilable dilemma, and one best not to think too much about now; one to worry about in ten years' time, once we've had a decade of Champions League football. You never know . . .

The home game against Fulham on New Year's Day qualified as one of those matches newly promoted to the 'We ought to beat this lot' category in my mind. Watching Spurs on New Year's Day has always been a bit of a toss-up in the past. I've seen some shockers, when it looks to all the world as if the team hasn't been to bed the night before, and some crackers. This one was somewhere in between, but at least we did the business thanks to Bale getting his head in the way of a bullet-like free kick from van der Vaart.

'Do you think he meant it?' Amici asked.

'It didn't look like it,' I replied.

'I'd give him the benefit of the doubt,' said Justin.

'Who cares?' Robbie said.

True. We'd got the lead, and we held on to it for an ugly win. We had beaten one of the teams we ought to be beating. Which wasn't one of our hallmarks. It had been a game of few highlights, the most memorable being David Ginola's annual reintroduction to the crowd at half-time.

Ginola and I hadn't got off to the best of starts. There was a time when footballers knew their place – which was to look like Dave Mackay or Gazza – because then fans were free to enjoy the game without any outside distractions. But by the late 1990s, every footballer had had a makeover and you couldn't go near a match without over-hearing some woman wittering on about how gorgeous such and such a player was. And the unspoken assumption was always 'and you're not'.

Footballers had become sex gods, and the worst offender of all was the silken-haired Ginola, who couldn't even restrict himself to the pitch and the sports pages. Not content with waddling up the catwalk modelling the latest Cerrutti designer clothes, Mr Parfait, the man who had been booted out of the French team four years ago for single-handedly ensuring it didn't qualify for the World Cup finals, was also the new TV face of L'Oréal, advertising haircare products.

All this was vaguely tolerable so long as he was playing miles away up in Newcastle. I even grew to appreciate his Renault Laguna ad – the one where he swaggered around saying 'non' to everything but the car – because I felt reassured that he wouldn't dare show his face outside the north-east. But it turned out that the man who couldn't be bought could be bought after all. *Quelle surprise!* By us, so he was in my face the whole time.

But I came to love him. He could be a lazy sod, hanging around the halfway line, but then, just when you were about to give up on him, he did a little shimmy and a flashy run here, a wonder goal there and I was swooning along with all the women. For several years, he was the one star in a mediocre team and the main reason many of us kept coming back. Other than habit.

So, it's always a pleasure to see him again. He walked out on to the pitch, his hair a lot greyer but still as long and silky, his Gallic eyes just as soulful, looking every inch the porn star he always had done, a man who still looked as if he believed women's legs would open up before him just as easily as opposition defences. He was probably right.

***

1901, 1921, 1961, 1981, 1991: all years ending in a one and

all years in which Spurs have won the FA Cup. And this was 2011. Spurs have always had a reputation for being a good cup team – partly because we've won the FA Cup eight times, partly because it's hard to claim to be a good league team when you've only won it twice, the last time fifty years ago – and whenever the year ends in a one the hype always goes into overdrive. 'It's our year.' Of course.

I'm not sure how or when the 'one' thing started. It can't have been in 1901 or 1921. It can hardly have been in 1961 either, as there had been many more years ending in a one when we hadn't won than when we had, and even the most loyal fans aren't that myopic. And by the beginning of the 1970–71 season, fans were more likely to be thinking it was our destiny to win the First Division title as we'd won it in both 1951 and 1961. So I'd guess it was 1981, the year of the replay against Manchester City and That Ricky Villa Goal, a game that will for me for ever mark the split between individual and collective memory.

I watched that match alone on a tiny black-and-white television in the bedroom I rented from Alex, one of the few friends who hadn't got totally fed up with me by then, though he would soon after when I kicked in the front door. I was certainly totally fed up with me. I was a miserable nightmare. It's a time of my life I try hard to forget, and might well have done so long ago, but for those magical few seconds of Ricky's individual brilliance that led to Steve Perryman lifting the trophy into the Wembley night. The triumph of my team that night is a permanent reminder of my own decline.

After winning the FA Cup in 1991, the 'one' thing had become as much of an established law to most Spurs fans as Einstein's Theory of Relativity was to physicists, so there was general bewilderment when we were beaten by Arsenal in the semi-final of 2001. It can't have happened. In fact, it almost certainly didn't, judging by the reaction when we were drawn against Charlton at home in the third round a decade later. 'The year ends in a one. It's our year,' everyone said. Probably even myself. It wasn't something to get excited about, or something to be debated; it was a statement of entitlement.

I've always loved the FA Cup, mainly because it generally represented our best chance of winning something. But even I hadn't been wholly immune to the feeling which had crept in over the previous ten years that the competition was no longer as interesting or important as it once had been. There had been a time when the final was an unmissable sacrament, regardless of who was playing, but I hadn't bothered to watch one in years. Chelsea versus Everton, Chelsea versus Portsmouth – who really gave a toss one way or the other? I couldn't even summon up the enthusiasm to support the underdogs. Well, not enough to spend ninety minutes in front of the TV.

But I had remained a big fan of the competition as long as we were still in it, and would happily come over all pious whenever any Manchester United, Chelsea or Arsenal supporter suggested the FA Cup was a bit of a chore. So it was disturbing to discover that after just eight games of Champions League football and with more to come, I could detect similar feelings of grandiosity in myself. I wasn't exactly flatlining at the thought of a home game against Charlton – the old adage that any Spurs game is better than none still held – but neither was the pulse quickening. I was in danger of becoming the sort of supporter I despised. I wasn't the only one.

'Who are we playing?' asked Robbie.

'Charlton.'

'I think I'll pass.'

I discovered from Anna a while later – apparently he'd given her permission to tell me as he felt it was too embarrassing to tell me himself – that Robbie had just started going out with a new girlfriend. So in hindsight, he's excused. If I'd been lucky enough to have a girlfriend when I was fifteen, I'd have made the same call.

Matthew had no mitigating circumstances.

'I'm away with my wife and kids in Dorset that week.'

'So?'

'So . . . I don't think she'd be very pleased if I came up for the day.'

'And?'

'And . . . obviously I don't want to rock the boat.'

Obviously untrue, coming from a man who had rocked the boat countless times before to make sure he didn't miss a game. What was obvious was that neither Charlton nor the FA Cup was not enough interest to him.

It was much the same when I got to the ground. It felt a bit like going to an away match, as half the regular season-ticket holders weren't there. There was no Justin, no Amici, no Trevor, no Andy . . . almost no one, really; they'd all either not taken up their right to buy a ticket for the game – the FA Cup was not automatically included in the season ticket – or had given it to someone else for the day. Still, I did have Patrick with me. Not Patrick, the Arsenal season-ticket holder; there was as much chance as getting him to sit with me at White Hart Lane as there was of me sitting with him at the Emirates. I had Patrick, the Norwich fan who reserves all his football hatred for Ipswich, and so was quite happy to come along.

Patrick is one of my more unusual friends, not because he's funny and bright, but because he'll invariably try to look for the positive in any situation. So when I tell you his half-time observation was, 'It's all a bit disjointed, isn't it?' you'll have a fair idea of just how desperate the first half had been. Everything we'd done had been a bit half-paced and half-arsed. There was no sense of passion. The game was just a job to be ticked off the list, and at 0-0 there was a great deal more to be done.

Harry clearly felt the same way. He had rested a number of our top players, but for the second half he put on Luka Modrić. He was simply a different class to everyone else, and within fifteen minutes of coming on to the pitch, he had created enough chances to put us 3-0 up. Modrić is a bit of a one-off: a footballer who always looks as if he's genuinely pleased to be playing in front of 36,000, a man who doesn't take his talent or the fans for granted. He is loved at White Hart Lane for that. We used to call him Gollum as he does look a bit like the malevolent Hobbit in *The Lord of the Rings* films, but we've stopped that. He's now just 'Luka'. Or sometimes Moddle. Respect cuts both ways.

The match died on its feet when the third goal went in, and for the last thirty minutes both sides just played out time, with Charlton merely intent on keeping the score-line respectable and Spurs on not doing anything too strenuous. Thanks to one player's efforts, it had turned out to be just a job to be ticked off, after all, for everyone concerned; I went home pleased we had won, but relieved I wouldn't ever have to watch it again.

There was more of a buzz the following weekend. Then we were home to Manchester United; it's strange how there's so often an inverse relationship between a game's importance and your chances of winning it. We hadn't beaten United at home for ten years, though we'd had our chances: 3-0 up at half-time only to lose 5-3, 1-0 up with just seconds of injury time left and we concede a soft equaliser – yes, it had been a long time since we had avoided at least partial heartbreak. And the match was all the more irresistible because of it, something that didn't go down too well with Tors, whose fortieth birthday party I missed as a result. The thank-you card for our present was pointedly sent just to Jill, 'the one who didn't think a football match was more important than my birthday'.

It wasn't irresistible to everyone, though. One season-ticket holder had found himself being taken away to Spain for the weekend by his wife to celebrate their wedding anniversary. I bet he found a great bar that just happened to have Sky Sports on the Sunday afternoon; I just hope they didn't have the same row Jill and I had when I took her to Barcelona for our twentieth wedding anniversary, and we ended up in some dive watching the World Cup final between France and Italy. She stormed off down the beach and threw another wobbly when she got back.

'It's not my fault the game has gone to extra time,' I pointed out.

'Is there nothing you can't ruin?'

Probably not.

But then, someone's loss is often another's gain, and the winners for the Manchester United game were Adrian and Matthew, who were delighted to take up the two season tickets the lovebirds couldn't use, though Matthew got the better deal. Adrian is a Manchester United fan, and the prospect of ninety minutes among the Spurs hardcore did have its downsides.

Much of the build-up to the game had been dominated by David Beckham, who had let it be known he wouldn't mind joining Spurs for a short while before he went back to play for LA Galaxy in the United States. There was a surprising amount of enthusiasm for the idea from the club, and it was even suggested he could make his debut against his old club. Some of the fans were quite keen on the idea, too. Matthew was one of them.

'It would give us a bit of glamour, and get people talking about us,' he said. The old Spurs inferiority complex at work again.

'But he's even slower than David Bentley, and we're trying to flog him,' I replied.

'He's a great dead-ball specialist.'

'We can't just bring him on to take free kicks.'

'He's a much better crosser of the ball than Aaron Lennon.'

'But we haven't got any strikers who can score. So what difference would he really make?'

'He'd sell a few more replica shirts.'

I couldn't argue with that. Though clearly he wouldn't flog enough shirts for a deal to be reached, as the legend remained unsigned. Instead, it was announced he would be training with the club on an informal basis. Honour satisfied on all sides.

Despite Robbie's usual moans about leaving far too early, we'd planned to make a day of it and meet for lunch before the game in a pub in Stoke Newington. Matthew put the kibosh on that; something to do with taking his kids to Sunday school, aka getting them into the local Church of England primary school. So instead we arrived at the pub just in time to watch Adrian eat a huge Sunday roast. It looked delicious, and Robbie was gutted to have missed out.

'I'll buy you a ratburger at the ground,' I said.

'Fuck off, Dad.'

As for the game? It was the same old, same old. We didn't actually lose, but United were there for the taking: they hadn't been playing well, had been down to ten men after Rafael was sent off midway through the second half and were just hanging on, but we couldn't take advantage. It felt like we just didn't believe we could beat them, as if some kind of divine cosmic order would be broken if we did. United have been playing on that for years, squeezing out results from matches they should have lost, and it worked again as the match ended goalless. We could learn from them. But at least Adrian didn't get any satisfaction. Like all United fans, he takes winning for granted.

'That was a bit shit,' he said.

'At least you got out of the ground alive,' I replied.

'There is that.'

'I fucking hate Lennon,' Matthew said on the way home in the car.

Where did that come from? It wasn't as if Lennon had had a particularly bad game. Matthew just needed someone to blame. And he always picks on Lennon. Just as I pick on Crouchie. And Jermaine Jenas. Then nobody likes him much. A few games ago, Amici had said, 'We need to bring on J.J.'

Justin and I had looked at him in amazement.

'You're right,' he conceded. 'I can't believe I just said that.'

Everyone needs one player to be their fall guy, and Lennon is Matthew's. Personally I love the guy. I know he's a rubbish crosser, but his pace is sensational and he makes me believe something might happen.

'Azzer wasn't that bad,' I said.

'I don't care. I still fucking hate him.'

'You can't believe that Beckham would have been better?'

Clearly he did.

We signed Steven Pienaar from Everton later in the week. From the glimmer of Goldenballs to a rather more prosaic squad player in the space of a few days. Reality always kicks in sooner or later.

***

For a while now there's been a conspiracy theory doing the rounds of the more paranoid Spurs supporters that the head of London Underground is an Arsenal supporter. Spurs and Arsenal play their home league games on alternate weekends to avoid congestion and/or trouble, and the suggestion is that the Victoria line closures for 'essential engineering works' are made far more often on those weekends that Spurs are at home. As I never take the tube to Spurs unless it's unavoidable, I can't really say if there's any truth in it. But I do know that almost any national train journey you take at the weekend is guaranteed to take almost twice as long as you expect. I guess it's for the best that the rail network discovered large sections of its track was falling to bits and decided to fix them rather than letting any more trains get derailed, but it does turn an away game to Newcastle into an endurance test.

Matthew and I were somewhere near Doncaster when there was an announcement that the rest of the east-coast line was closed and we would be making a scenic detour at about 25 mph along a few side lines until we reached Newcastle. Matthew didn't care one way or the other as he had already dozed off, but I had finished the book I had to read for work and had nothing to do but stare out the window. Still, it did give me my first ever look at Hartlepool, and left me wondering how on earth the Labour party members of this depressed north-eastern town got conned into adopting Peter Mandelson as their parliamentary candidate. It was hard to think of anyone less likely to fit into the constituency.

'Fuck,' said Matthew, just waking up as we pulled into Newcastle. 'We're over an hour late.'

'Well spotted.'

'No harm done, though. We've still got loads of time. And I do feel incredibly rested.'

Well that's all right then.

St James's Park is right in the centre of the town and just a fifteen-minute uphill walk from the station. The closer we got to the ground, the more we were approached by suspiciously orange-looking women in their late teens, wearing next to nothing in the middle of January and handing out flyers. We took a couple. Flyers, that is.

'Upstairs in the Rose & Crown: Topless Barmaids Every Home Matchday. Special Drinks Promotion'; 'Foggo's Pre & Post Match Football Show. Every NUFC Home Game. Plus the Finest Topless Dancers. Pints from £2.40. 4 Pint Pitchers from £8. Vodka Energy Pitcher £8' These were offers all too easily refused. I don't drink. A Spurs shirt might not have gone down too well among a pissed-up Toon Army. And topless teenagers hot from the tanning booth don't really do it for me. But it did get me thinking the following day when the *News of the World* ran their story about Sky presenters Andy Gray and Richard Keys rubbishing the woman assistant referee off air, that it was probably only middle-class liberals like me who thought they were out of order. I doubt anyone in the centre of Newcastle on a match-day afternoon could work out what all the fuss was about.

They keep the away fans tucked well out of earshot up at the very top of the Sir John Hall Stand at St James's Park. So I daresay any of the Tottenham Hotspur directors who had made the trip to Newcastle would have missed the tuneless chant the 3,000 visiting supporters started well before kick-off and kept up throughout the afternoon: 'North London is ours, North London is ours, Say no to Stratford, North London is ours.' But even if they did hear it, it's hard to imagine they gave it a moment's thought.

For some years now, Spurs had been talking about redeveloping the stadium: a ground capacity of just over 36,000 was a severe limitation with 35,000 supporters on the season-ticket waiting list. If we were to maximise revenues and attract and keep the kind of players who would guarantee us a diet of Champions League football, then we needed a bigger ground. We needed to be more like Arsenal, who had abandoned Highbury in favour of the Emirates. That was the idea, anyway.

The initial plan had been to redevelop the Northumberland Park site, right next door to White Hart Lane, and now and again the club would put press releases on its website about the 'exciting new development' that would ensure everyone was just as close to the action in the new ground as they were now. With predictable sentimentality every fan vox pop and survey came back, 'Thanks, but no thanks.'

From myself included. Even though no part of the ground is the same – apart from the golden cockerel – as it was when I first went to White Hart Lane in the 1970s, I have managed to delude myself that it is inherently unchanged, that the soul of the club has been kept. I have an aversion to the idea of some new megastructure, with corporate lounges and hospitality areas, where football tourists come from around the world on pilgrimage. I basically want to be able to sit in the same uncomfortable seat with limited legroom until I die. And despite the current team being unquestionably the best and fittest I've ever seen, I'd actually be happier still watching the team of the 1960s which I first watched in black and white on the TV, battling a heavy ball on a mudheap of a pitch. Fandom is rarely a rational process.

Then the club threw a spanner in the works, by putting forward a rival bid to the one West Ham had already made to move to the new Olympic stadium seven miles away in Stratford, east London, as an alternative to the Northumberland Park development. Most fans saw this as a warning shot: 'If you keep on being this stroppy, then look at the alternative.' No one fancied Stratford, and Northumberland Park suddenly became very attractive.

The club's strategy appeared to have paid off when Haringey finally gave the Northumberland Park development proposals planning permission, and we were once more given glimpses of our new golden future with a further series of press releases and images on the club website. And then, it seems, the Spurs directors started to do their sums. They worked out that the Northumberland Park option would cost £450 million, while they could effectively dismantle the Olympic stadium and rebuild the seating for about £250 million. At which point Plan B suddenly became Plan A.

Both Mat, a native north Londoner for whom bragging rights over Arsenal overrode all other considerations, and Matthew were warming to Stratford. They believed that notions of Spurs' spiritual identity being rooted in N17 were hopelessly outdated. They reckoned most fans live outside the area in Enfield, Edmonton, Essex and Kent – or in my case, Streatham; that most local people didn't actually like having their high street invaded by 36,000 fans on a weekend and would like having 60,000 even less; that the already crap public transport infrastructure around the ground would collapse, even with the odd refit here and there. Most of all they thought we were already punching above our weight in a pint-sized stadium, and that sooner or later the club would disappear beneath an ever-richer Arsenal.

I didn't feel the same way. I didn't think the club would necessarily invest any savings in players. Nor that choosing the more expensive option meant the club would be forced to sell off our best players partially to fund the difference: the club would sell them both regardless at some point, if the price was right.

There were also questions of morality and identity. I couldn't justify bulldozing three-quarters of a £450 million new-build structure in a major recession, even if it was a white elephant. Nor could I square away the move east to a location that was undeniably more West Ham than Tottenham. As unlovely as parts of Tottenham might be, they still have more appeal than a five-minute high-speed rail journey from King's Cross to a long-forgotten former Olympic theme park. I couldn't get that worked up about financial muscle and having a stadium as big as the Emirates, either. We've had good years, bad years and indifferent years: that infuriating unpredictability was my real Spurs identity.

If change was inevitable, then paying £450 million to stay in the area seemed a price worth paying. It was certainly a price the club was prepared to pay before Stratford came along, so it could hardly argue that the cost was now prohibitive. Mat tried to argue me out of it. 'If we move to Northumberland Park and get crippled by debt,' he said, 'the chant "North London is ours" is going to have the same hollow ring as Tranmere Rovers fans singing "Merseyside is ours".'

'Possibly,' I replied. 'But that's all "if this" and "if that". Besides, isn't self-delusion really what it means to be a Spurs fan?'

'Sure,' Mat snapped back. 'And so is grandiosity.'

Not that either of us would have any impact on the outcome. The Spurs board knew most fans were against Stratford, and they weren't that bothered. The directors reckoned that no matter how much the fans moaned, when push came to shove most would take the pain and follow the club. They're probably right. I would. Albeit reluctantly.

But being ignored was no reason not to join in the singing at St James's Park. It was certainly more interesting than the game. All season, Spurs fans had held their breath after Bale was hacked down by one defender after another, wondering if he was going to emerge unscathed. And time and again he had. So when he rubbed his back ruefully after an innocuous challenge ten minutes into the game, no one paid much notice until he asked to be substituted. It was to be the last any of us saw of him for six weeks.

Bale's departure exposed Spurs' attacking limitations and the game drifted into an error-strewn midfield struggle. From the top of the stand where I was sitting, I could look out over the ground towards the Tyne and the sea, and I spent as much time looking at that as at the game. Only when Newcastle went a goal up midway through the second half did Spurs begin to start playing, and it looked as though we were going to come away empty-handed until Lennon fired in an equaliser deep into stoppage time.

There's always something glorious about late goals – if it's your side that's scoring them – and Spurs had become late-goal specialists this season. But there's something extra special when you score them away from home. It's not just the result, it's the silence of the home crowd. There were over 50,000 spectators in the ground, and 48,000 of them were gutted when Lennon scored. *Schadenfreude* may not be an attractive quality, but it's written into the DNA of every fan.

Matthew was beside himself. 'The lucky shirt worked again,' he said.

It was time to test him.

'So. Do you still fucking hate Lennon?' I asked.

'Of course.'

The journey home was just as long as the journey up, though rather more entertaining as Matthew unexpectedly managed to stay awake throughout. Then it would have been hard for him to have slept, as we found ourselves in a carriage surrounded by remnants of the Yid Army. The singing, if you can call it that, was relentless.

In one corner, there was a group of lairy teenagers who were going for it big time. At first they were quite funny, and the conductor went easy on them. But after one bloke, who can't have been more than fifteen, got so drunk he pissed himself – 'I neffa. I just spilled my drink' – the conductor told them he'd have them slung off the train if they didn't keep the noise down. Within five minutes the volume was back up.

'I warned you,' said the conductor. 'Next time you're off.'

'Well, you can fuck off then,' said one of the fans.

'That's it. You're off at Peterborough.'

'That's so unfair, you cunt.'

'You were warned. You blew it.'

'Do we all have to go?' asked one of the others.

'No. Just your abusive mate.'

When the conductor left to call the transport police, the whole gang rounded on the one who had overstepped the mark.

'What the fuck did you do that for? Now we've all got to get off.'

'No you don't.'

''Course we fucking do. We can't leave you on Peterborough station. And how the fuck are we going to get back to London at this time of night? We're banned from the trains, there's no bus and a cab will cost us a fortune.'

So they did all pile off at Peterborough. I suppose there

was something noble about their 'all for one, one for all' team spirit – not a trait you always see on the pitch – but it was all so pointless and inevitable. It certainly wasn't my finest hour as a fan. I hadn't stood up to them, told them to keep their mates in order and that they were embarrassing themselves and the rest of the Spurs fans on the train. Had it been an act of tribal solidarity or abject cowardice that I had kept my head down, hoping they would have the wit to get their act together and leaving the conductor to take the flak when they didn't? I fear it was the latter.

There wasn't enough time for Matthew to have a proper snooze before we reached London, so he started listening to his iPod instead.

'What are you listening to?' I asked.

'What do you think?'

Silly me.

'Did you know that Journey were one of only three rock bands to make the top one hundred of the UK singles charts last year?' he continued. 'And they were the highest-ranked at twenty-five.'

'You're kidding. You're the only person I know who likes Journey.'

'Let me tell you that as well as me, my mate Paul and fifty million Americans, there's a whole new generation of fans who have got into them through hearing "Don't Stop Believin'" on *Glee*.'

'I've never heard of "Don't Stop Believin'".'

Now it was Matthew's turn to be amazed.

'You can't seriously have never heard of their huge 1981 hit that became the most downloaded song in history after it was played in the final episode of *The Sopranos*?'

'I seriously haven't.'

'It was my wedding song. The most moving bit of the occasion.'

It was time for detente. I had to hear this song.

'OK, then. Let me listen to it on your iPod.'

I wanted to like it. I tried to like it. But it started off a bit bland and just got blander.

'What did you think?' Matthew said eagerly when I took off the headphones. 'Have you seen the light?'

'Well, it was OK . . .'

'You didn't like it much, did you?'

'I'll tell you what. Why don't I play you something on my iPod?'

'What?'

'Leonard Cohen.'

'I can't stand him,' he groaned.

'You haven't heard the recording of him live at the O2. It's superb. I'll play you "Anthem".'

Less than three minutes into the six-minute track, Matthew removed the headphones.

'I really can't listen to any of more of this. Did he really just ask will the dove event be free. I couldn't give a shit whether "the dove will ever be free" or not. If it was down to me, I'd strangle the dove.'

We carried on tormenting each other with our differing tastes in music until we arrived back at King's Cross, over an hour later than scheduled. It was enlightening in a way. Matthew and I have travelled round England and Europe together, but there will always be some things on which we disagree: Journey, Leonard Cohen and Aaron Lennon.

**

A fourth-round FA Cup draw away to Fulham was no gimme, but I was happy enough. We'd beaten them home and away earlier in the season, we'd beaten them en route to our FA Cup semi-final exit the previous season, and it meant another afternoon of organic burgers at Craven Cottage with Robbie. I was even starting to feel some of the passion for the FA Cup that had been missing from the Charlton tie; which was more than Matthew was.

The previous season he'd blagged a ticket from a friend who is a Fulham member, and I assumed he'd be doing the same this year. 'Uh, no, John,' he said. 'I think he's taking someone else.'

'Have you asked?'

'No, but I don't want to be too pushy.'

Code for he couldn't be bothered, the Champions League was far more important, he might get interested once we reached the semis and was more than happy just to watch it on TV.

There were still several thousands of Spurs fans who still believed enough, if not always wholeheartedly, in the magic of the FA Cup, and the away-supporters end was sold out. However, the Spurs team gave every appearance of having reached the same conclusion as Matthew, and decided to not really turn up. The team offered nothing, not even any pride.

We were 2-0 down within ten minutes after the usually reliable Michael Dawson made two horrendous mistakes that ended in penalties. The second got him sent off. By half-time, Fulham had doubled their lead, not through brilliance, but just by playing averagely competent football. Even a Second Division team would have beaten us that day. At half-time there was a mixture of disbelief and anger among the fans. A feeling we had been betrayed.

'This is awful,' said Robbie.

I nodded. I couldn't remember a worse performance.

A large number of fans cut their losses and left before the restart. Many more drifted away throughout the second half, as it became clear there was to be no Inter Milan-like second-half renaissance and we were intent on playing just as badly as we had in the first. Throughout the game we didn't have a single shot on target; Fulham could have played the whole ninety minutes without a goalkeeper and still kept a clean sheet. As one fan said to me on his way out, 'I'd rather watch a TV documentary about badgers mating than this rubbish.'

I stayed until the end, both out of a ghoulish curiosity to see just how few Spurs fans would stick it out, and to look at the players' faces as they left the pitch. Either they were expert poker players and used to giving nothing away, or they weren't that bothered.

As we listened to the Radio 5 phone-in on the way home in the car, the irritating Alan Green did what he always does. He acted the calm rationalist who knows football better than everyone else and urged angry Spurs fans 'to see the big picture; every team has an off day, and losing will allow you to concentrate on the Premiership and the Champions League'.

I switched him off. 'Thanks for nothing, Al,' I shouted at the radio. 'There are off days and off days. If Spurs didn't really fancy the FA Cup this year then they should have bloody well said so and I wouldn't have gone. As it is, I've just been conned out of £70 for two tickets.'

There was a moment while Robbie caught his breath. 'Calm down, Dad,' he said, eventually. 'It's only a game.'

Was it? It didn't feel that way. It felt more like a betrayal.

Still, at least 'the one thing' had been put out of its misery for another ten years.

February

THERE'S A POINT IN every season when I find myself pompously saying, 'The next few games are crucial. They will define our season.' To be strictly accurate, there are several points in every season where I find myself saying, 'The next few games are crucial. They will define our season.' But because collective short-term amnesia is part of the football supporter's general condition, no one will ever point out that I've said that already. This is mainly because they too were having exactly those conversations themselves, but also because whatever crisis may have sparked the previous outburst must have turned out not to be so critical after all, as there would be no need to repeat it otherwise, so therefore no one probably ever said it. Well, if they did, they didn't really mean it like they do now.

At any rate, now was one of those moments when I, along with most of my Spurs friends, was saying, 'The next few games are crucial. They will define our season.' After a decent run over Christmas and New Year that had taken us back into the mix for a Champions League place the following season, we'd stalled against Manchester United and allowed the wheels to come off completely against Fulham. To make matters worse, our best three players – Bale, Modrić and van der Vaart – were all out injured and our next three games, Blackburn and Sunderland away and Bolton at home, were all fixtures we had shown ourselves more than capable of losing in the past. Especially in winter, when it gets a bit cold and our players think nobody much is watching.

They were also three games I would be missing. The midweek game in Blackburn was always going to be a non-starter. We all have limits, and that was well past mine. I wasn't the only one to find it missable; everyone else clearly did too as it wasn't being shown live on Sky, so there was only one thing for it. Live streaming via an illegal overseas website.

I say live streaming, but the only thing that happened in real time was the chat forum and I could have done without that. Quite why people from around the world feel the need to get together to share observations like, 'I hate all Yids,' 'Fuck off, Yids are the best. COYS,' 'Northerners don't know shit,' 'Have you seen Rafa's missus? She is well fit,' and 'Yeah, I would, would you?' is beyond me.

The action on the pitch was inaction on the screen as the website repeatedly stalled for several minutes at a time after less than ten seconds of live football. And when it restarted the ball wasn't just in a different place on the pitch, it was in a different time zone. I was probably the last person supposedly following the game to realise we had taken the lead after just three minutes, and it was only several hours later when I caught up with the highlights later that night on TV that I got to find out how.

There were only two people I knew who hadn't completely given up on Crouchie; Justin and the manager. Everyone else had become completely bewildered that he kept getting a start ahead of Defoe and Pav. What was the point of a striker who didn't score goals? Admittedly, Pav and Defoe hadn't been scoring goals either, but we all felt they were marginally more likely to find the net than Crouchie and, at the very least, we could do with watching a different striker not score, if only to give us somebody else to moan about. So what did we know? Because Crouchie jumped above Samba – just about the only Premiership defender nearly as tall as him – to head home. It was every bit as much of an eye-opener to me as it must have been to Blackburn, because I couldn't remember ever having seen Crouchie jump before. Crouchie doesn't do jumping. I knew that and Samba knew that. Which is presumably why he hadn't bothered to jump for the ball himself.

About halfway through the first half, I got fed up with only having watched about two minutes of football and did what I had done so often in the past; I followed the match on the Sky Sports news channel instead. It's far more engaging than it sounds, even if it is merely substituting one form of torture for another, as I found myself in a different psychic limbo, torn between willing there to be a goal flash from Ewood Park that gave us a two-goal cushion and praying to hear nothing in case there was an equaliser. As with so many games where we take the lead, I rather wished I could have been given a general anaesthetic and woken up when it was all over. But I couldn't, and I had to guts it out. As did the team, who unusually hung on to their lead for the remaining eighty-seven minutes.

I wasn't nearly so sanguine about missing the Bolton game. When Terry had sent out the invites for his wife's fiftieth birthday party before Christmas, I hadn't given a second thought before accepting. I hadn't even looked at the date because it just hadn't occurred to me he could do anything so stupid as to arrange a party on the same day as a home game. This might sound like a small oversight on his part, but it was a completely unnecessary one. The fixture lists are printed in the summer, precisely to avoid cock-ups like this. To compound the felony, he had chosen the only day in the whole of February when Spurs had a home game. Any other Saturday would have done. His wife's birthday wasn't even on the weekend he had chosen. Nor was there any wriggle room, as Terry had timed the party to start at 2 p.m., eighty miles west of London. Open as I am to the possibility of bilocation – I've lost count of the number of times I've set off for an appointment at the very moment it was supposed to start – there could be no shuffling in late or sloping off early this time. It was the party or the game, and as I was already in deep shit for missing Tors's birthday the previous month, the party it was.

Not that it stopped me making a few half-hearted attempts to get out of it.

'I've just realised Terry and Ianthe's party clashes with the Bolton game,' I said to Jill one evening.

'Oh dear,' she replied, grinning. 'Then you are going to have to miss it. It's only Bolton.'

Since when had she become an expert on whether Bolton was missable or not?

'But it's in the run of three crucial games that will define our season.'

'Every game is in a run of three crucial games that will define your season.'

Terry was just as stubborn.

'It's only Bolton. You're just going to have to miss it,' he said.

'That's all very well for you to say. You don't have a ticket.'

'Get over it.'

'Do you really think Ianthe would mind if I didn't come?'

'Yes.'

'What would happen if I didn't?'

'Well, for a start, I can guarantee that you will never bat higher than ninth or bowl more than two overs again.'

'How would I know the difference?'

'You're coming. End of.'

'I don't suppose there's any chance of changing the date?'

Click.

Matthew couldn't believe his luck when I offered him both season tickets for the game.

'That's fantastic.'

'What is? That I can't come?'

'Er, no. Obviously that is very sad. Very, very sad.'

'I want text updates, OK? Not just the score, but what's going on.'

'Yeah, sure, whatever.'

The party was a top bash with forty people treated to a sit-down lunch. I'm just not sure the people seated either side of me between 3 p.m. and 4.55 p.m. will have had a particularly fun time, as I nervously checked my phone for automatic score alerts every five minutes or so. It's amazing how little effort it takes to spoil something for those around you. I cheered up and became tremendously chatty when we went a goal up, and then became morose and twitchy when Bolton equalised early in the second. My body was in Wiltshire but my mind was at White Hart Lane, imagining the best and fearing the worst. As my watch moved on to 4.50 p.m., I had given up and was just waiting for the buzz on my phone that would come in with the final score of 1-1. It came, only it wasn't the final score but a ninety-third-minute winner from Niko Kranjčar, a player who had been brilliant for us the previous season until he got injured and who, for no very obvious reason, had been sidelined this season. He'd hardly even had a chance as a sub. I'd always take a goal from any player, but I've never lost that extra thrill I used to get as a child when one of my favourites scores. It's somehow all the sweeter. It's as if there's a special connection between you and that goal. It feels like you've scored it yourself.

I tried to make up for my mental absenteeism by being extra charming for the remainder of the party. It was hard to tell if I got away with it, as most people were either too pissed to have noticed or too polite to comment. Back at the hotel, Jill was unamused at being forced to watch the highlights on *Match of the Day*.

'I can't miss the Kranjčar goal,' I said.

'I can.'

'I'll make a compromise. I'll turn off the TV after the Spurs game.'

It was the last match shown.

The following morning, I remembered Matthew had failed to text or ring me once during the game the previous day, and I'd had to rely on the automatic alerts. I called him.

'So what happened?'

'I forgot. Sorry. It was all a bit tense.'

'So was I.'

'At least we won. It was a crucial game.'

'Precisely.'

Call me a lightweight, but I had no qualms about staying at home for Sunderland. Even for a proven masochist, this was a Saturday too far. A late kick-off, no chance of a train home that night – even assuming I was prepared to hang around for hours on several different platforms if there was one – and, crucially, it was on TV. And again we got a result, coming back from a goal down to win 2-1. As usual, it was an agonizing last half-hour. Why couldn't we ever do what other teams do from time to time, sneak a two-goal cushion and give the fans a break? But if there's an easy way and a hard way, you can generally put money on Spurs taking the tough option. And a win is a win, even if you need several hours of therapy to recover from it, especially a win at the Stadium of Light, which generally brings nothing but darkness for us. Best of all, the winning goal had once again been scored by Kranjčar.

***

Nine points from three games. Games I'd decided were crucial. Games that were all too losable. It was remarkable. All the more so given my mental state.

For a good fifteen years now, I've had recurring bouts of depression. Not every year or even every two years, but regularly enough to know that another one is never too far away. And it's time had come again. In some ways I've got better at dealing with it – there's no longer that feeling of 'what the fuck is going on?' I experienced when it first happened to me – but the sense of abject powerlessness never gets any easier. The symptoms are often quite subtle to start with. My sleep will become slightly worse than usual, my anxiety levels will rise, I'll start to catch myself wondering if that funny pain I sometimes get is cancer and I'll become less engaged than usual. All normal stuff for me. And every other Spurs fan, I should think.

Sometimes it stops at that; but not often. Usually what happens next is like falling off a cliff. After a couple of weeks of hanging in, of trying to hold it together, of trying to cope, of trying not to let Jill see that everything is on the verge of going tits up because I know how scary she finds it, all hell breaks loose. Crippling panic attacks, complete insomnia and an overwhelming sense of futility; even getting out of bed feels too hard. At this point I call in the artillery.

I have an ambivalent relationship with my psychiatrist, not helped by the fact that he only usually sees me when I'm in crisis. He thinks his job is trying to keep me well enough not to need to go into a mental hospital, but part of me – obviously not the well part – can't think of anything better than going into a mental hospital, because I was sent to one when I was first diagnosed with depression and I quite enjoyed it. Not the being ill bit, but the being in the hospital bit, because it's one of the few places I've ever been where I felt totally safe.

No one had any expectations of me – if I said I wasn't up to doing very much, no one so much as raised an eyebrow – and the other patients were some of the loveliest people I had ever met. They were bonkers, of course, but then who was I to judge? There were the depressed, the manic, the manic-depressed, the schizophrenic, the ones who couldn't stop sleeping, the ones who couldn't stop talking and the ones, like the New Zealand dentist, who couldn't stop doing both at the same time. It was also the only place I've ever been since primary school where I was congratulated for knowing the capital of France. Every afternoon, the nursing staff would try to hoover up as many patients as they could and make us interact in some kind of communal activity. Usually a quiz. Most patients were sensible enough to duck out of this, but I couldn't resist as I've always been a competitive bastard.

'What's the capital of France?' a nurse would ask.

I'd say nothing, not wanting to look too pushy. No one else would say anything either, though for rather different reasons. They were either too catatonic to speak, or felt no need to bother with such a ludicrously trivial question. So it would inevitably always be me who broke the silence.

'Paris.'

'Well done, John.'

And so it would continue until the nurse decided enough was enough. At which point I would ask for the final score.

'John, 23. Everyone else, 0.'

I never got bored of that bit.

There were downsides to being in hospital. Apart from being mentally ill. It was inconvenient, it was worrying for the family, it interrupted my work. And my football. It's surprising how vocal people who have done nothing but stare at the wall all day can become when someone suggests watching something on TV they don't like. It was also an eye-opener to discover that not everyone wanted to watch football. I had thought it was only Jill.

Not necessarily for all the right reasons, then, I'd steered clear of being an inpatient since the first time

I'd been seriously depressed and, on balance, I wasn't that keen to try it again just now. Spurs were playing AC Milan in the last sixteen knockout stage of the Champions League and, after telling Jill how I couldn't possibly not go to Milan the previous November to see Inter as there might never be another chance to see Spurs play in the San Siro in my lifetime, I had tickets to return less than three months later.

Within an hour of the draw being made before Christmas, I'd booked the flights for Matthew and me and emailed the two Marcos to see if they were up for a repeat night out. I never heard back from Marco G.; the trauma of finishing second to Spurs in the qualifying group combined with the suggestion of watching his least-favourite team – AC Milan – play his newly appointed second least-favourite team must have crashed his laptop. But Marco A., a lifelong AC supporter, replied within minutes. He would love to come to the game, and he would love to have us to stay again, despite Matthew's snoring. Sorted.

I just wasn't sure if I was up to it. I liked the idea of being there; I just couldn't imagine me getting there. It felt too far, too difficult. I could barely make it to the end of the road to get a paper in the morning. How was I going to make it to Milan? So when I saw my shrink a few days before the game, I was half hoping he was going to let me off the hook and tell me to stay at home.

'I've got this other problem,' I said towards the end of the session. 'I've got a ticket for the Milan game, and I was wondering if it would be a mistake to go.'

'Are you mad?' he replied.

'I wouldn't be here otherwise.'

'You're right. Sorry.' Never underestimate the value of

a shrink with a sense of humour. 'I meant, "How could you not go?" If I could get off work, I'd go myself. I've been a Spurs fan for decades and it's a once-in-a-lifetime opportunity.'

Who would have thought it? A shrink who understood that a once-in-a-lifetime opportunity could come round twice in three months. Perhaps we were both certifiable.

Even with the same complicated itinerary as before, the journey to Milan was a lot less stressful second time round as we'd done it already, though I could have done without the scariest-looking Spurs fan and his sunbed-orange girlfriend deciding that the two seats next to me on the plane were just the ones they were looking for. As he necked three or four cans of lager before breakfast while repeatedly jabbing his elbows into my ribs, or standing up to talk to his nearly-as-scary mates in the row behind, I was reminded of just how much of a lightweight I really was. 'Fuck this,' I whispered to Matthew, who was looking annoyingly smug in the seat across the aisle at having avoided the neighbours from hell. 'Next time we're flying BA. Whatever it costs.'

There wasn't much thinking to do, though, because Pete had done it all for us. After the previous trip to Milan, Pete's Independent Spurs Supporters Official Football Firm aka Piss Off Tours had gone upmarket. Instead of the few photocopied sheets he had knocked up for the game against Inter, Pete had now produced a glossy brochure, 'AC Come, AC Go', for the return, complete with every piece of travel information you could possibly need along with a review of every bar in Milan which Matthew and I didn't need, as neither of us drinks. But Pete didn't hold that against us – even if he didn't necessarily see quite why we were here if we weren't going to get arseholed for thirty-six hours – and he was happy to include us as associate members of Piss Off Tours.

'We've got a couple of hours to kill before the train leaves for Milan,' he said. 'There's a nice café-bar in the piazza across the road from the station. Come and join us.'

Matthew quickly downed two double espressos. His coffee habit has to be seen to be believed.

'You just don't understand,' he explained. 'Life's really tough when you've got twins under three. You're fighting extreme fatigue on a daily basis. You're lucky. Your kids are in their teens. You could have a lie-in any day you liked if you weren't an insomniac.'

'So part of the attraction of these away trips is to get away from your kids and catch up on a few zeds?

'That's a typically negative way of looking at it, John. I prefer to think of it as an act of heroism. That despite my acute exhaustion, I'm prepared to tear myself away from my family to put my body and bank account on the line for the sake of the team.'

'Silly me. Talking of which, have you told your wife how much all this is costing?'

'Not exactly. I did say the flights were quite cheap.'

'What did she say?'

'That presumably that meant everything else wasn't. How about you? What have you told Jill?'

'As little as possible. I'd led her to believe the Champions League would be over by Christmas, so I didn't tell her I was going until the weekend, and then I pretended I'd told her ages ago and that she must have forgotten.'

'Did it work?'

'I'm here, aren't I?'

The Italian train was the same as before; fast, on time and comfortable and, once we arrived in Milan, Pete made sure we had the right metro pass and vaguely knew where we were going before he and the rest of his crew headed off to the bars downtown.

'Just one more thing,' Pete said as he left us.

'What's that?'

'If anyone asks you who you're travelling with, just say, "Piss off".'

After a couple more detours to refuel Matthew with double espressos, we arrived at Marco A.'s apartment where the caretaker let us in. We had planned just to dump our bags and explore the city for a few hours, but it was pissing with rain, Matthew needed a snooze and I wasn't feeling that wonderful myself. Having expended all that nervous energy fighting off the anxiety of getting to Milan, I was going to have to do it all again the next day to get home. I closed my eyes and concentrated on just breathing for the next few hours. What a state. Reaching the last sixteen of the Champions League was supposed to be fun, not a mental test of endurance. One that I was worried I was losing.

Marco A. had made it even easier for us to reach the San Siro this time round by sending his twenty-year-old son, Giorgio, to the apartment to take us to meet him near his office. Giorgio was everything I would have liked to have been at twenty. Or fifty. Apart from supporting AC. He was good-looking, intelligent, fluent in three languages and a model of metropolitan sophistication. He didn't even blink when Matthew demanded his usual double-espresso stop. When I was twenty, I could barely speak to people my own age and would certainly not have dreamed of starting a conversation with my parents' friends on the grounds they were bound to be boring, yet Giorgio chatted to us about this and that in English as if he were pleased to meet us. Remarkable. The only time his guard dropped a little was when we reached the stadium.

'Can you tell me where I can get one of those half-and-half scarves?' I asked.

'You mean the souvenir ones with AC, Tottenham and the date on?'

'Yes.'

'Why would you want one of those?'

It was one of those moments when a deep footballing truth couldn't be covered up by politeness. Only a football bumpkin would want to buy that kind of tat; and to Giorgio, Spurs and their fans were bumpkins. For AC, reaching the knockout stages of the Champions League was completely unremarkable. If Giorgio were to buy a scarf for every knockout game AC played, his bedroom would be knee-deep in rubbish. He was part of an established football elite, and we were arriviste chancers. We may have taken Inter by surprise, but there was no way we would get lucky again. Not that he said so, of course; but if he had, I'd have agreed.

Giorgio quickly recovered his poise and found me a scarf, and we agreed to meet at the same stall at the end of the game. He and his dad were off to sit in their usual seats at the opposite end of the ground to Matthew and me.

'You know what?' said Matthew, the moment they were out of earshot. 'The San Siro doesn't feel nearly so imposing second time. In fact, it looks a bit tatty . . .'

'Don't start up about Stratford again.'

Matthew had bought the Tottenham directors' dream

wholesale, and for the last couple of weeks he'd done nothing but fantasise how, if we won the Olympic stadium bid, our new ground would be the last word in concrete, modernist neo-fascism and that clubs from all over the world – and especially elsewhere in north London – would be sick with envy and mentally crushed before a ball had been kicked.

He was right about the San Siro's tattiness, though. The stadium was showing its age; even at White Hart Lane the roof doesn't leak when it's raining. But it was still one hell of a ground. Back in October, the ground had been little more than half-full and the Inter fans had been indulgent towards the pockets of Spurs fans who were sitting in the neutral seats. This time there were more than 75,000 in the stadium and everywhere, except for the Spurs end, was decked out in red and black. We had missed the loyalty-point cut-off and were back among the neutrals: only it didn't feel very neutral.

'Fuck me,' said Matthew. 'We'd better keep our heads down.'

When I'd seen our team sheet, it hadn't occurred to me our heads would ever need keeping up. Bale and Modrić were both still out, our squad looked like the walking wounded, we were relying on Sandro and Palacios to control the midfield – not something they had ever looked like doing before – and I had switched to the usual auto-pilot defence mechanism of 'I just want not to be embarrassed and have something to play for in the second leg.'

But then the incredible started to happen. It was AC who looked nervous, Sandro and Palacios were immense and, while we didn't create too many clear chances, we didn't look to be in any great trouble. We were totally comfortable at 0-0 at half-time.

'I can't quite believe this,' I said. 'We could get a result here. Imagine coming away with a draw.'

'It's astonishing,' Matthew replied. 'Bolton gave us more trouble than this.'

Inevitably AC came harder at us in the second half, but Gomes made two stunning saves and they couldn't break us down. With fifteen minutes to go I was experiencing the familiar agony that comes with daring to allow yourself to believe: the dread that hope would be rewarded with disappointment. With ten minutes to go, we took the lead. Lennon ran from the halfway line, beat a couple of defenders and squared the ball to Crouchie, who slid it into an open net. I couldn't help myself from standing up and started yelling, 'Ye-e-e-e-s.' Immediately, I felt Matthew tugging on my arm.

'Sit down, you fucking idiot.'

I looked round to find I was the only person standing in the whole of our section of the ground. I smiled sheepishly and tried to pretend I'd only stood up to stretch my legs. Amazingly, I got away with just a few disapproving glares. Either the AC fans were a lot more forgiving than most or they were all numb with cognitive dissonance, incapable of accepting that what had just happened, had happened. It hadn't been in my script, so it was unlikely to have been in theirs.

Nor did we throw it away, though AC did get the ball in the net in injury time, only for it to be disallowed for a push on Dawson. Better and better. We'd never have got that kind of decision in our favour if we were playing at Old Trafford with an English referee. Thank God for the Champions League, then. It seemed to be a great deal easier than everyone made out. Against all the odds and expectations, we had played the perfect away leg and beaten one of the best teams in Europe, one that had won the Champions League seven times, on their own pitch. I was stunned, unable to move from my seat, and it was only when most of the AC fans had left the stadium that I could find any words.

'You do know that Crouchie scuffed it,' I said.

'Of course he did,' Matthew replied. 'You didn't imagine he hit it cleanly, did you?'

'Amazing.'

'Amazing.'

Scuffed or not, Crouchie had scored. And he would probably become a Spurs legend on the back of it. It made me wonder how selective my memory really is. How come I only remember Ricky Villa for his FA Cup final goal? Could he not also have had dozens of horrendous misses that I have successfully managed to block from my mind? If I'm still alive, perhaps in thirty years' time, Crouchie's newly published ghosted autobiography, *Stooping to Conquer*, would be my Christmas book highlight and I would be boring anyone who would listen with stories of how I was there on both occasions when Crouchie scored two of the most important goals in Spurs history – the one that beat Manchester City to get us into the Champions League, and the one that secured us victory in the San Siro. Perhaps. Perhaps. At any rate, I loved Crouchie that Tuesday night. Fickle? *Moi*?

Marco A. was grace personified when we hooked up afterwards.

'Congratulations,' he said. 'You deserved to win.'

Giorgio was anything but grace. He might have been cool *savoir faire* before the game, but now he was so angry he could barely speak, reduced instead to swearing to himself under his breath. He had said he would come back to the apartment for some late-night pasta, but he got off the tram early, pleading tiredness and an early start the next day. I think he just needed to kick something. I felt closer to him than I had all day. We were more alike than I had thought.

For Matthew, the reality of what we had achieved began to sink in on the train back to Bologna early the following morning. Aided by several large espressos.

'I know gloating is wrong and all that,' he said, 'and I do feel a bit bad that we've repaid the two Marcos' hospitality by coming here and fucking over both their teams . . .'

It didn't seem quite in the spirit of the moment to point out that we had actually lost to Inter in Milan, and there was still a second leg of this tie to come. Still . . .

'We did lose to Inter . . .'

'Do shut up, John. We've stuffed the pride of Italy within a few months. The Milanese will never forget us now. Life can't get any better.'

It would be a while before it properly sank in for me. I was still anxious and depressed, and it felt as if there was a disconnect between me and reality. It was like I had been there, yet not really been there. Maybe if we'd have lost it would have seemed more real. I was certainly more at home with the Spurs fans from Nottingham we met at the airport than with Matthew's reawakened megalomania.

'Amazing game,' they said.

'Amazing,' I agreed.

'You know what, though?'

'What.'

'We all reckon Crouchie scuffed his shot.'

***

Spurs were soon to be off on a rather more extended mini-break of their own, courtesy both of their own incompetence in the FA Cup giving them a weekend off, and the FA's annual ritual of scheduling next to no league games in late February and March in order to turn April and May into an attritional battle to find the last player still standing among a condensed fixture list. With time to kill, the club had decided to take the team to Dubai for a little warm-weather training.

I might have been more sympathetic to the training value of such a trip if the Blackburn Rovers team hadn't turned up to the hotel in Dubai where we were staying on holiday for a week in 2006. My reservations weren't based on Robbie Savage pushing his way to the front of the breakfast queue, or Craig Bellamy assaulting guests by the pool bar; both players were never less than well behaved in public, signing autographs for anyone who asked. Even for my son Robbie, then just ten, whom I had begged not to.

'You can't ask them,' I had said. 'They're Blackburn. You can't do anything to make them feel important and good about themselves. Just try to ignore them.'

'I can't, Dad. They are Premiership footballers. I've got to get their autographs just to prove we were in the same hotel.'

Robbie's interest waned the moment he had the

autographs – he managed to lose them within a couple of hours – but mine didn't. I was fascinated to see what they were actually doing in Dubai, and I used to watch them from my bedroom balcony while they were training in the morning on a small piece of AstroTurf. The manager, Mark Hughes, would order someone to set up a few cones and there would be a bit of running, a bit of passing and a great deal of chat for ninety minutes. And that would be it for the day, apart from the occasional informal game of keepy-uppy on the beach, designed more to impress the female guests than improve ball skills, in between snoozing on a sun lounger and cooling off in the sea during the afternoon. I was working harder on my fitness in the hotel gym.

This wasn't a training camp, it was a holiday camp, albeit a very effective one as Blackburn went on to finish sixth in the Premiership and qualified for the UEFA Cup. But it was a holiday nonetheless. And Spurs were shortly to depart for Dubai, where they would presumably be following a similar routine. Now, I've nothing against holidays. We all need them from time to time. But the thing about holidays is that you generally have to pay for them yourself. I'm not moaning about how much I earn – I do OK – but there are a number of Spurs players earning more in a week than I do in a year, and it was me and 36,000 other fans who were going to be paying for the Dubai trip.

Mind you, if Jill had known Spurs were going to Dubai and that I would be indirectly paying for it, she would have been a great deal more upset than me. My grumpiness was more about the double-think of describing a holiday as training; and if it resulted in Spurs winning the Champions

League this year, or qualifying for the competition again the next, I'd probably have been prepared to bung them an extra £100 if they had asked. Jill's displeasure was rather less petty, as she had been trying to arrange our own spring holiday. She had just handed in her notice at work, was taking a month off before starting her new job and wanted us all to go away for a week.

'I can't afford to take the time off,' I had pleaded.

'It's amazing you've managed to go to Milan this month, then.'

'It is, rather.'

There wasn't much point trying to explain the difference between sneaking abroad for the night to see 'The Most Important Game of the Season'™ and trying to find a convenient seven-day stretch in the second half of April when Spurs weren't playing – a near-impossible task, given the danger of postponed games being rescheduled. Or of me just cocking things up as I had four years previously, by failing to check on the UEFA Cup dates and finding myself with no internet or mobile-phone access in the middle of a South African game reserve, rather than at White Hart Lane for the quarter-final tie against Seville.

This year, thankfully, I had a rather better reason for being obstructive. My depression. Every cloud has a silver lining, I suppose. You might have thought that a holiday would be just what you need to cheer yourself up; Jill had once thought that when she booked a holiday to La Gomera, one of the least-inhabited of the Canary Islands, while I was depressed. I sat by the pool for a week, either reading a book about the fire-bombing of Dresden or staring catatonically into space, while she tried to entertain the kids with the island's two-star attractions: a piece of uneven concrete doubling as a crazy golf course and the German nudist beach. We hadn't tried that again.

That didn't stop Jill finding me annoying, though. Living with someone who is depressed must be almost as bad as being depressed. There is no standard rhythm or logic to depression; you know you're losing touch with reality, you can't be talked out of it and you just have to hold on as best you can through the white-knuckle ride until it lifts. And you have no idea when that will be, so there's no point making any major plans for when you might be well again. Even more infuriating for her was that, beyond just about holding my job together – I had a lot of holiday held over, so I went on a two-day week – and trying to deaden the panic attacks in the gym, the only thing I could really manage was going to the football. She thought it typically perverse of me.

It may well have been, but it wasn't deliberately so. She saw me as someone putting himself into her twin visions of hell: Ryanair and a huge crowd of football fans. I saw myself just doing something that had to be done, something that required nothing of me beyond showing up. I could shout or stay quiet as I pleased, and no one would judge. Or notice. At the best of times, the idea of milling with crowds of shoppers on the high street makes me anxious and homicidal. Yet even when I'm nuts, I feel safe in a football crowd: over and beyond a common sense of purpose with everyone else, I feel as if I'm in a bubble where there's nothing getting in between me and the moment. All the other worries that are invading my psyche 24/7 – 'You're going to die, John, it's only a matter of when' – dissolve for a few hours. There is no me; only football. It's the most perfect time off, time out from myself. Knowing there are football matches – and there-fore moments like these – ahead is one of the things that helps me survive those days when every minute feels like an hour.

A still more surprising side-effect of my depression is that it took a period of mental illness to inject a temporary note of sanity into my football-watching. Like every fan, I want to believe that my being at a game somehow has an impact; that if I wasn't there, something different would have happened. To an extent this is true; my driving has almost certainly caused the blood pressure of other road users on the M40 and M6 to spike from time to time – though not Matthew's. But what my attendance definitely hasn't done is altered the result. Any correlation between me wearing a lucky shirt, shouting at a referee to give a penalty or booing John Terry to make him lose his rag and get sent off is accidental. And yet part of the collective delusion of being a fan is the notion that your participation and involvement can make an incremental difference. By willing something enough, you can get what you want. It's like being an American for ninety minutes.

I hadn't noticed the mismatch between cause and effect so much in previous depressive episodes – princi-pally because it wasn't particularly evident, as my negative mood was generally reflected in a negative series of results. But this time, despite my repeated pre-match predictions of disaster, we had won four tricky games on the bounce. Even I couldn't escape noticing I had no control over events; it was almost a relief, in a dull sort of way. There was even some good news off the pitch, though this was rather less unexpected than beating AC Milan. West Ham had been chosen as the preferred bidder for the Olympic stadium. Matthew was apoplectic, as he saw his dreams of crushing the 1,000-year tyranny of the Arse under hundreds of thousands of tons of concrete that he'd already christened the Death Star of our own evaporate. 'Back to the same old lovable, useless Spurs,' he chuntered.

The away game to Blackpool proved Matthew right. Despite Blackpool having had a dreadful run since the beginning of the year, despite this being, on paper, the easiest game of the year, despite us creating more than ten clear-cut chances, we were 3-0 down by half-time. A consolation deflection by Pav in the second half wasn't really much consolation. Disturbingly, the defeat also began to make me wonder if maybe I didn't have some influence over Spurs' performances after all. It was a worrying time for both me and Matthew.

March

THE LANDING WALL OUTSIDE my study has become a Spurs 'Hall of Fame'. It started out as a few pictures and just, well, grew really. Several times Jill has placed me on a final warning not to add anything more as 'it's hideous and my wall, too' and every time I've ignored it. If there's something worthy of inclusion, up it goes. When she's out. I'm still not sure if she hasn't noticed there's very little blank space left on the wall, or if she actually doesn't care that much and just wants to give me a hard time when she remembers.

There are photographs of important goals; and yes, the ones Crouchie scored against Manchester City and AC Milan are up there, too. You can't say I'm not fair. There's the original cartoon from the front cover of the programme for the Second Division match Spurs played against Oldham on 19 December 1931. All Spurs programmes had cartoons on the front of a rather grubby-looking bit of brown paper back in those days: this drawing is of a Santa Claus standing next to a Christmas tree with 'FA Cup 3rd round draw' written on the base, handing over an owl with a Sheffield Wednesday tag attached to its ear to a grateful Spurs player with a cockerel for a head, above the caption, 'Thank You, Father Christmas'. Which rather proves that hubris really is written into the club's DNA, as we only drew the home tie the following January and lost the replay 3-1.

There's also handbill flyers for old games, and even a couple of outsized, pictorial cheques drawn on the club's bank account: one from April 1907 for £2/15/- made out to Nurse Morrall, the other from October 1925 for £3/13/6d made out to the London Football Combination. No one but me, and possibly Trevor, can understand why I've bothered to have them framed and given them wall space. But pride of place goes to a fabulous black-and-white photo of eight members of the team carrying captain Danny Blanchflower on their shoulders around Wembley, after completing the double by beating Leicester to win the FA Cup in 1961. It's signed by all the players. Except for one.

Rob White has similar photos in his home. His, too, are unsigned by the same player, only it's rather more poignant for him because the player was his father. John White is a Spurs and Scotland legend. He was a key member of the team that won the double in 1961, the FA Cup the year after, the European Cup Winners' Cup in 1963, and was capped for his country twenty-two times. Yet, to a large extent, all these achievements have been overshadowed by his death; at the age of twenty-seven he was struck by lightning while out playing golf in July 1964.

For those who are old enough, John's death is a football JFK moment; they can remember exactly what they were doing and where they were when they heard the news. I'm not quite old enough. But I did find out about him a few years later when I started reading football magazines as his name was still often mentioned, never in less than reverential terms and almost always accompanied by the word *tragic*. And I became fascinated by his story; I wanted to know all about him, and on the rare occasions some old newsreel clips of the early 1960s Spurs side were shown on TV I'd try to pick him out. But there were no pause or rewind buttons back then, and the picture quality was so poor and the footage so short, I still can't be certain I was actually looking at the right person.

If Greavsie and Big Chiv were the figures of my conscious present and future, John White was the figure of my subconscious present and past. He didn't have a nickname. Not Whitey or Chalky; to me, he always was and always will be just John White – a mark of respect for the dead, and a sign that we didn't know each other that well. I certainly wasn't mates with him as I was with Greavsie and Big Chiv. There also seemed to be frustratingly little to know about him; almost every story I read about him gave as much prominence to the manner of his death as to his brilliance on the field.

Maybe that was the attraction. His death was a guilty, ghoulish window into the growing awareness of my own mortality that was slowly penetrating my eleven-year-old mind, while his life was sufficiently sketchy for me to mould his story to fit my own narrative. Unlimited by too many facts or points of reference, I could, through him, connect to the Spurs prehistory of the early 1960s that I had missed by just a few years.

More than forty years later, nothing much has changed really. Every now and again, members of the double-winning team are introduced to the crowd during the half-time interval at White Hart Lane; their numbers are dwindling, though, as time catches up with them. Those that do appear are ageing fast – well, everyone but Cliff Jones, who is still ridiculously spritely – and as they drag their creaking bodies on to the pitch, it's almost like watching my memories, imagined or real, dissolve in front of my eyes. It won't be that long before there are no survivors of the double team. None but John White, that is, who will always symbolize that side because by never having been alive for me, he had never really died. He always has been, and always will be, preserved as a youthful legend in black and white on my wall.

And in my cupboard, because I've also got squirrelled away the ticket and programme for the memorial game played between Spurs and a Scotland X1, the programme for the match played at Hendon in September 1964 between the Maccabi Association London and an Ex-Spurs All Stars XI in aid of the John White Benefit Fund, and the programme for the last game John White ever played for Spurs against Leicester. None of this is very valuable, but it is precious. I did also come close to buying a silver-plated tankard from Trevor that had been given to another Spurs legend, Maurice Norman, as a thank-you for playing in the memorial game against Scotland; but it was just too expensive and I wasn't feeling flush. I still rather regret not buying it, as I can't imagine I would have done anything much more useful with the money.

It may seem strange to have these bits of John White clobber knocking around the house, but I don't think I'm particularly unusual in my feelings about him. Almost every other Spurs fan I know who is roughly my age has a more intimate relationship with John White – I still can't bring myself to call him either John or just White – than any other player of that era; it's as if he has come to represent the more tender, private part of the psyche of a whole generation. So when I was sent a copy of a new biography of him, *The Ghost of White Hart Lane*, written by his son Rob and journalist Julie Welch, and asked to interview the whole surviving White family – Rob, his elder sister, Mandy and his mother, Sandra – it was rather like being asked to write your own job description.

But I did feel uneasy. I was still feeling depressed, and I hadn't seen anyone but family, friends, work colleagues and tens of thousands football fans for weeks. I certainly hadn't been to the house of someone I had never met, whose father I admired and on whom I wanted to make a good impression. I was worried I would come across as an awkward combination of monosyllabic and intrusive. And that was the upside: the down was having a panic attack in the middle of their kitchen.

Rather more importantly, I was feeling guilty. Mandy was only two years old when her father died, Rob just six months, and the chapters he had written were a moving account of his search for the father he had never known. Both he and Mandy were too young to have any memories of their father; their only experience of him was his absence. Rob had grown up with an emptiness in which there were thousands of people who had stood on the terraces for week after week watching his father, and seemed to have a closer relationship with him than he did.

I hadn't stood on the terraces in the 1960s, but I was one of the many who had subsequently annexed Rob's past and reclaimed it for my own. I'd never really given much thought to the impact John White's death had had on his family before. He had been a footballer and therefore public property, someone at my disposal to reconfigure at will. Unintentionally, I had been part of Rob's problem. It must be tough enough having a living footballer for a dad, let alone one who had died so young. Who is there to teach you bloke stuff? Who is there to be angry with? How can you ever hope to match up to a dad whose image has been preserved as an icon for so many?

Rob, Mandy and Sandra couldn't have been more welcoming. Rob's daughters made me a cake, and for the couple of hours I was with them, my anxiety and depression melted away. We talked and talked, Rob showed me his father's old boots – a tiny size seven – and a Scotland shirt he had worn that would be way too small for my own son, Robbie, and I felt a weird and almost embarrassing sense of belonging. Rob had set out in writing his book to reconnect with and make sense of his own childhood; bizarrely, he had also in the process helped me do the same with mine, both through being a physical bridge between a bit of my past and present that had never previously been fully joined up, and as a reality check.

As a child, I'd always rather wished my dad had a different job. He'd gone from never being around that much when he was in the Navy – he'd stayed in the service after the Second World War – to being around the whole time, when he decided to become a vicar in the early 1960s. In time, I came to be proud of my dad for doing a job he believed in and thought mattered, but I couldn't help wishing he'd chosen something a bit cooler. Of all the identities I had ever imagined for myself, vicar's son came somewhere near the bottom. Everyone in the village where my dad lived knew who I was, while I had little idea of who they were. With the spotlight came expectation; a vicar's son is expected to be either a geek or a fuck-up. I generously fulfilled both these obligations.

One of the parallel fantasy careers I had mapped out for my dad was professional footballer. Rob made me see something I should have always known; that all careers come at a price. Not of death – that was just a horrible, tragic accident – but of insecurity and taking things for granted. Football genius he may have been, but John White was still plagued by doubts and anxieties about his form and fitness, about others being better than him, and saw little of the glamour in his life that those of us outside football imagined there to be. Do anything for long enough – however well you do it – and it will always end up being just another job. As I left Rob's house, I thought that, not for the first time, the White family had given me a great deal more than I had ever given them.

***

The imagined world still has its advantages, though. I know we're all supposed to lament the passing of the era when footballers lived like the rest of us – a friend once told me how he had been taken by his dad to a Spurs versus Arsenal game in the 1950s, and they bumped into goalkeeper Ted Ditchburn on the way home on the bus. His dad said to Ditchburn, 'Can you let my son see your hands, please?' Ditchburn held out his hands for inspection, and his dad said, 'See, I told you they were huge.' However, there are definite pluses to footballers conducting most of their off-field life behind gated mansions, tinted windscreens and the ropes of VIP lounges. It's every bit as important for fans to keep their distance from the players away from the pitch as it is for players to steer clear of the fans. It helps preserve the mystique.

It's also true that the older I've got, the less I've become interested in the players' off-field personas. Or, to put it bluntly, in them as real people. There was a time when I could imagine myself being friends and hanging out with them – I doubt I'd ever be on Crouchie's Christmas-card list, mind, though I much appreciate being on Spurs members' list as the card from the club is invariably the first to arrive and gets pride of place on the mantelpiece. I also like sending Spurs Christmas cards to all my Chelsea- and Arsenal-supporting friends, though that's another story – but now I really only care about what they do on the pitch. If they try hard and show brilliance, they get my love and support; if, after a suitable period of benefit of the doubt – between ten seconds and a year, depend-ing on my mood – they look like they aren't trying or are being particularly useless, they forfeit both temporarily. And sometimes permanently.

Their only real off-field value to me is comedy – their idiocies and indiscretions, which, thanks to the Premier League's ever more Stalinist PR – I can no longer be bother-ed to read official interviews with players more because they are unspeakably dull and never reveal anything – and super-injunctions, are increasingly hard to tease out. Mostly, I have to rely on unsubstantiated gossip for my kicks. But not always. Twitter does turn out to have its uses after all.

I've had my own Twitter account – @digestedread – for well over a year, but I've never really thought of anything worth tweeting. I've made about nine posts in total, the most interesting of which was that I'd just seen my friend

Patrick pick up a piece of cheese that someone had slung in a dustbin and eat it. Despite this, I still get the occasional notification that someone new is following me on Twitter; it's very flattering, but I can only assume they are doing so because they enjoy the silence.

Many of the people I follow also seem to have equally little to say.

You have to have a lot of time on your hands to read Aaron Lennon's infrequent tweets, like this one from March. 'Good session 2day a bit of gym work now!!! Cheltenham starts as well any tips send my way lool be lucky!!!'. Tom Huddlestone and Younès Kaboul tweet in much the same style. As does Rafa van der Vaart. Except when he's tweeting in Dutch.

For Twitter gold, I turn to Jermain Defoe, because in between the mundane 'I can't wait for the big game tomorrow' and 'What a nice weekend', he regularly reveals a nice sideline in mysticism. Like 'Yesterday is history. Tomorrow is a mystery. And Today? Today is a gift. That's why we call it the present' and 'Don't put off today for tomorrow, as you never know what tomorrow will bring.' How true. It rather looked as if Jermain was preparing for a career outside football as head of his own cult TV station. Which would not be such a bad move under the circumstances, as he was looking hopelessly out of form.

Defoe is a natural goal-scorer and, I hasten to add, a favourite of mine – a player to whom I accord a great deal of slack. But we were now into March, and he hadn't scored a league goal all season. He had been injured for a couple of months, but he had had plenty of time to regain match fitness and hadn't found it. Nobody would have minded so much if he was looking sharp and creating chances from which the other strikers were scoring, but he wasn't; though even if he had been creating chances, the other strikers would have missed them as they were just as badly out of form. But it still wasn't any real excuse.

One of Jermain's most recent tweets was preying on my mind. 'Being the person you want to be, not the person others want you to be,' he had posted. The fans wanted him to be one of the best strikers in the Premier League; he clearly just wanted to be a philosopher. So we were all losing out. Couldn't he settle for being a hybrid? Albert Camus had managed to be a philosophical goalkeeper; was it asking too much for Jermain to be a philosophical goal-scorer? The impasse needed to be resolved quickly. Preferably against Wolves; the team's inability to score – most of our goals had come from our midfielders, and our goal difference was what you would expect of a mid-table side – was costing us and we were making hard work of qualifying for the Champions League again.

There are probably huge geographical and cultural differences between Wolverhampton and Birmingham if you live in the Midlands, but in the Londoner's footie map of England, a trip to Wolves basically counts as another day out to Birmingham. It's just the way it is. I'm sure fans from outside London lump all London clubs in together when planning their trips south. So after Matthew had finished his weekly Sunday-morning Faustian pact of trying to get his twins into the local faith school at the expense of the salvation of his own immortal soul, we headed up the M40 once more.

Surprisingly, he was still awake by the time we reached High Wycombe. I sensed an opportunity for conversation.

'So what Journey tracks have you been listening to recently?' I asked.

Matthew sighed deliberately and audibly.

'I don't just listen to Journey, John. Obviously, I'm very passionate about Journey, but I do listen to other stuff as well. Do you only listen to the fucking dove man?'

'Er, no.'

'Precisely.'

'OK, OK, I'm sorry. What are you listening to, then?'

'As it happens, I'm playing a lot of Yacht Rock on my iPod.'

'What the hell is that?'

'It's a bit sophisticated for you, John. Think southern California in the late 1970s and early 1980s. Imagine it's early evening, and the sun is falling into the ocean as you relax on your yacht. Your chick has just gone home . . .'

'Would that chick be blonde with large fake tits?'

'Don't be stupid, John. Of course she would. Now where was I? Ah, yes. You're all alone, and your shiny shoulder-length hair is gently fluttering in the breeze, though your immaculately cropped beard stays effortlessly in place. As do the tight creases in your bright white suit. For a moment or two, you think of making yourself a pina colada or breaking into your kilo stash of cocaine. But instead, you reach for your guitar and break out into some smooth grooves of limitless depths. That, John, is Yacht Rock.'

'It sounds like every mindless identikit West Coast band I've always done my best to forget.'

'No one can forget Loggins and Messina or Christopher Cross.'

I had until he mentioned them.

'You're seriously telling me you like this shit?'

'What's not to like?'

'The fact that it's all so bland and dull.'

'You just haven't been listening to it properly. You have to get past the veneer of blandness and dullness to find the layers of intricate soulful sophistication.'

'OK,' I said, doubtfully. 'And are there any British bands that qualify as Yacht Rock?'

'Certainly not. You have to have the Californian vibe in your DNA.'

'Not even . . .' I scrabbled around for the dullest, blandest British band I could remember. '. . . Dire Straits?'

'Don't be ridiculous. Dire Straits are far too British for Yacht Rock. There is a sub-genre of Yacht Rock called Marina Rock that is slightly more gritty, but Dire Straits don't qualify for that, either. Look, why don't I plug my iPod into the stereo and I'll give you a blast of Ambrosia's album. "One Eighty"?'

'Maybe on the way back, Matthew.' Or maybe not. 'Why don't I put Five Live on the radio to see if we can get any team news? There's a possibility Bale might be back.'

There were two surprises awaiting us at the ground. The first was the food. Having sniffed around various burger stalls, Matthew decided that 'Mr Tikka – The Only Mobile Tandoori Oven in Britain' was the place for lunch.

'This is really good,' I said, tucking into tandoori chicken and salad wrapped in naan bread. 'And cheap.'

'I know,' Matthew replied. 'It's disappointing, isn't it? I don't come to a football ground to eat well.'

The second was our seats. Usually clubs make a point of giving the away fans the worst possible seats in the ground. I know we do at Spurs. But after studying the Molineux layout on the back of the tickets, it looked as if we were sitting three rows from the front virtually on the halfway line.

'What's going on?' said Matthew, as we made our way through the turnstiles. 'Are you sure we're in the right place?'

'Definitely. I can only imagine most Wolves fans aren't prepared to pay for anything except the cheap seats behind the goals.'

We were still quite some way from the action, though. Whoever had designed the Steve Bull stand appeared to have no idea where the pitch was, as it was set back about ten metres from the touchline. There wasn't even an athletics track to blame. I could now see why the Wolves fans chose to sit behind the goals. Welcome to your world, West Ham, if you move to Stratford.

There was a minute's applause for Dean Richards, the Wolves and Spurs defender, who had died the week before, and at the end there was a joint chorus of 'There's only one Dean-o, there's only one Dean-o'. A bloke behind me tapped me on the shoulder and asked, 'Why are we all singing for the Irish cunt? He doesn't even play for us any more. He's gone to West Ham.'

'It's Dean-o, not Kean-o. It's for Dean Richards.'

'Whoops. Sorry.'

It was an easy enough mistake to make. The chant was almost identical.

Everything was only too familiar once the game got under way. As so often with teams whose names begin with W, we looked as if we thought we only had to turn up to win. Within twenty minutes we were a goal down and being run ragged by a side playing with a much higher level of commitment. And then in the space of five minutes we were ahead, courtesy of two goals from Jermain Defoe that were conjured out of next to nothing. The man who couldn't score had just done so twice. He could philosophise all he liked now, as far as I was concerned.

Not everyone saw it the same way.

'Oh fuck,' said the bloke who had mistaken Dean-o for Kean-o. 'Now I've got nothing to moan about.'

He soon did, as Alan Hutton gave away an unnecessary penalty to leave the scores tied at 2-2 at half-time. Within ten minutes of the restart we were ahead again, as Pav also remembered what he was paid for and found the net with a long-range strike of his own. We should have buried them at this point. Bale came on and tore them to shreds, we created chance after chance and Defoe missed a tap-in for his hat-trick. Then Wolves started pressing. We got lucky when they had a goal wrongly disallowed, but justice was done when Dawson got outjumped five minutes from the end and it finished 3-3.

I would have been much happier with rank injustice, though. The lucky shirt had seen off a league defeat but a draw, especially one where all three points looked to have been – and should have been – in the bag, against a team near the bottom of the league, was no kind of result. No sooner had our strikers rediscovered their touch than our defenders had lost theirs. It was as if there was some new quantum law running through the team.

Matthew had his usual snooze on the journey home, leaving me to mull over the 'if onlys'. As we reached London, he woke.

'You know something, John?' he said.

'What?'

'I don't feel I've suffered enough today.'

'Are you mad? We've just tossed away two points.'

'Oh, I know that. I expected it. It's the other stuff I was thinking of. The food and the seats. It was just all a bit too high-class.'

'Don't worry. There will be plenty more suffering to come.'

Starting with the AC Milan Champions League return on the following Wednesday, a match that would be all the more stressful as we would be starting favourites after our 1-0 away win in the San Siro. Many fans, myself included, have got fed up from time to time with the residual tag of 'plucky underdogs' that we've acquired over the years, but it does seem that more often than not we play a great deal better when not too much is expected of us.

This game had even more riding on it than usual. Having unexpectedly lost the Carling Cup to a last-minute cock-up goal that was eerily reminiscent of the one that had cost us the FA Cup semi-final the previous year, Arsenal had been knocked out of the Champions League without registering a single shot on goal against Barcelona the night before our game against Milan. It had been a great night to be a Spur, one that would be immeasurably spoiled if we were to throw away our own advantage the following day. Surviving an extra twenty-four hours in the Champions League does not secure you any real bragging rights.

'I'd almost rather we had drawn the away leg 0-0,' I found myself saying to a couple of friends before the game.

Usually this is the opportunity for them to round on me for my abject negativity. Instead, there was barely a murmur of dissent. Everyone felt the same way. It was the latest 'Biggest Game in the Club's History'™ and everyone just wanted to be put out of their misery before the game had even started. Just wake us up when it's over and tell us if we've won or lost. I'll get on with the celebrating or grieving then. It's the living through the 120 minutes of not knowing that's unbearable. The tension had even got to Robbie, normally the most upbeat of all Spurs fans, the one to whom defeat always comes as a surprise.

'How are you feeling?' I had asked him on the way up in the car, wanting him to tell me he was feeling great and reassure me that we were going to win and all would be well.

'Fucking tense, Dad. I'm bricking it.'

Was this the moment when he made the transition from boy to man, when the egocentric certainties and optimism of childhood get replaced by the alarming randomness of adulthood? Or was it the moment when he finally became a true, lifelong Spur, steeped in the tradition of suffering?

'Me too. I feel sick.'

At least I only felt sick. I got a text from 'Even Gloomier Than Me' Bob to say that a mutual friend of ours had thrown up on the tube on the way to the game, and had returned home to watch it on TV from under the duvet.

What happened next is largely a matter of interpretation. If you listened to the post-match interviews, or read the newspaper reports the following day, you would think Spurs had put on a masterful defensive display and had again shown the unexpected tactical savvy of European football to contain Milan to a 0-0 draw to reach the quarter-finals of the Champions League at the first attempt.

Everyone who was sitting near me – and indeed everyone I later talked to who had been at White Hart Lane – had watched a rather different game. The idea that a Spurs team could transform themselves overnight into the masters of *catenaccio* (which means 'door-bolt' and accurately sums up the way Italian teams have defensively shut up shop for years) and deliberately set out to play for a goalless draw was too absurd to contemplate. Anyone who had watched us over the season – or over a lifetime, for that matter – would know that we can never bank on keeping a clean sheet. Our strength has always been in going forward, not defending in depth. That's why so many fans always worry when we go ahead too early in a game, as the team tends to go into 'We Must Now Try To Play Like A Serious Premier League Side' mode and get men behind the ball to protect the lead. Which is frequently the cue for an equaliser.

So as a tactic, playing for a 0-0 draw was a non-starter; far better to try and get an early goal and make Milan score twice. Then there was the game itself. In the first-half, the Spurs players looked to be even more nervy than the crowd, overawed by the thought of what they might achieve, and could scarcely string two passes together. Only a Gallas goal-line clearance and Milan's own jitteriness near goal had kept the scoreline blank by half-time.

Who knows what went on in the dressing room at half-time, but when the second half got under way it looked as if Harry had decided to make a virtue out of a necessity. Having sensed there was little he could do about the collective anxiety, and that our scoring a goal was probably out of the question, he rearranged the formation to block up the midfield and give us a better chance of containing the Italians. Which – to the manager's and the players' credit – they did, though it wasn't until there were only twenty minutes left that anyone near me began to believe we might just get away with it and hold on.

'Fuck me,' said Amici. 'I've been expecting Milan to score all game, and now I've started to think we might hold on, they probably will.'

No one thought we stood a prayer if Milan did score and it went to extra time or penalties, so I spent the last quarter of the game with one eye on the digital clock above the south stand and one on the field. It was only when the game reached the last minute of injury time with Bale holding the ball up near the Milan corner flag that White Hart Lane dared a celebratory, 'Spurs are on their way to Wembley.'

It had been an unbearably tense ninety minutes. For me, at least. 'That's the dullest game I've ever watched,' my Chelsea friend Kevin texted me afterwards. I didn't bother to reply, but then I always reach a point with Kevin when I don't reply. His football texts always start off quite friendly, signing off with an 'x', but as the exchange continues he becomes increasingly unpleasant until you don't answer. He's actually a lovely bloke and a great head teacher. I guess it's supporting Chelsea that does it to him.

I couldn't get to sleep for ages that night. I was a wreck. But Spurs were now officially one of the best eight clubs in Europe, and I was seeing my therapist at seven o'clock the following morning, so I'd probably survive. Though not for long, if I had to watch too many more games like the home league game against West Ham that followed ten days later. This was another 0-0 draw, though one with no conceivable redeeming features. The Hammers had been rooted near the bottom of the table all season, and any team with pretensions to being one of the best in Europe would have been looking at three points at home as a formality.

It was the same problem we had been suffering from all season; the inability of our strikers to find the net. Jermain Defoe was all ready to reveal the '100 Goals' vest he was wearing under his match shirt to celebrate his 100th Premier League goal – his tally now stood at 99 – but even his two goals against Wolves failed to remind him where the goal was, as he missed several clear chances. Perhaps he was worried about the automatic yellow card he would get for taking off his shirt. We did have most of the possession and hit the bar three times, but as the object is to aim the ball between the posts, and not at them, we only had ourselves to blame.

'I hate games like that,' Matthew moaned on the way home. 'It wasn't bad, it wasn't great, just rather disappointing. It's too much like real life, and I don't come here for that. I'd much rather have a gigantic fuck-up or a tragic loss.'

He'd almost certainly get one or both before too long.

***

To be a fan of a Premiership club is to understand hierarchy, as there's even less mobility in football than there is in society in general. Unless your club gets lucky with an overseas billionaire with no real interest in the game, your place in the pecking order is pretty much set in stone. You may have the good or bad season, but over a decade things will even themselves out. That's why there's a Big Four, a collective of Bubbling Unders and a bunch of clubs whose sole aim will be to avoid relegation.

However much we may tell ourselves we deserve to gate-crash the Big Four, every Spurs fan implicitly understands our place as one of the Bubbling Unders. It's how we define ourselves in relation to the world, and how we shape our likes. And, more particularly, dislikes. There are ancient, historic reasons for hating Arsenal, but there are also more pressing recent ones. We hate them all the more because they've done so much better than us over the past twenty years. The same applies to Chelsea. There are no real territorial reasons for hating Manchester United, just their consistent success and smugness.

There's only so much hatred anyone, even a football fan, can carry at one time, so I'm fairly indifferent to every other club when we aren't playing them. I only care what happens to them in as much as their results impact on Spurs. Or if they are playing one of Arsenal, Manchester United or Chelsea. Then I become a temporary fan. It's like being in a little bubble of Spursdom. So it always comes as a surprise to be reminded that other clubs have their own hierarchy of hate.

West Ham are a case in point. We don't care that much about West Ham one way or the other. As they are a London club, we'll give a half-hearted, knee-jerk cheer if we hear they are losing at half-time, but that's about as far as it goes. It's condescension of the highest order. Over the years they have been more of an annoyance than a threat. But Hammers fans dislike us intensely. To them we are deadly rivals, second only to Millwall in their ranking of hate, and their joy at getting an away 0-0 draw at White Hart Lane was out of all proportion to the result.

'I don't quite see why they hate us so much,' Theo said, after we had navigated the taunts of some West Ham fans on the way out of the ground. 'I know their best players come to us, while we dump ours who are over the hill on them, but we can't help it that we're better than them. I suppose they just want to be us.'

Hierarchy shapes your identity. It informs your outlook and manages your expectations when you start to get above yourself; however much I might have been crowing about Spurs being one of the eight best teams in Europe, our league form was telling me what I had always known deep down – that we were, at best, only the fifth-best team in England. Which is no bad feat in itself, but not exactly the message we wanted to publicise. So it was looking increasingly likely that my identity would not be under threat from Champions League football again the following season.

It was under threat from another, even more unexpected source, though. There's another writer with the surname Crace. His name is Jim Crace, a brilliant writer of serious prize-winning fiction. Rather better than me, in other words. And although he doesn't know it, I've always suspected that I owe him my career.

I'd never had any burning ambition to write; in fact, I'd never had a burning ambition to do anything very much ever since I'd realised, while doing a postgraduate degree at the London School of Economics, that I was too stupid to become an academic. That was probably part of the problem. I only started writing in my thirties because I couldn't think of anything else to do.

So I wrote a rather worthy story about a charity and faxed it – there was no email in the early 1990s – to the features desk of the *Independent on Sunday*. It was an OK story; not bad, not brilliant, the sort of average story that must arrive unsolicited on editors' desks every day and get promptly binned. Yet three days later I got a call. The editor liked the article and said she would pay me £400. I just said, 'Thank you,' and assumed it was the going rate.

It was only when I sold a second article to her that I realised £400 was the paper's celeb rate for 1,000 words, as she made a point of telling me that from now on I'd be on the normal freelance rate of £200 per 1,000 words. We never had the conversation, but I couldn't help feeling the only reason she must have picked out my fax from her slush pile was that she had seen the name Crace and assumed it must be Jim. By the time she realised her mistake, she'd come to the conclusion I could write well enough and there was no need to cause any extra embarrassment to both of us. So Jim unwittingly gave me a career, as I doubt I'd have continued writing if that first article hadn't been accepted. I'd have thought, 'Sod it, that's another thing I'm no good at.' I wasn't very good at rejection back then. I'm still not.

There have been several occasions since that first article when something I've written has appeared under Jim's byline – curiously nothing he's written has appeared under mine – but we had only spoken once when I was asked to do a short telephone interview with him. He had been a laugh and had told me we were distantly related, but I hadn't paid too much attention as I had been far too excited that someone I admired was being nice to me.

We'd finally met at the Bath Literature Festival. I'd been thinking of pulling out as I was still getting horrendous panic attacks, and the prospect of speaking to a couple of hundred people seemed unlikely to improve my mental state, but I was appearing with my friend John who would take care of me, so I went anyway. Jim had his own event, and we met by chance beforehand. It was like meeting someone I already knew, the formalities and awkwardness of a first meeting bypassed by a shared kinship. And we were family. Jim had studied the Crace genealogy and we could all be traced back to one seventeenth-century Crace. Every Crace in the UK is related to every other Crace in the UK, and Jim and I were cousins. How distant, neither of us was sure.

What's more, this first Crace had been Jewish, with the name probably being borrowed from the Polish city of Cracow from which he had come to England to escape persecution. So I was a bit Jewish. The knowledge didn't leave me with a new feeling of cultural attachment as the Jewish element was just an added dilution to a bloodline that already incorporated English, German, Australian, Scottish and God knows what else origins, and I'd always made a point of resisting affiliation to a particular ethnicity. But I did feel more Spurs. Having Jewish blood, however thin, somehow bound me tighter to the club. It sounds ridiculous, but Theo understood exactly what I felt.

'You're so lucky,' he had said when I told him. 'I've always wanted to have some Jewish blood, too. In fact I'm sure I might have, as my maternal grandmother looked just like Alan Sugar.'

That's the first and last time looking like Alan Sugar is likely to be seen as a blessing.

It turned out that Jim had also been a Spurs fan all his life. Had we both intuitively channelled our Jewishness into our allegiance? Of course not. Get a life. It was just a wonderful, happy coincidence. Another thing we had in common.

Being a bit Jewish did make me think again about the word Yid. Was I more entitled to chant it? I thought I probably was. Did I feel any more uncomfortable when a moment of joyous brilliance was welcomed with 'Yiddo'? No. It still felt overwhelmingly empowering. It was something – or rather someone – else that made me think twice about that.

I'd met David Baddiel at a bookshop event back in January. We'd got on quite well in the few minutes we chatted, and he told me about *The Y Word*, a short film he and his brother had made about anti-Semitic abuse in football. His argument was that Yid was a no-go word. No exceptions, not even for Spurs fans. I disagreed, suggesting he might feel differently if he experienced the chant from inside the Lower East stand at White Hart Lane, rather than from the Matthew Harding stand at Stamford Bridge. We parted amicably.

A month or so later, I was invited to the film's launch. I couldn't go, but soon found myself in a protracted email debate with David, which ended with my being backed into an intellectual corner. I couldn't escape the conclusion that whatever right Spurs fans had to use the word was outweighed by the legitimacy it gave fans from other teams to use it against us abusively.

My friend Alex, a Jew and non-Spur who has been to White Hart Lane countless times with me over the years, was shocked by my conversion. 'I can't believe it,' he said. 'I've never felt my identity celebrated so positively as when the Yid chant starts.'

Matthew and Theo were equally horrified at what they

saw as my *Guardian*-ista wishy-washy liberalism. 'You can't let a Chelsea fan tell us what we can and cannot sing,' they said as one. 'He's got no fucking idea. We reclaimed that word from the racists, so he can't stop us saying it. What's he expect us to do when the Arse and the Chelce make gas-chamber noises at us? Just sit back and take it?'

That's precisely what I proposed to try and do. I wasn't convinced that the Arsenal and Chelsea fans would stop their anti-Semitism if Spurs fans dropped the Yid chant – after all, we had adopted it in response to their anti-Semitism in the first place – but if there was the smallest chance that they might, then morally I was obliged to give it a go. And if the Arsenal and Chelsea fans did continue, then they would be more openly exposed for the racists they were.

I didn't think it would be easy, though. 'I'll do my best,' I wrote to David, 'but when Gareth Bale scores another wonder-goal to defeat the Arse, I can't promise that years of operant conditioning won't kick in and I'll be chanting "Yiddo" along with the rest of the crowd.'

'I quite understand,' David replied conciliatorily. 'But if you do join in, just try to be conflicted about it.' That I could manage. Conflicted is the default position for every Spurs fan.

April

THAT 1901 FA CUP final ticket. It turned out it did exist. I was wasting a few minutes leafing through the football auction catalogues, as I do most months, and there it was. Lot 625, 'Ticket for the Final, 20/04/01, Tottenham v. Sheffield United in front of 110,820 at The Crystal Palace. Ring Seat ticket, some creases. *Fair-generally good. Estimate: £3,300 – £3,500.*'

It was a moment I'd imagined for years, though I never imagined it was one that would make me feel sick. I now had to put up or shut up. The ticket hadn't ser-endipitously come up for auction at a time when I had a £5,000 Premium Bonds windfall sloshing around my current account; if I was going to buy it I would have to stick it on the credit card and pay for it in instalments. It felt like a turning point. A true obsessive wouldn't give it a second thought, as there might never be another chance. If I didn't take the hit, I'd have marked myself out as a part-timer.

I dithered for days. I called Chris the auctioneer to see what I could find out about the ticket, and whether there were likely to be any more coming on to the market. Chris was non-committal, only saying it had come from the collection of an elderly gentleman in the north-east. On the day of the auction, I was no clearer about whether I was actually going to bid for it or not – or how much I was willing to pay – though I had registered to bid online. Just in case.

When the auction got round to Lot 625, my hand was poised over the onscreen bid icon. The price reached £3,100, but I just couldn't bring myself to make that final click of the mouse. Even though the selling price was below the estimate, I couldn't justify spending that much money on a ticket I would never be able to tell Jill about. I tried to rationalise the decision by telling myself I had been 'unusually mature', and that the final had ended in a 2-2 draw and the ticket really worth having was the one for the replay a week later, but I regretted it immediately. I felt as if I had bottled it. I'd have rather the ticket had never come up for sale, than it had continued its meta-existence as an elusive object of desire whose purpose was in the longing, not the realization, a fantasy to be endlessly re-visited but never fulfilled.

Still, I did buy the ticket for the 1901 FA Cup semi-final later in the auction. I hadn't known that ticket existed either, and technically it should have been a bit rarer as there was only a crowd of 20,000 for that game. I also bought it for a lot less that the final ticket, though I still thought better of telling Jill about this particular triumph and I'm counting on her to have stopped reading this book long ago for her ignorance to remain intact. I did tell Adrian, though. When he stopped laughing, he said, 'Look at it this way, John. The semi was played before the final, so the ticket is actually a couple of weeks older. You've got a bargain.' And then he started laughing again.

At least Trevor understood, though he had problems of his own. He was in the middle of a lengthy negotiation with some bloke in Serbia to sell a Jimmy Greaves silver tankard. Trevor wanted the cash, the Serbian was offering cash and part-exchange of a couple of rare tickets – the away leg of the 1963 European Cup Winners' Cup semi-final in Belgrade and the away league game against Bolton from the 1960–61 double-winning season. 'Do you want them?' Trevor asked me. We agreed a price. It was a lot, but not that a lot. All double tickets come at a premium, and none more so than the Bolton away.

'You do know Bolton is the trickiest of the lot, don't you?' I said when we met later. 'The programme from that game goes for silly money.'

Trevor groaned. 'You mean I could have got a lot more on eBay?'

'Probably,' I grinned.

I didn't feel that sorry for him. I'm sure he'd made a decent enough mark-up.

***

I also missed out on the away game at Wigan. Right from the start of the season, Matthew and I had set our hearts on going to this fixture, as it ticked all the right suffering boxes – unglamorous, miles away but still reachable without changing trains and with the near certainty of a terrible game – and by the time the away ticket application opened in March it had become even more attractive, as it looked fairly likely that Wigan were going to be relegated and there would be no chance of going the following season. So I was probably one of the few people in London who was genuinely pleased when the tickets arrived.

Then I checked the date. It was Jill's birthday. Well, not literally – her actual birthday was three days earlier, hence my error – but it was as good as the actual day because she insists her official birthday celebrations last for a minimum of a week. And there was no way I could get back from Wigan in time to take her out on the Saturday night. It briefly occurred to me to suggest I took her up to the north-west for a romantic weekend, but I thought better of it. She puts up with a lot, but her tolerance has its limits. It was a rare moment of self-preservation. I never did find anyone to take the tickets off me.

Just occasionally things work out regardless. Even at my gloomiest, I hadn't banked on the game being quite so awful. I followed it via the internet and radio with a growing sense of relief that I didn't have a four-hour journey home to look forward to. I could just switch off and walk away, which was pretty much what Spurs seemed to have done before a ball had even been kicked. The inability to score goals that had been all too self-evident throughout the season and had not been dealt with in the transfer window was now killing us. We had turned the opposition's penalty area into a no-fly zone, and the lack of confidence among the strikers was starting to seep into the rest of the squad. And you couldn't blame them. What was the point of a midfielder making a sixty-yard run to create a chance that would be poked feebly wide? You'd be better off staying where you were and saving energy.

The team may also have had both eyes on the away leg of the Champions League quarter-final against Real

Madrid. I certainly had. This was my dream draw. I didn't want us up against Manchester United or Chelsea, as it would be unbearable to be knocked out by an English club; we'd already played Inter Milan, and I was a bit blasé about a third trip to the San Siro; and Shakhtar Donetsk and Schalke 04 were just too boring; which left Real Madrid and Barcelona, and as no one in their right mind would want to play Barça until the final, Real were the ideal opponents.

Who could resist going to see Spurs take on the crème de la crème of European football at the Bernabéu on a warm spring night? Terry, for one, as he had been shown a red card for Madrid. There would still be three of us going, though. Theo had miraculously worked out that there was a really important client he had to see in Madrid that day, and he could pretend it was work. He managed to fool himself, if nobody else.

It had been a simple reflex response to decide to go to Madrid, even though I was still depressed when the draw was made. No trips to the shrink to question my sanity this time, or telling Jill until a few days beforehand, by which time it was a fait accompli, as she had been less than impressed with the impact the Milan trip had had on my psyche. While I thought I had got away with it fairly unscathed at the time, she wasted no opportunity to tell me over the following weeks that every panic attack I got was a direct result of my having gone to the San Siro. So best to avoid that one. Besides, as Matthew pointed out, having failed to tell his wife he was going to Madrid as well, 'What kind of weird world would it be where you had to ask permission to go to the Bernabéu for the Champions League quarter-final?'

Getting to Madrid was more of a problem. Within seconds of UEFA finally deciding on which day the game was going to be played – for some reason it took them a couple of hours of 'It's tricky; Tuesday or Wednesday? How about Wednesday? On second thoughts, Tuesday is better. Are you sure?' after the draw to work it out – direct flights to Madrid that had previously been only £40 were now over £600. Pete from Piss Off Tours emailed me his 'The Real Deal' itinerary: Easyjet from Luton to Amsterdam and then a direct flight from Amsterdam to Madrid. But by the time I got round to checking availability, even Easyjet was an arm and a leg. The route we ended up probably didn't work out much cheaper: British Airways from Gatwick to Barcelona – I told you I wasn't going Ryanair again – and then a high-speed train from Barcelona to Madrid. Factor in the hotel and match tickets with a face value of 135 euros each, but costing rather more, and we could have had ten days in a four-star hotel in Majorca for the same money.

'Did she want to know how much it was costing?' I asked Matthew after he had finally revealed his travel plans to his wife a week before the game.

'This time I told her we'd got a really good deal on the hotel,' he said.

'Did that work?'

'No. She just said "I suppose you're overpaying for everything else again, as usual".'

The panic attacks had finally stopped, though it had taken me a while to notice, as expecting them is almost as debilitating as having them and it takes me at least a week to believe that some kind of normal service to my psyche has been resumed. By normal, I mean above-averagely neurotic.

'Phew,' said Theo, as we cleared a queueless airport security. 'Thank fuck you made us arrive three hours early for a 6.30 a.m. flight.'

'I know what you mean,' Matthew agreed. 'I'd have hated to cut it any finer.'

Personally, I thought my travel arrangements were working out just fine. And so they were when we arrived in Barcelona with four hours to kill before our train. It proved to be only just enough time as, when we got to the barrier at the station, it turned out that the tickets Theo had bought in advance – the train was the only bit of the itinerary that someone other than me was responsible for, I'd like to point out – were for the day before.

'Um, sorry guys,' he said, leaving Matthew and me hovering near the platform entrance. 'My fault. I'll go off and see what I can do about it.'

'The good news is that I've managed to get us on the train,' he said when he reappeared just a few minutes before it was due to depart. 'The bad news is they wouldn't exchange the tickets and I had to get new ones. And as second-class is fully booked, we're in first-class. Still, apparently we get lunch included in the price.'

This wasn't quite as wonderful as it sounded as we'd just had a big meal while we were hanging around. An expensive trip had just got that bit more expensive. Still, first-class was very comfortable and as the train raced through the bleak, sunburned Spanish interior, I thought it would be fun for me and Theo to take the piss out of Matthew.

'So tell me a little more about Yacht Rock,' I said. 'I'm still not exactly sure what it is.'

'It's the sound of winning, John.'

I sniggered.

'You're right,' said Theo. 'Which do you prefer, Matthew? Early, mid or late Michael McDonald?

'You mean there's a difference?' I interrupted.

'You're a very bitter man, John,' Matthew said. 'You will have to get over missing Kranjčar's wonder-strike against Bolton sooner or later. I'd say mid-McDonald is the authentic sound of Yacht Rock.'

'I think you're probably right,' said Theo. 'What do you reckon to Rupert Holmes?'

'Too Marina.'

I couldn't believe it. Finding even one person who knew about, let alone liked, Yacht Rock seemed absurd. To be hurtling towards Madrid at 300 km/h in the company of two seemed to be beyond coincidence. Was Yacht Rock some Spurs thing I'd managed to miss out on? Was there another version of 'We're on Our Way to Wembley' somewhere on YouTube, with Glenn Hoddle and Ossie Ardiles chilling out in spotless white suits somewhere off the West Coast of America?

The cab took us past the Prado.

'What's that?' Matthew asked.

'One of the most famous art galleries in the world,' I pointed out. 'I thought we might go and have a look round tomorrow morning. We ought to do something cultural while we're here.'

'Why?' said Matthew.

'What do you reckon, Theo?'

'Reckon to what?' He hadn't looked up from his iPhone since we'd arrived in Madrid, and was busy tweeting something. Presumably that he hadn't looked out the window and didn't have a clue where he was.

When we reached the hotel, Matthew announced he was exhausted and needed a snooze, Theo had some more urgent twittering to do, and I managed to find a Spanish TV station showing highlights of the Wigan versus Spurs game the previous weekend. They didn't last very long.

I wasn't the only one who liked to get to the ground early. There were thousands of Spurs fans milling around outside the Bernabéu by the time we got there two hours before kick-off. The difference was that they were pissed and we weren't, so the two hours probably felt a great deal longer to us than it did to them as there wasn't much to do after buying the obligatory half-and-half scarf from a vendor who barely knew that Tottenham was a football club. It was another Inter moment. This may have been 'The Biggest Game in the Club's History'™ but it was a run-of-the-mill European fixture for Real that the whole of Madrid expected them to win fairly comfortably. There were even posters stuck up all around the ground telling supporters how they could get tickets for the semi-final against Barcelona.

The inside of the Bernabéu was breathtaking, unquestionably the best stadium I've ever visited. Where the San Siro had a grandeur that was crumbling beneath your feet, the Bernabéu was a temple to inherited wealth; even the toilets had attendants and individual urinals. Inside it was more magnificent, with the stands steepling into a night sky that itself appeared newly painted. It was an amphitheatre of dreams. Though not one where dreams came true.

I'm not sure at what point Matthew, Theo and I had decided Real were beatable, but we weren't alone. Every other Spurs fan I had talked to over the previous week had come to a similar conclusion: that it was our destiny to win. Real might have José Mourinho as their manager, but they weren't as good as all that; they had been beaten 5-0 by Barcelona earlier in the season and they were there for the taking.

This delusion lasted until kick-off. Aaron Lennon had been named in the side, but in the fifteen minutes between leaving the pitch at the end of the pre-match warm-up and the start of the game, he had dematerialised.

'Where's Lennon?' I asked Matthew.

'Fuck knows,' he replied, not nearly as concerned by Azzer's absence as me.

There was no announcement, and rumours began to circulate that Lennon had bottled it. Terry then texted me from England to say that Sky was reporting Lennon had been feeling ill all week and had felt worse just before kick-off. If so, his original selection had been a hell of a gamble for everyone to take for such an important game. As it was, we had used up one of our substitutes before the start and sent out an unprepared team, playing a hastily rearranged formation with no attacking threat on the right-hand side.

It felt as if we were playing with ten men when nobody bothered to mark Emmanuel Adebayor, Spurs' arch nemesis when he used to play for Arsenal, at a corner and Real went a goal up after three minutes. Within fifteen minutes we really were playing with ten men as Crouchie got himself sent off for a second yellow-card offence. He hadn't attempted a tackle all season but now he had made two hopeless, unnecessary lunges in Real's half of the pitch, and his sending-off was a formality. A friend texted me to say he reckoned Crouchie must have had an early date with Monica Mint. She did live in Madrid.

'Have you realised the Spanish bloke sitting next to you has been smoking dope throughout the game?' Matthew said at half-time.

I really hadn't.

'If we can keep the score down to one or two, we'll still be in with a shout for the return leg,' I said.

We couldn't. Madrid ran us ragged and romped home 4-0 winners. Long after most of the crowd had left, we remained in our seats, each of us lost in a private grief. The very worst had happened. We had been outclassed on and off the pitch. The Real supporters even had their own cheerleader, who orchestrated their singing and kept his back to the action the whole time. It wouldn't surprise me if he was on a club salary. Worst of all, José Mourinho had been really, really nice about us – something he only ever does when he doesn't respect you.

The extent of our humiliation was brought home by the absence of any crowing texts from Kevin. Normally he can't resist, but this night he was abnormally respectful, as if he understood this was a bereavement more than a loss. Though I'm sure he couldn't resist having a laugh with his Chelsea mates. I did with my Spurs mates when Chelsea got beaten by Manchester United the following night.

Eventually Theo broke the silence. 'How did we ever come to imagine we would win?' he asked. 'Look at their substitutes. Kaká, Higuaín, Benzema . . . Most of our team wouldn't make it on to their bench.'

We nodded, saying nothing.

'Never mind,' Theo continued. 'I'm being taken out

to a flash restaurant by a client. Enjoy some tapas and the rest of your miserable evening, and I'll see you both at 9 a.m. in the hotel for breakfast.'

'Thanks.'

'Think nothing of it.'

Matthew and I shambled around aimlessly outside the Bernabéu for half an hour before accidentally bumping into Bob from work, who had also come out for the game.

'Do you fancy joining us for something to eat?' I asked.

'I can't,' he replied, gloomily. 'I'm being given a lift back to Alicante by a bloke who has been done for murder.'

'See you back in London, then.'

'I do hope so.'

At least someone was shaping up to have a worse night than us.

The next morning I woke up to find Matthew sitting on the edge of his bed, staring out the window. Not, like me, staring into an abyss. His headphones were jammed on tight and in his mind he wasn't in Madrid, but 8,000 miles further west in Santa Monica. Sometime in the 1980s.

'What are you listening to?' I asked.

'Smooth grooves, John. I'm in a place where the hot tub is always bubbling and Cheryl Ladd is waiting for me.'

'Who is Cheryl Ladd?'

'There's no hope for you.'

I couldn't really argue. I felt as if someone had been kicking me all night. All plans to combine the football match with a bit of cultural tourism were instantly shelved. You could forget the Prado. And you could especially forget a stadium tour of the Bernabéu that Piss Off Pete had tentatively suggested the previous day. Why would I want to go back so soon? Madrid was a tainted city. The streets that had felt so interesting and welcoming when we arrived now felt hostile. I just wanted to get away as soon as possible, which wasn't as big a problem as it might have been as Theo had also bought our return tickets for the wrong day, so we were now free to get any train we wanted. So long as we paid for it again.

'Shall we just bugger off back to Barcelona?' I suggested. Going to the Catalan capital, Real Madrid's biggest rival, felt like an act of defiance and liberation.

'Suits us,' said Matthew and Theo. 'We can't wait to get out of here, too.'

It did feel like Matthew was taking retaliation a bit far when he refused to give the cab driver a tip after dropping us at the station.

'Why did you do that?' I asked.

'Because he was definitely trying to rip us off. He took us the long way.'

'How would you know? You've never been here before.'

'I could just tell.'

'Well that's odd. It cost an almost identical amount as it did yesterday from the station to the hotel.'

Theo tried to mend relations with the city by being super-friendly with everyone else with whom he came into contact. Principally the rather attractive woman working at the train ticket office. I never knew buying a ticket could take quite so long.

'I wasn't flirting,' Theo later protested. 'I was just trying to hold up everyone behind us.'

Going to Barcelona proved a wise choice as we did feel less oppressed by defeat, though I could have done without Spurs showing their usual exquisite sense of timing by sending me an email inviting me to renew my season ticket while I was on the train. Getting to the airport four hours early was no bad thing either, though it cost Theo £60. He had a guilt attack in duty free, and rang his wife to see if there was anything special she wanted. There was. I bought chocolate for Jill, Anna and Robbie, though I had eaten half of it before we took off. Matthew bought his family nothing, nada. I'm only saying.

There were several other Spurs fans travelling back from Madrid on the same flight. In the row in front of us were Tony and Jared who we'd talked to on the way out. But there was no sign of their mate Ross.

'Where's Ross?' I asked.

'He's moved to the row in front,' Tony said. 'He's chatting up a Spanish woman.'

'Does he do that often?'

'Always. He can't help himself. The man is a legend. He's got huge ears and is the ugliest man alive; yet women find him irresistible because he's interested in whatever they've got to say.'

Four days later I got an email from Tony. Ross had been out on a date with the Spanish woman. It was the closest any Spurs fan came to a result in Spain.

***

Bye-bye, Europe. If we had only lost 2-0, I'd have been able to conjure a semblance of a chance in my mind. Or possibly, if my denial levels were particularly high, 3-0. But there was no coming back from a 4-0 scoreline against the Madrid *Galácticos*. All that was left for the second leg was the salvaging of some pride. After waiting a lifetime to see us play Real in the top European club competition, the reality would almost certainly end up having all the passion of a pre-season friendly.

It was only after there was no hope left that I realised I must have once had some. The drip-feed of pessimism with which I had poisoned my veins all season – 'It's all going to end in tears, We don't stand a chance' – hadn't actually offered me any protection against the feelings of disappointment when my gloomy predictions were realised. As in so many areas of my life, I'd conned myself into believing that Zeno's dichotomy paradox might actually be true and that the moment of arrival, or more usually ending, and the feelings that come with it could be postponed indefinitely through an infinite division and stretching of time.

Sometimes this isn't too traumatic; I always get some sense of relief on getting back from a holiday to find the house hasn't been robbed. Ordinarily football can be accommodated somewhere in the middle of the 'Don't care–Devastating' spectrum with the thought that 'There's always next season'. Only it was looking increasingly unlikely there would be a next season in the Champions League as our Premiership form was so ropey. And I was surprisingly miserable at the thought that our European adventure might have to be filed under 'Holiday of a Lifetime' rather than the beginning of 'Business as Usual'. I rather wished I'd enjoyed it more at the time. I'll probably be saying much the same on my deathbed.

It did make me wonder if I wasn't even more of a hypocrite than I had imagined. For someone who had gone on and on about the soul of the club, and not wanting to turn into a Manchester United, Arsenal or Chelsea, I was unhealthily attached to the status and glamour of the Champions League after just one exposure. The thought of trudging off to watch us play some Europa League game against Aalborg of Denmark, a fixture that had once seemed attractive, no longer appealed. Perhaps, underneath my mask of dogged, soulful integrity I was just another sold-out, corporate glory boy after all. I'd watched my friend, Simon, a Manchester City fan, wrestle with the same problem. After years of self-identification as the fan of impoverished football-*vérité*, he was rather enjoying the success – and the absence of being patronised – that an Abu Dhabi billionaire can bring. The only real difference between us was that it now seemed likely he would have to live his feelings of self-betrayal for much longer than me.

The defeat to Real also forced me to confront another unwelcome truth: that the season was closing in on itself. I know the players needed a rest, but I have a rather more complicated relationship with endings. I'd much rather everything continued on a seamless loop: then I would neither be so conscious of the gaps that punctuate the passing of time nor have to experience so fully the losses, as everything would merge into a shapeless, timeless blur.

Some final whistles are more welcome than others, though. A case in point being the one that ended the home league fixture against Stoke – a game, it goes without saying, that had become the latest, and almost certainly not last 'Most Important Game of the Season'™ if we were to hang on to any hope of requalifying for the Champions League. It was also yet another game that would be filed under 'I wish it had finished at half-time'.

The first surprise had been that Harry had chosen to start with Crouchie up front after his disastrous fifteen minutes against Real midweek. All that could be said was that he couldn't possibly be tired. The second was to find a four-year-old boy there instead of Amici.

'He's away on holiday,' said Justin. 'So I've brought along my son for his first game. I reckoned you wouldn't be able to give me so much abuse for Crouchie with him in earshot.'

Remarkably there was no need, as within ten minutes Crouchie had headed us in front. I'm not sure who was more amazed; him or 36,000 spectators. When we scored a second ten minutes after that we were cruising, playing some of our best football of the season and making Stoke look leaden. It was all too easy, too comfortable. So not Spurs. Which is probably why we let Etherington run from the halfway line to score. In a bid to reassure himself the first goal wasn't a fluke Crouchie got his head to another cross to restore the two-goal cushion, before we gifted Stoke a second to make it a breathless 3-2 at half-time.

That's the way it finished, though I'd rather not have suffered the second forty-five minutes as chances went missing at both ends, and for long periods a draw looked by far the better bet than a home win. But sod it, a win was a win and we needed it badly. And if frayed nerves were the price, I'd take it for the team. Robbie wasn't so sure.

'I'm done in, Dad,' he said. 'Does it always have to be so tense?'

'I know what you mean,' Mat replied. 'How many people do you reckon have died of a heart attack in the ground this season? There must have been at least one or two. The club should include an organ-donor card with the season ticket next year.'

There would be little danger of anyone dying at the return game against Real. I've seldom felt less tense before a game. A few weeks before, Trevor had been gutted to find that his wife had booked a holiday that straddled the home tie.

'What can I do, John?' he had asked. 'I can't tell her to unbook it. Or fly home. The ridiculous thing is we're going to Spain.'

I nodded sympathetically and made reassuring noises. It didn't seem the moment to suggest that the timing of the holiday was almost certainly not coincidental. It had all the hallmarks of deliberate sabotage. Besides, the holiday was now looking a reasonable option.

But as Robbie and I drove up to north London, I found myself thinking the absurd. Maybe we could do it. Sneak a couple of goals in the first half, hope Real start to panic and who knows? Whatever it takes to get you through. Even a condemned man is allowed to pray for a power cut. It quickly became clear there were going to be no miracles. Madrid were too well organised, our strikers had flicked the switch back to misfire and even a single goal for a consolation victory was beyond us. We didn't deserve to lose, though, and we wouldn't have done but for Gomes palming a speculative thirty-five-yard shot from Ronaldo – why did it have to be that diving little shit? – that went straight at him over the line. The Brazilian keeper had mixed the sublime with the ridiculous all season, and the fans had been getting increasingly fed up; everyone had long since stopped singing to invite him to shag their wives as they had done earlier in the season. When the goal went in there was just silence.

A chorus did begin about ten minutes before the end, as the crowd went through the team chanting one player's name after another. It was a way of saying thank you to the team for having done so well in Europe and for lasting in the competition longer than both Arsenal and, by twenty-four hours, Chelsea. Mainly, though, it was an act of defiance for the TV cameras, a performance to remind everyone else that Spurs fans weren't a fickle bunch who rounded on their team the moment things went tits-up. I sang along, though my heart wasn't in it. Neither, judging by the expressions on the faces of those around me, was anybody else's. It was just something that needed to be done. More importantly, it needed to be heard to be done.

Away from the cameras, the recriminations started.

'I've had it with Gomes,' said Robbie.

We'd all had it with Gomes.

'I've had it with Crouchie and Pav,' Mat added.

Agreed.

'Well, I've fucking had it with Corluka,' said Theo. Where had that come from? I'd never thought of the Croat right-back as one of the worst offenders. 'He can't run and he plays like a doddery old man.'

Yeah, what the hell? Theo was right. I'd had it with Corluka, too.

'I've had it with Lennon,' Matthew said gratuitously. Old habits die hard.

***

JOHN CRACE

I'd never been that close to my sister, Veronica. The six-year age difference had seen to that when we were children, and when I was old enough for the gap not to matter so much, my lifestyle did. Veronica was just one of many who would rather have had open-heart surgery than spend any time in my company. By the time my life had been rearranged into something recognizably less antisocial, too much had passed to be easily forgiven. We still loved one another, but it was a love sustained by duty rather than warmth: birthdays and Christmas was contact enough.

It was football that brought us back together. As far as I remember, Veronica had never shown much interest in football when we were young. She had briefly declared herself a Manchester United fan as a teenage homage to George Best – my other sister, Sue, had a crush on Colin Bell and chose Manchester City – but I'm fairly sure neither of them consistently checked how their team was doing. Still, it probably tells you all you need to know – that the three of us supported different teams. We did briefly unite in the year Swindon won the League Cup and promotion to the Second Division, but even that was half-hearted. As soon as we were through the turnstiles at the Town End, my sisters ditched me for their own spot on the terraces, while I joined the other boys at the front behind the goal. Or maybe I ditched them. Soon after that season Veronica left home, and football was barely mentioned again until about five years ago when she announced she was an Arsenal supporter.

Given our history, you might think this was an act of provocation. But it wasn't. Veronica is not like me; she's a nice person. She'd chosen Arsenal because one of her

254

best friends was a Gooner and she had been gradually indoctrinated over many years. Had this been Jill or Anna declaring an allegiance to the Dark Side, I'd have found it rather more difficult. Imagine having to sleep under an Arsenal duvet cover. But as it was Veronica, I didn't take it too personally. Any team was better than none, and football proved to be a side door to healing wounds that had often seemed too raw to get near in the past. The restrained politeness of our relationship gradually gave way to something more real where we could start to take the piss out of each other again. Especially when Arsenal lost. And the annual league derby at White Hart Lane had become a fixed point in the calendar of our relationship.

When we had first started going together, Veronica hadn't minded so much about being stuck among the Spurs with me, but over time her support for the Arse had become more hard-Arsed. And it made life more difficult, not because she was concerned for her safety, though I continually reminded her of the knife edge she was walking – 'You do know I could have you killed at any time' – but because it's quite hard to enjoy yourself when 35,000 fans are shouting for your downfall. And the loudest of them all is your brother.

We went mob-handed that night. Terry had come up from the sticks and Matthew had got a late call-up after Theo's dad, one of the most antisocial men alive, had discovered the match was being shown on Sky and was therefore saved the effort of having to spend a couple of hours with his son. For one night only the rhythm of the season was put on hold; every other game is seen through the prism of its wider meaning – league position, etc. – but these all take second place for the Arsenal. The result is everything. You'd almost rather lose every other game to win this one.

Adrian called me just before kick-off.

'I've got more money in my Paddy Power account than in my current account,' he said. 'What do you reckon on the result?'

'A 0-0 draw looks a sound bet. We can't score and neither can they.'

Within three minutes Arsenal were 1-0 up when Theo Walcott ran through our defence. Three things happened simultaneously. The chants of 'You're Just a Shit Aaron Lennon' were temporarily suspended; Adrian texted me to say 'Thanks' and Veronica whispered, 'That's very good, isn't it?'

She stopped smiling briefly when Rafa, who always seems to run a yard faster for the big games, threaded in a great near-post finish to equalise, but it returned when Arsenal scored twice more before the half-hour was up. I couldn't bear to catch her eye. Arsenal were in control and our midfield looked outnumbered, principally because the Thudd was having one of those games he'd rather forget. He's never been the quickest of individuals – Justin, Amici and I have an ongoing bet on how much he will weigh by the time he is forty; the lowest bid is over twenty stone – but normally his lack of pace is disguised by the quality of his passing. Not that day. Everything he tried to do went wrong – apart from blasting home a left-footed volley from outside the area just before half-time to pull one back. He looked as surprised as everyone else.

The second half was all Spurs. We equalised through

a Rafa penalty – he didn't miss! – and had several good chances to win it, but it finished all square at 3-3, a result that suited both Manchester clubs a great deal more than it did either of the two that had been playing. Veronica and I hugged one another and agreed it was good we could both go home happy. But that was just for public consumption, like two politicians shaking hands. She had been spitting murder – 'Aren't we at least going to try and fucking win this?' – when Wenger brought on Bendtner and Arshavin, the Arsenal equivalent of Crouchie and Jenas, for the last ten minutes, and was cursing her side for surrendering yet another two-goal lead. And while the team that comes from two down is always going to be a bit happier with a draw, I couldn't help feeling we should have nicked it. I'd felt the same way several years earlier, when Berbatov had missed a last-minute open goal that would have given us a 5-4 win over the Chelce after being 4-2 down. It wasn't about the victory or the extra two points. It was about the laughs.

On the way home, Matthew went into one of his periodic Glenn Hoddle trances. In his memory, Hoddle is the greatest footballer who ever lived, a player who never put a foot wrong. Admirer that I am of the Hod – he did have moments of sublime brilliance – I can also remember some of his weaknesses.

'Weren't you ever pissed off that he never made a tackle?'

'No.'

'Or that he never tracked back?'

'No. A genius like that shouldn't have to bother with anything like that. A manager should just pick a whole team to play around him.'

It all became clear. Alex has a theory that people's tastes stop evolving when they fall in love. They wear the same clothes, keep the same haircut and listen to the same music for as long as they stay in that relationship. Matthew had never, ever stopped loving Glenn since the mid-1980s. No wonder he had a passion for Yacht Rock. It wasn't Christopher Cross who was being moody out on deck; it was Matthew and the Hod. And the chick they were waiting for was Eileen Drewery.

**

Friendships are a complicated business. They are predicated on opening up to other people and sharing ideas, feelings and interests. Yet most of us tightly control the amount we choose to disclose to any one person; there are layers of access to our hearts. Splurging everything all in one go is just too much information – a sure-fire way of making sure no one ever speaks to you again: if the revelations themselves aren't too off-putting, then the underlying neediness will be. So we incrementally release bits of ourselves into our relationships, testing them every step of the way to make sure everyone is comfortable with the status quo. And they all find their own level: some remain shallow, some become more significant. It's a deliberate, considered process. Except sometimes you unintentionally reveal far more than you ever intended.

John is by far my most intelligent, most knowledgeable friend. He's bailed me out of countless intellectual scrapes where my ignorance was about to be exposed, looked after me when I've been falling apart and kept me laughing with the dryness of his humour. He also reads people as sharply as he reads books, so I should have been prepared. Before we became friends he'd had a second-hand interest in football, but now he'd developed pleasing signs of becoming a Spur. He'd make a point of watching their games on TV, and after most of them I'd get a text or an email asking what I'd made of it. The only time he'd ever been to White Hart Lane was for a lukewarm pre-season friendly so, when Robbie had to drop out of the West Brom game with a school commitment, John was an ideal man to bring off the bench.

'Are you sure you're OK?' he said to me at half-time, with the score at 1-1. 'You look terrible.'

'It's too stressful,' I replied. 'We've been struggling to beat teams like this all season.'

'Can I get you some water or something?'

'No, I'll be fine. Thank you.'

'Try to calm down a bit. It's going to be fine.'

It would have been had West Brom not grabbed a late equaliser to cancel out a great Defoe strike midway through the second half. The most depressing thing about the draw was its predictability. Spurs looked shot of inspiration, and the fluency they'd shown earlier in the season had vanished. We may have still been theoretically in the mix for a Champions League place, but we were playing like a mid-table team.

'I was rather worried about you,' John said on the way home. 'You seemed so upset. I couldn't really enjoy the second half as you looked so miserable. I kept trying to think of ways to cheer you up.'

What was particularly disturbing about this was that I didn't feel as if I had been behaving particularly abnormally. No one could claim the disappointment was in any way unexpected after the way we'd been playing for the past couple of months. Also, if anything, I'd tried to make it appear to John as if I wasn't too bothered, that I was the kind of bloke who could take my team's failings with a wry detachment. Above all, I didn't want him to think I was a nutter. Yet not even affecting nonchalance could disguise my psychosis; I'd unwittingly shown John a side of myself I'd meant to keep hidden. During the match itself and for a couple of hours afterwards, all pretence at normality was suspended. I had to hope he learned to tolerate it as well as some of my other friends.

***

From the very first game of the season, both fans and experts try to impose their own narratives on events in an attempt to explain what's happening and to give a sense of deep purpose to something that in reality has very little. Subsequent events almost invariably prove these narratives fictitious and most die quietly and unmourned along the way, as no one has a vested interest in pointing out they have been proved wrong. The ongoing Spurs narrative was that since we'd had a remarkable series of victories against Arsenal, Chelsea and Manchester City after caving in to Portsmouth in the FA Cup semi-final the previous year, we were bound to repeat the feat in the same coincidental series of fixtures that followed our thumping by Real Madrid. Strangely, the narrative was still alive and well despite us having only drawn against Arsenal; apparently pyrrhic victories also now counted. Call it a plot twist. The narrative was finally killed off at Stamford Bridge. But it was done by the referee and the linesmen, rather than by Chelsea.

Robbie stopped coming to the away game at Chelsea a few seasons back when he was thirteen. We'd had seats in the away end of the Lower Shed, too close to the Chelsea supporters for comfort, and at one point an overweight Chelsea fan in his mid-thirties had leaned over towards our section and screamed at Robbie, 'Fuck off, you Yid cunt.' It's probably splitting hairs, but it was the screaming, the fuck off and the cunt that Robbie took exception to rather than the Yid, and when we got home he told me he'd never go to Stamford Bridge again. So well done, Chelsea fan. You must feel proud. Anyway, Robbie's self-deselection meant Matthew now had the automatic nod for this game, though getting hold of him proved to be tricky as he'd managed to drop his mobile phone down the toilet.

Terry also got a call-up from Theo, whose dad had once again decided he'd rather watch the game on TV than with his son, though Terry was at first undecided whether to go.

'I've said I'd go and watch my son Pete play cricket,' he said. 'And I don't really want to let him down.'

'You've never hesitated to let your family down in the past,' I replied.

'Good point.'

We met several hours before the game for a burger at the Bluebird café on the King's Road, an undeniably more upmarket venue than anywhere on Tottenham High Road, though N17 does have the advantage of carrying no risk of an unwelcome sighting of Earl Spencer, who marched through the café with his nose thrust in the air. But it was a warm, sunny day, the food was good, the girls on the street were pretty and, despite not having won at Stamford Bridge for decades, we allowed a wave of optimism to break through.

'You know,' said Theo, 'once we beat Chelsea and Blackpool, we'll be right in there with a shout for Europe. I'm definitely going to get a ticket for the away game against Man City.'

'Me too,' Terry said. 'In fact, I'll get one for Anfield, too. Let's do the lot.'

We looked like doing Chelsea. We were 1-0 up and cruising after Sandro, one of the buys of the season and a key player since February, hit a glorious volley past Čech from outside the area. Chelsea were going nowhere, with the home fans on their back, when in the final minute of the first half Lampard hit a long-range shot straight at Gomes, who let it dribble backwards through his legs. It was yet another calamitous piece of goalkeeping from the Brazilian, but it wasn't a goal as the ball never crossed the line. But the linesman, who was out of position and couldn't tell one way or another, bottled the decision as the home fans screamed for a goal and a goal was given. We never really recovered from the injustice and struggled during the second half, intent on holding out for a draw rather than looking for a victory. And we would have got it had the other linesman not also been so keen to prove that he wasn't keeping up with the game either, by allowing Chelsea a late offside winner.

The post-match reactions were predictable. John Terry claimed the official Chelsea photographer had told him the ball definitely crossed the line, though the snapper remarkably chose to keep that image to himself when he could have made a fortune out of it. Frank Lampard talked meaningless platitudes about 'deserving' the goal, as if trying hard and not having a goal awarded against Germany in the World Cup were new criteria for deciding matches. The match officials admitted nothing and apologised for nothing.

Most telling was Harry Redknapp's response. He was just so damned reasonable. 'These things happen,' he said. That's not what any Spurs fan wanted him to say. We didn't care if he was liked by the media or not. We wanted him to have a Fergie-style rant and cop a touchline ban from the FA. It would have shown how much he cared, that we were a serious team who couldn't be carelessly jerked around. Just as importantly, it would have thrown down a marker for the future. As Fergie well knows, keeping the officials in a state of fear makes them less inclined to give the difficult decisions against you in the future.

I was furious. I'd paid £55 for a ticket for a match that had been decided by incompetence. I don't know if the players felt cheated, but Matthew, Theo, Terry and I did. That was £220 none of us were going to see again, for a result whose only relationship to the truth lay in the updated league table. There are some injustices that are just too much even for a Spurs fan, one of which is having to be nice to my Chelsea friend Kim on the Fulham Road immediately afterwards as he struggled not to look too pleased when saying, 'I feel I should apologise.'

Walking back to the car, I was confronted by two teenaged Chelsea fans.

'Yidd-o, Yidd-o,' they yelled at me.

Normally I'd have kept quiet to avoid a beating. But I was so pissed off generally, I no longer gave a shit.

'Ra-cist, ra-cist,' I shouted back.

The two Chelsea fans had the grace to look sheepish. They kept their mouths shut and their fists in their pockets. It was by far the cleanest victory of the day.

May

WITH JUST A FEW weeks and four games left, the end of the season was taking on its familiar rhythm: Jill was getting more and more fed up with football. All those weekday nights when I had insisted I had to watch a match on TV – 'It's really important. Chelsea might get knocked out if Spartak Moscow beat Marseille'; all those weekday nights when I had lost the battle for supremacy of the TV but had still flicked over to the football every time there was an ad break or she left the room; all those weekends spent in N17 or on the motorway had taken their cumulative toll. Whatever tolerance or benign indulgence towards my football habit she might have shown earlier in the season – the summer months do help her forget how much she hates football – had long since dissipated. At this time of the year, football was just a constant source of irritation and difference, a symbol of something we didn't share.

In my defence, it wasn't me who didn't want to do the sharing. I'd have been quite happy for Jill to have watched loads of football with me on TV. On several occasions I've also suggested she might want to come to a game with me, but every time she's found a good reason – 'I've got to feed the cat' – to not go. I'm not sure how I would have felt if she'd said yes, but that's beside the point. Jill can't accuse me of not showing willing. Nor can she claim that football is my way of avoiding spending time with her; it would be tough to argue that I've been going out of my way to avoid spending time with her since I was nine.

But football is undeniably my escape from myself, and for that reason it's probably healthier for both of us if she keeps her distance. To have your partner colluding in your madness does tend to normalise and excuse it. So it's for strictly therapeutic reasons, I'm sure, that Jill often makes a point of not asking me the score when I get back from a game. But all therapy has its mental blocks, and neither of us can claim football isn't a source of friction between us. She thinks I'm being casually dismissive when I lose concentration halfway through a conversation; I think she's being deliberately provocative to try to talk to me when I'm checking a football result online.

Mostly, though, we negotiate this minefield successfully. Indeed, I've sometimes wondered if there isn't something in it for her, too. Would Jill really want a man who was physically present and emotionally there for her the whole time? I think not. It's held up as the idealised image of reconstructed man, but I think she'd get fed up with me pestering to know how she feels every few minutes. She likes her own space, too, and it's convenient for me to be labelled the mentally more unstable partner. And given my medical history, it's a hard charge to refute.

What gets to her as much as the attritional nature of the nine-month football season is the indecision it generates as I find it increasingly hard to commit to anything in case there's a fixture clash. This season it had been particularly bad because Jill had switched jobs and was taking a four-week break in between finishing the old one and starting the new one in May. Her attempts to get us to take a holiday together, just the two of us, were met with stonewalling.

'Be spontaneous,' she said.

That was a bit rich, coming from her.

'I'll see what I can do.'

Not very much as it turned out, apart from a great day out at the garden centre; it wasn't my fault I had a lot on at work and couldn't be certain Spurs weren't going to make it to the Champion's League semi-final at that point. And though Jill did later admit she had a much better time going walking in Andalucía with a couple of her women friends than she would have done with me, my inability to leave home still rankled.

'You owe me,' she said later.

'Fair enough. What do you want?'

'You can book the summer holiday.'

'Where do you want to go?'

'Anywhere. You decide.'

'When do you want to go?'

'End of July, beginning of August.'

Half an hour later, I had the holiday sorted. It's amazing what you can do when you are sure of your dates.

Spurs' on-field problems were proving more tricky to resolve. Manchester City had thrown us a fourth-place life-line by losing to Everton, which we immediately spat out by drawing at home to Blackpool – and we only got that much through a late, late goal from Defoe.

The game was our season reduced to ninety minutes: plenty of possession but very little to show for it, with our strikers' lack of confidence spreading to the rest of the team. Our midfielders decided to save the strikers the effort by hoofing the ball over the bar themselves. Meanwhile, Bale's season came to the premature end we had all been expecting. All year, referees seemed to have come to an understanding with our opponents that everyone was allowed to have one free reckless assault on the Welshman without getting a yellow card, and time and again Bale would end up face down on the turf. This time he didn't get up, and was stretchered off with knackered ankle ligaments after a dangerous foul from Charlie Adam that didn't even get a yellow card because of the one-free-foul rule.

Gomes's season was enshrined in just ninety seconds. First he saved an Adam penalty, then he needlessly clattered a Blackpool player to give away a second penalty from which Adam scored. The Lord giveth and the Lord taketh away and everyone near me, even Robbie, wanted Gomes taken away.

Unlike earlier in the season, there were no boos for another unsatisfactory performance. The fans had got too used to them by now and couldn't summon the effort. Justin and Amici hadn't even bothered to turn up. After the game, Harry delivered his standard Orwellian Newspeak about how there were no easy games in the Premiership and how we'd actually done really well, considering.

Once more, it seemed as if there were two separate football universes: the one inhabited by those inside the game and one inhabited by the rest of us. There are easy games if you are Manchester United, Chelsea and latterly, Manchester City; and we hadn't done very well, considering. Yes, we'd had a great time in the Champions League and we were very grateful for that, but in the Premiership our squad hadn't performed to its potential and we'd carelessly tossed away a good eight or nine points – points that would have made qualifying for the Champion's League again a formality.

Matthew was unusually vocal. 'Harry goes on as if he has single-handedly saved the club,' he said. 'We were near the bottom of the Premiership when he arrived but we weren't exactly Northampton. We'd had a crap run of nine games and needed sorting out but the squad was basically sound. We'd won the Carling Cup and come fifth twice in the previous three seasons, for fuck's sake. And the way we're playing right now, we'll be lucky to finish fifth again.'

I'd never heard Matthew speak for so long or so eloquently. I was also fairly confident it wasn't likely to be repeated on the trip north to Eastlands, which meant we were probably in for another quiet trip as Theo and Terry's pre-Chelsea sunshine euphoria had subsided into inertia. I had suspected as much when Theo didn't reply to my first email. So I sent him a second reminder.

'I don't want you to think I'm not coming just because we're shit, which we are,' he wrote back. 'But I've got a big family do I can't miss.'

Terry was just as blunt.

'A bit of treachery to report, I'm afraid,' he said. 'I'm not going to make it to Eastlands. I've got something else on.'

'What?'

'I dunno. I'll think of something. And while I'm about it, I'd better fess up to another treach. I'm not going to Liverpool, either.'

This is the way it always is. You start out with the highest hopes and the best of intentions – all for one and one for all – and come May, you're lucky to find one man still standing once the season has unravelled. That man was Matthew, who was coming along for the nobility of the futile gesture. As was I, though I had another reason for going as well.

Someone had once asked John why he thought it was that people's outlook seems to become more limited as they grow older. He considered the matter for a while before suggesting the question was arse-about-tit; what was really going on was that old people were dispensing with all the trivia with which they had cluttered their lives to concentrate on the only really serious thing. I'd never thought of it before, but he was so clearly right. There is nothing more serious than one's own mortality. And in a manner of speaking, that's what was at stake for Spurs at Eastlands.

Any fool can bust a gut in the early half of the season when they are full of hope and anything is still possible, and any fool can fight to the death at the end of the season if there's a trophy or the threat of relegation at stake. But it's how you play when there's nothing at stake that really defines you, because that's how most of us will die. We won't go out tragically early, nor will we go out in a blaze of late triumphant glory; rather we'll just gradually grind to a halt as our arteries thicken or a cancer spreads. The only question is how we face the inevitable: do we roll over meekly and die, or keep on playing as long as we can? That's why I was going to Eastlands. To see how this Spurs team was going to die, to see who was going to fade away, who would struggle for one final breath, to learn about myself. Their death was a glimpse of my own.

Even by my own low standards, I've seldom felt such an absence of hope on the way to a game, a despair born largely out of my sentimental attachment to symmetry. Virtually to the day the previous year, Matthew and I had travelled to Eastlands for the game that would decide who got Champions League football the following season. Mathematically we were playing for the same stakes this time round, but the points and mental gap were now far larger. City was a team finding some edge; we were a team losing ours. It made me wonder if Spurs weren't, at heart, like me, more comfortable with the familiar pain of missing out than the burden of achievement. There was one other noticeable difference between the two trips. This time it was me that was half an hour late, though as I was picking up Matthew from his work he'd have been struggling to be late himself under any circumstances.

'I remember the journey up last time,' said Matthew. 'God, I was tired. The twins were only two then and I just felt shattered the whole time. Now they are a year older I feel much more match-fit.'

'Really? Can't say I'd noticed.'

'No, really. I reckon I'll stay awake the whole way to Manchester this time.'

He was asleep by Oxford.

'I wasn't technically asleep, John,' he said somewhere after Birmingham when I woke him up by putting on the radio. 'There's a difference between just closing your eyes and losing consciousness.'

'Maybe. But I don't think you were in a position to tell.'

The Spurs fans end wasn't full this time round. The website had said we'd sold out our allocation, so I guess some fans had decided it was too much hassle to travel up on a Tuesday night. Those that did come seemed resigned to the inevitable. When Crouchie took a long-range shot that slowly billowed high and wide of the goal, all the fans near me just laughed. We'd stopped expecting him to score goals or create chances: now his value was only in his comedy. Within minutes the humour became a lot darker as the man who couldn't score for us turned the ball into his own net to put City one up. The poignancy was inescapable: it had been Crouchie who had scored the goal that had guaranteed us Champion's League football. Now he had scored the goal that all but handed the same prize to City.

I couldn't not feel sorry for him. No matter how useless he'd been, he didn't deserve that burden. It was almost too painful to watch. We all screw up massively from time to time, but few of us ever get to have our limitations so ruthlessly exposed on such a public stage. 'Why me?' he must have thought. 'Why not Dawson or Rafa, someone the fans love?' Bathos demanded it was Crouchie. It wouldn't have been much comfort to him, but Crouchie's disaster made 45,000 people feel a bit less inadequate.

Ten minutes into the second half, it suddenly occurred to me we were playing quite well.

'So we are,' Matthew said when I pointed this out.

We had both been so lost in an inner catastrophic world that neither of us had noticed we had been dominating the game and it was City who were looking panicky and short of ideas. Judging by the noise levels, most of the other Spurs had also been in much the same suspended state and it was only for the last thirty minutes that we really got behind the team. Hope is a dangerous feeling. Scoring a goal remained as elusive as it had all season, and City held on.

There were no police to hold us in after the game this time. It was the City fans who stayed behind to celebrate, while we sneaked away unnoticed. We were out of the car park and on to the M62 in record time. As with so many games this season, I was left with the feeling of being robbed, that we had been the better side and justice had not been done. But no one gets robbed that frequently without having to wonder if they aren't a bit of a mug or have *victim* writ large on their backs. We were probably a bit of both. There was also the guilty realization that I was quite relieved it was all over. There was no more anxiety to be had, no more looking at the league table and thinking, 'If this happens and that happens then we might just have a chance'. We had opened our exam results and we had failed.

On the way home, the Radio 5 Live pundits talked their usual mindless post-match air-filler platitudes, and for a quarter of an hour Matthew and I amused ourselves by chatting to one another in the same nonsense footiespeak.

'The Premiership is becoming more competitive every year, don't you agree, Matthew?'

'Yes John, the Premiership is becoming more competitive every year. I can't believe how competitive it's become.'

'You're right, Matthew. If you don't have the money then you just can't compete. The teams without the resources are always going to struggle.'

'That is so true, John. You've got to have some sympathy for your Blackpools and your Wigans, because realistically they've got no chance against your Manchester Uniteds and Manchester Cities.'

'Spurs fans that criticise Harry Redknapp just don't know what they are talking about. The manager has done a brilliant job, considering.'

'Outstanding, John, outstanding.'

We got bored at this point, and lapsed into silence. It was Matthew who broke it.

'There's something I've been meaning to tell you.'

'What?'

'I can't make Liverpool on Sunday.'

'Why the fuck not?'

'Er, because my wife has to be away and I've promised to look after the twins.'

'So she wasn't going away when we still had a chance of fourth place and now we don't she is?'

'Yes. I know it looks bad, but I promise you it's true.'

'Why can't you get someone else to look after them? Can't your mother do it?'

'She's seventy. Twelve hours is too long.'

'She can't do a worse job than you.'

'I've already promised the twins I'll take them out.'

'Where?'

'To a sheep farm.'

'To a sodding sheep farm? How miserable is that? Do you want your kids to hate you?'

'They think sheep are cute.'

'Are you serious?'

'Totally. I have to do it. I've made a promise and there are times in the season when you have to put your family first.'

'Do you think it's a coincidence that you, Theo and Terry suddenly find your families utterly fascinating when we're out of the running for fourth place, having ignored them for the previous nine months?'

'Yes.'

And then there were none.

Matthew dozed off for over an hour, finally waking up near Thame.

'Can we turn off this shit?' he asked.

'It's not shit. It's Radio 4.' I'd had enough of Radio 5.

'Blah. Blah. What have I learned from Radio 4 today? That some German environmentalist's sister has had an eye operation and that Betty whatshername . . .'

'Boothroyd.'

'. . . Boothroyd said something dreary in the House of Lords. That's it. The reason I spend so much time asleep in your car is because Radio 4 knocks me unconscious.'

'What would you rather listen to?'

'Magic FM.'

'No.'

'More music, less talk, John. You can't beat it.'

We switched over to hear a presenter reading out a letter from a listener who wanted her to play something soft and smooth to help her come to terms with the fact that her boyfriend didn't understand her feelings.

'I don't blame him,' I said.

'It's a very moving story, John.'

It was also a story that demanded a playlist of Labi Siffre, Cyndi Lauper, Rod Stewart and Bryan Adams ballads. Matthew was rocking out. He was as good as his word; I'd never seen him so fired up. I, on the other hand, was in danger of falling asleep at the wheel.

***

Auctions are the ideal antidote to any end-of-season ennui as they are not bound by the football calendar. They just keep on rolling, minute by minute on eBay and month by month elsewhere; if you're not happy with the way the present season is going, you can just as easily live in another one. I was temporarily living in the summer of 1951, soaking in the triumph of Spurs first Division One title.

I've mastered the art of speed-reading an auction catalogue. I scan each page quickly, looking for the word Tottenham, and make a mental note of any lot that looks as if it might be worth following up. Very rarely does something stop me dead in my tracks: twice in two months was unprecedented. First the 1901 FA Cup tickets, and now the menu for the 1951 celebration banquet at the Savoy. It was an unnerving feeling. My heart caught a beat, and I had to go back to reread the entry to make sure I hadn't made a mistake. Then the type seemed to go up a point size and be written in bold. Here was another piece of football social history that was only of interest to me and about five other people in Britain. One of whom was Trevor.

'It's a great item,' he said on the phone.

'I know.'

'It's the seating plan that comes with it that makes it so special. There will be quite a few guests who kept the menu, but very few will have bothered to save the seating plan, too.'

I hadn't noticed the seating plan was included.

'Are you planning on bidding for it?' I asked.

'No. I'm saving my pennies this month. You go for it.'

I did. The bidding uncannily stopped at the upper limit of what I was prepared to spend. This has happened so often now that I've begun to wonder whether auctioneers can read my mind. Even when I'm a hundred miles away behind a computer. I wasn't too bothered, though, as the

menu itself gave a better glimpse of the past than any pho-
tograph. It had a picture of the trophy on the inside page
above the words 'Many Happy Returns', despite us never
having won it before, and told of the evening's delights:
the post-war rationing menu of Le Consommé Madrilène
en Tasse au Sherry, Le Dindonneau Roti Washington with
Les Pommes Berny followed by L'Ananas Voile Savoy; the
toast by the Marquess of Londonderry; and the entertainment from Flack and Lucas ('England's finest step-dancers
from the Palladium'), Jack Train ('the universally popular
comedian'), Leslie Welch ('the famous Memory Man
from Tottenham') and the Beverley Sisters ('the glamorous harmony trio').

But, as Trevor predicted, it was the seating plan that was
the real gold dust. Great Spurs names, such as Alf Ramsey,
Bill Nicholson and Ted Ditchburn were seated alongside
Major-General G. T. W. Horne, Sir Bracewell Smith and
H. J. Hampden-Alpass. Representatives from Harwich &
Parkeston FC shared a table with those from Newcastle
United. They did things differently sixty years ago. I doubt
you'd have found many wags.

The adrenaline rush spurred me on to buy a signed
menu from the 1995 Football Writers' Association dinner – Jürgen Klinsmann had been voted player of the year
– along with signed Spurs calendars from the 1986 and
1988 seasons. As I've said, Matthew is the only person who
has ever expressed any interest in my Spurs collection – if
anyone I knew was going to be interested, it was him – but
when he saw it he greeted it with the same mixture of con-
tempt and fatigue as everyone else, so I never volunteered
any information about my latest additions. But sometimes,
when he fancied a laugh, he'd ring me up to ask if I had

bought anything, and when I mentioned the calendars, his tone changed.

'That 1986 calendar,' he said. 'What month is Glenn Hoddle?'

'He's January.'

'Is it signed?'

'Oh yes.'

'Do you . . . Do you think you might sell it to me?'

'Well, it's terribly difficult to work out just how much it's worth, as I got it in a job lot with the 1988 calendar.'

'How much did you pay for them both?'

'Twenty-two quid. But it doesn't mean they are worth £11 each. The 1986 could be worth £15. Or more. I'll have to think about it.'

It would be good to make him sweat after years of taking the piss out of me.

Purchasing the menus and calendars would have been even better had I been able to sneak them into the house unnoticed. Robbie caught me at the door, signing for a special delivery.

'What's that?' he asked.

'Nothing much.'

'Oi, Mum. Dad's just wasted a whole lot more money on some football crap.'

***

Far from making the journey up to Anfield on my own, I ended up with a full car. Alex was the first to sign up. He'd never been to Anfield, and he fancied a day out. His partner thought he was mad.

'What do you want to do that for?' she had asked.

'Because it will be a fun day out.'

'No it won't. It will be really boring and you'll be stuck in traffic jams for hours.'

That conversation ran for a solid forty-eight hours up until Alex left his house on the Sunday morning. It might have ended there, too, had he not run off with his partner's car keys by mistake.

Andreas was the next signature. Like Alex, he had no real loyalty to Spurs, but he is Uruguayan and had his heart set on seeing his fellow countryman Luis Suarez in the flesh. Things were looking up, so I reckoned it was worth giving Matthew one last chance to change his mind.

'Did you know that the Spurs ticket office has some late returns from lightweights like you who can't be bothered to go now we can't finish in the top four?' I said.

'Really? It's tempting. My wife isn't going away, after all.'

'I never thought she was.'

'You're so cynical, John.'

'Are you coming or not?'

'I'll have to think about it. I don't want to break my promise to the twins to take them to the sheep farm.'

I still hadn't heard back from him by the following day, which meant he must have committed himself to the sheep. It was time for a last throw of the dice. I forwarded him an email from a Spurs fan saying he had a spare ticket that could be collected outside the ground at the game. That had to appeal to Matthew's natural inertia. No need even to pick up a phone to the ticket office. Just get in a car and go. There was an almost instantaneous reply.

'You're evil.'

'So you're coming, then?'

'You're worse than a dealer.'

'What about the poor little sheep?'

'My wife is taking the twins to see them. I'll make it up to them another day.'

'Shouldn't be hard.'

There are few more dismal places on the Premier League football map than the streets around Anfield. Houses are boarded up or burned out, and only a few are still occupied. I asked a local why this was. He shrugged and said, 'It's north Liverpool.'

Andreas was horrified. 'Imagine how Suarez must have felt when he first arrived,' he said, never one to miss the big picture.

'Quite. You'd have thought his agent would have insisted the club regenerate the whole area before letting him sign,' I replied.

'Actually, Andreas has a point,' Matthew said. 'I'm told that David Ginola's wife sobbed all the way back from St James's Park to the airport after he signed for Newcastle. She couldn't face the idea of living there.'

'She must have been thrilled when he came to us, then. N17 is so much classier.'

Outside the Bill Shankly gates super-inscribed with 'You'll Never Walk Alone', Matthew took a picture of me making a 'Whatever' gesture. It was as childish as it sounds, but there's something particularly irritating about the mythologies other clubs invent for themselves. As readily as I can still buy into the illusions Spurs creates for itself – 'The Spurs Way' – I can see through those of other clubs. The more corporate the Premier League becomes, the greater its attachment to sentimental notions of the past. I can't see Liverpool's previous owners, Gillett and

Hicks, or its present ones, Fenway Sports Group, for that matter, walking with anyone but investment-fund managers. Maybe nostalgia is the last resort of every disempowered supporter.

We had barely discussed the game once on the way up. There wasn't any need, as Anfield has been a graveyard for travelling Spurs fans, with just a handful of victories in a hundred years. You have to be feeling ridiculously optimistic ever to imagine a draw at the best of times, and given that Spurs had been making their way down the table while Liverpool had been travelling in the opposite direction, hope was in even shorter supply than usual. Besides which, it felt as if there was nothing riding on the game, as I wasn't that bothered whether we finished fifth or sixth. Having spent many of the previous seasons sweating over the permutations that would get us into the UEFA Cup, its attractions had now paled. And even if we had wanted to avoid the Europa League's doubtful glamour by failing to get automatic qualification, we were in pole position to collect the arbitrary place UEFA awarded for winning the Fair Play League – a league Fulham had been rapidly trying to lose in recent weeks by collecting an indecent amount of bookings in order to avoid the six qualifying games they would need to play over the summer just to get to the first round proper.

It could well have been the prospect of these six extra games that inspired Spurs to their best league win of the season. Rafa opened the scoring after ten minutes with a stunning volley – a touch of genius that must have been a bittersweet reminder for some Spurs players of the gulf between artist and journeyman footballer – and a couple of minutes into the second half we were given a soft penalty that we didn't miss. We never looked like losing, and long before the end the ambivalent chant of 'Thursday night – Channel 5' echoed around the away supporters.

Matthew had a treat lined up for himself on the way back.

'We're going to listen to my 'Best of Yacht Rock' playlist,' he said, plugging his iPod into the car stereo.

'That would be just amazing,' Andreas chipped in.

'Not you, too?' I said. 'Surely you can't like that shit as well?'

'I love it. It's the sound of winning.'

Unbelievable. Not just the same taste as Matthew and Theo, but the same choice of words. How had I managed to surround myself with these people?

Alex shares my tastes for depressing songs about un-free doves and heroes in the seaweed, and was struggling to comprehend the overwhelming banality of what we were being made to listen to.

'This is truly shit,' he said after a couple of minutes.

'How can you say that?' Matthew replied. 'This song is a tribute to what $5 million dollars in the recording studio can buy you. There's not a hint of edge anywhere; it is the anthem of smooth.'

'It's like being in church,' said Andreas.

'For a funeral,' I said.

Despite Alex's best efforts to get Matthew to fast-forward through some of the drearier tracks – there did turn out to be levels of dreariness in Yacht Rock; every time I thought I'd hit rock bottom, Matthew and Andreas would find something else – we ended up with a fairly constant stream of 1980s West Coast revivalism the whole way home. And for the first time ever, Matthew didn't nod off for a second in the car. The journey must also have notched up a new benchmark for my masochism because, even with the musical torture, it had been one of the most enjoyable days out at the football all season. It had been a day in a bubble. There had been no anxiety about the result, because there was no future to be stressed about; the narrative was necessarily limited to the day itself. I had gone to Liverpool with some friends. Spurs had won, which was terrific. But not all-important, as it would still have been OK if we had lost. And we'd had a laugh on the way back.

Andreas must have been thinking much the same thing. 'We've got to do this next season for the away Europa League games,' he said.

I thought about the implications: wandering around minor European cities with Matthew, Theo and Andreas listening to bands I wished I never knew existed. It could be worse. I could be wandering around minor European cities on my own.

'OK,' I said. 'But I'm not going to eastern Europe. It's got to be strictly Italy, France, Spain, Portugal and Germany.'

'How about Scandinavia and Holland?'

'Yeah, probably.'

'Switzerland and Austria?'

'At a push.'

'That's a deal,' said Matthew.

***

For some clubs, the final game of the season is vital. It had been in the past to us, and it was to our opponents Birmingham, who were locked in a five-way fight to determine who was going to be relegated with West Ham. But this season there wasn't anything at stake except pride in finishing in fifth place ahead of Liverpool. Harry Redknapp had been contradicting himself all week in the press about whether he really wanted to play in the Europa League the following season. Theoretically it was possible to avoid the competition by losing to Birmingham and getting the whole team booked and three players sent off in the process, but it was a bit of a long shot. As it was, Liverpool made the matter academic by losing to Aston Villa and our home win – the first in ages – with the last kick of the game merely allowed everyone to go home happy. Though not Mat (or the Birmingham fans).

'See you for the 0-0 draw against Norwich on the first day of the season,' he said before heading to the pub. 'Stay in touch.'

I would. But I would miss the others: Trevor, Andy, Rick, John and the dozens of other fans I knew by sight but not name with whom I had shared hugs, laughs and moans over the previous nine months.

Mostly I would miss Justin and Amici. They hadn't turned up for the last three home games, and I wondered what had had happened to them. For their first no-show, I assumed they were both away; for the next, I began to worry and now I would have to wait till August to find out why they had been AWOL. Or not. If they didn't renew their season tickets, or moved to a different part of the ground, I'd never be any the wiser. Nor could I get in touch as I had lost the piece of paper Amici had given me with his phone number on it. I had meant to ask him for it again but had never got round to it. We were too busy chatting about other things.

I'm not good at endings, so I hung around at the ground for a while after the final whistle. The Birmingham City fans were distraught their team had been relegated, but I felt detached from their misery as I hadn't cared too much one way or the other which side had gone down. There was no joy or sadness to experience; just the slow realization that Wigan had survived, and I would have a chance to get to the JJB Stadium after all. It's always good to have some future regrets on which you can count.

Media pundits often talk of the unpredictability of the Premier League as one of its great attractions. But it's really its predictability that is the fans' lifeblood. Any Birmingham fan not in abject denial would have said at the beginning of the season there was a good chance of his team ending up in a relegation dogfight by the end. Just as the same Birmingham fan would probably have put money on Manchester United, Chelsea and Arsenal qualifying for the Champions League. Understanding your place is what creates a team's identity. And for Spurs, that is to be the nearly team. No one could say we'd had a bad season, but it hadn't been that good, either. There had been some stand-out performances, but we had lost too many games we ought to have drawn and drawn too many games we ought to have won. It had been typical Spurs, and pretty much what I had expected at the start of the season.

'So why bother?' Jill asked when Robbie and I got home. It was hard to explain what it was like to be hypnotised by men kicking a ball – however badly – or be left breathless by moments of transcendent brilliance. It was harder still to explain how empty I would feel without the friendships, and the constant endurance test of proving to myself that I can stick with something through both good and bad.

Football helps me navigate my life. Robbie had started the season more boy than man and had ended it more man than boy; his life was increasingly his own and he now came to games with me because he wanted to, not because he thought he had no choice or needed to keep me sweet. There was a loss in that, but a gain also. Robbie was surviving growing up rather better than I ever had, and I felt flattered he liked me enough to spend that amount of time with me. Spurs had become part of the glue that held us close.

As indeed it would be for me and Anna. By the start of the next season she would have left home to go to university in Manchester, and it would have been the first time in nineteen years she hadn't been living at home. I was going to miss her a lot. But Manchester had its advantages; it was a gateway to United, City, Blackburn, Wigan, Liverpool, Everton and Stoke.

'I have a feeling you're going to be seeing a fair bit of me next year,' I told her.

'Not too much, I hope, Dad.'

Football has also helped me deal with the smaller stuff. Mostly my life is a succession of unheroic failures, of things that I haven't done quite as well as I should have done, of being a bit late for something or turning up in the wrong place. Which is just like watching Spurs. Imagine how inadequate you must feel to support Barcelona; inch-perfect passes relentlessly pinging around the pitch from first to last. It would get to me in the end. I need a team that goes from the sublime to the ordinary in a blink. It helps to keep me sane. Or insane, depending on your viewpoint. Spurs fail so that I don't have to.

Then there are the equations you don't know how to balance. Was my shirt lucky or not? It didn't make it through the season unscathed. It crumpled at Fulham in the FA Cup, was cheated at Chelsea in the Premiership and came unstuck thanks to a Gomes howler at home against Real Madrid. But due to the club not getting the new strip on sale till September, it avoided the home defeat to Wigan and made it through the rest of the Premier League season unbeaten at White Hart Lane. I'd say that was fairly lucky. It's now joined all the other old Spurs shirts on a cupboard shelf. It won't get worn again.

Some collectors keep a detailed record of how much they've paid for an item. I don't. It would involve far too much admin and be far too incriminating if anyone else in the family found it. Far better to keep these things vague. So there will never be a detailed profit-and-loss account of the tickets, programmes, menus and calendars. Well, the calendars maybe. Had I paid too much, the right price or got a deal on everything? Probably too much, though my pension was larger than it would have been otherwise.

The one inarguable gain was that I was still alive, something you may take for granted but I never have. I had made it through another year. It's good to have a few constants in my life. After my mum and sisters, Spurs is the longest relationship I have ever had, and it's an infinite source of enrichment: Spurs show me how to win and lose, how to say hello and goodbye. From ninety minutes to a lifetime.

The players would change: some would definitely go – Trevor had bought a painting of Robbie Keane from the club shop that had been reduced to a fiver on the last day of the season in anticipation of his transfer; some might go – no one could say for certain if van der Vaart, Modrić and Bale would definitely still be at Spurs the following season. And some new faces, as yet unknown, would come in. But as long as there were Robbie, Matthew, Mat, Theo, Terry, Trevor, Rick, Justin, Amici, Andy and the 36,000 others with whom I share my weekends, the club was guaranteed to stay pretty much the same.

I didn't have everything completely nailed, though. Despite years of practice, I'm still not entirely sure what to do in the summer.

'Don't worry,' Matthew said. 'I've sent you a link to a YouTube video of every Spurs goal from last season.'

'That takes care of three minutes.'

'It's a start, John. It's a start.'

Acknowledgements

THIS BOOK HAS TAKEN the best part of forty-five years to write. Inevitably over that long a period of time, the cast list of those who deserve my gratitude has become a little hazy, so to the many who have been accidentally left off, my apologies. Thank you first to Jill, Anna and Robbie for putting up with both my absences and my presences. Thanks, too, to my mum and dad, my sisters, Veronica Robinson and Sue Crace, Matthew Hamilton, Andreas Campomar, John Sutherland, Theo Delaney, Adrian Sington, Mat Snow, Terry Blake, Kevin Jones, Angela Martin, Hunter Davies, Richard Williams, David Baddiel, Mike Leigh, Phil Cornwell, Tim Parks, Justin, Amici, Trevor Jones, Rick Mayston, Andy, Pete Crawford, Pete Haines, Patrick Barkham, Steve Chamberlain, Simon Hattenstone, Bob Granleese, Tom Pool, Alex Benady, Tom Butler, Briony Byrne, Chris Williams, Celia Locks, Rob White, Mandy White, Joanna Briscoe, Theo Briscoe, Will Woodward, Ollie Jones-Evans and Patrick Butler. And finally, thank you to the players, managers and supporters of Tottenham Hotspur. Life wouldn't be the same without you. COYS.